**Prague 22: A Philosopher Takes A Tram Through A City**

First published in 2024 by Philosophy Now Books, an imprint of Anja Publications Ltd, who are also the publishers of *Philosophy Now* magazine.

**ISBN:** 978-1-3999-7381-6

**Layout by** Andrea Bölinger

**Cover photo:** Prague tram  iStock.com/leezsnow

**Distributed by** Gazelle Book Services Ltd

**Printed and bound** in Great Britain by Clays Ltd, Elcograf S.p.A.

Raymond Tallis

# PRAGUE 22

*Philosophy Now Publications*

RAYMOND TALLIS

# Prague 22

## A PHILOSOPHER TAKES A TRAM THROUGH A CITY

———————

RAYMOND TALLIS

FOR THE LADY WHO LOVES A TRAM(P)

# Contents

**Preliminaries**

Overture

Preludes to Prague

CBA: A Statement of Principle.

**The Ascent**

Hop-On: To Ruská

Ruská- Krymská

Krymská - Jana Masaryka

Hop-Off: A Visit to Grébovka

Jana Masaryka - Námesti Miru

Hop-Off: Námesti Miru

Námesti Miru - I.P. Pavlova

Hop-Off: The Café Mistral

I.P. Pavlova - Stepánská

Stepánská - Karlovo Námesti

Karlovo Námesti - Neomeste Radnice

Neomeste Radnice - Národní trídá

Hop Off: The Riddle of the Sphincters

Hop-off: Caff and Kafka

Národni Trída - Národni Divadlo

Hop-off: Café Slavia

Legii Most (Národni Divadlo - Újezd)

Újezd - Hellichova

Hellichova - Malostranská námesti

(Mainly Virtual) Hop Off: Malostranská námesti

Malostranská námesti - Malostranská

Malostranská - Královsky letohrádek

## PRELIMINARIES

# Overture

"My dear fellow", said Sherlock Holmes as we sat on either side of his lodgings at Baker Street, "life is infinitely stranger than anything which the mind of man could invent. We would not dare to conceive the things which are really mere commonplaces of existence. If we could fly out of the window hand in hand, hover over this great city, gently remove the rooves, and peep in at the queer things which are going on, the strange coincidences, the plannings, the cross-purposes, the wonderful chains of events, working through generations, and leading to the most *outré* results, it would make all fiction with its conventionalities and foreseen conclusion most stale and unprofitable."[1]

In the beginning was the word and the word was 'Prague'. And in the end was the word and the word was still 'Prague' but the word had been changed by many encounters with its referent. Between 'Prague' and 'Prague' lay a web of intersecting journeys on foot and on wheels, on the ground and in the air, spread over two decades; streams of experiences that washed off and then restored those inverted commas cupping the city's name like a caught butterfly. A succession of visits unpacked the monosyllabic puff of air and the six-letter squiggle of ink into: buildings, streets, traffic, skies, cafés, conversations, worries, joys, trees, a river and rivulets, music, drinks, sunny hours with their million patches of light and shade, and lamps planting epicentres of radiance in shiny-cobbled gloom.

Start anywhere, start nowhere.

Or make anywhere Somewhere by starting there...

It is true to the spirit of Prague that this tale of one mind's experiences of the city, of a body propelling a head through streets, cafés, rooms, should begin with a sound like a pistol shot in the early hours of the morning. It originated from an apartment located in a mainly beautiful suburb. Its homely cause was a toilet seat crashing down, taking the narrator, the consciousness on the underside of this page, by surprise. The stream was intercepted and scattered by the smirking oval of the falling seat, making its 'O' father an 'Oh!'

The descent was particularly irritating. Much trouble had been taken to secure the seat in the upright position. Its wayward habits were well known to the inhabitants of our flat. A blob of Blu-Tack had been deployed to hold it upright. This magic stuff, whose composition is still a manufacturing secret, is one of the many tricks humans have devised to allow hands to outsource their grip, their handiwork. Blu-Tack has an honoured seat in the order of artefacts, taking its place along with glue, sellotape, drawing pins, and their more muscular colleagues, such as screws and nails (cousins of those that affixed Luther's theses – *vide infra* – to the Wittenberg church), string, rope, elastic bands, and bulldog clips. The list is endless – and includes those snap fasteners or poppers that we shall meet on another dark morning; but this small sample is a sufficient reminder of the many ways we promote the coherence of the world in the interval between the accident of our birth and the other accident that corrects it.

I dwell on this because it is a reminder of certain aspects of our consciousness that *Prague 22* aims to explore, an intention sometimes obscured by its more particular aims. The exploration – or inquiry or recollection or celebration – will borrow structural support from the stops punctuating one of the most beautiful tram routes in the city of Prague, indeed in the world.

The route in question is that of the 22 tram.

In the hour or so of insomnia following the crash, the spike of irritation softened into a more open kind of wakefulness. The sounds that I imagined spreading outwards into the surrounding suburb, staining the quiet, also moved inwards, awakening a sense of the city in which I was located and trying to imagine. (Nothing is more difficult than to imagine the place we are in. As Erwin Mortier observed, "It demands an equally intense labour to live in the present, as it does to evoke the past, or probe the contours of the future".)[2]

I like to think that the crash prompted a flock of memories to take flight. If so, among those memories there would be that of another pistol shot from a similar source fired on a sweltering August night on the island of Samos. The seat landed with the distinctive accent of plastic on porcelain, that happens to be the same in Greek as it is in Czech and in English.

Philosophers should always be on the lookout for reasons to be impersonally surprised by themselves – themselves as mere examples, rather than exemplars, of humanity. I might therefore have invited myself to be astonished by my ability to connect the two crashes; by the wormholes in time opened by memory, reviving the warmth of experience as a cold flame of factual recollection, re-kindling in a private darkness the light that had once belonged to a public space. I had sensed an opportunity to trace the internal stitching that, for many decades, has held together the (still) going concern that is Raymond Tallis and is more or less replicated by the 7.8 billion other going concerns with whom he shares the planet earth.

Out of these unglamorous origins came the idea that has unpacked itself into this book of tenuous connections celebrating "the drunkenness of things being various"[3] and the seeming sobriety of their coherence.

Toilet seats, Blu-Tack, autobiographical memory: glints of anyone, anywhere. Anyone, certainly. For, as noted, a philosopher should be interested in himself only as an instance of a general case. But *anywhere*? Prague is and is not anywhere. It is, of course, special but its specialness is necessarily dappled with ordinariness and that ordinariness sometimes conceals the specialness.

Perhaps I sensed this as I imagined the crash spreading into adjacent apartments, separated from, and connected with, the Tallis flat by flights of stone steps always ready to turn sounds into their echoes. I imagined the ripples of audibility, and followed the awakening idea of Norská (the beautiful suburban street in which we had our apartment) past the Buddha restaurant next door, the Vietnamese Potraviny or basement mini-market a few doors down, and across the road to where the decorative balcony at the level of our apartment was supported by a stone goblin, in mediaeval dress, on duty 24/7.

As I reached into the circles of sound, losing their identity in the low hum of the early hours, I hovered on the edge of a promise: that my mind would deliver a sense of the city.

'A sense of the city'? What on earth could that mean?

In Richard Powers' novel Generosity, one character invites another to pick a meeting spot. 'Anywhere in the city' he says. The city is Chicago:

She laughs at the blank check. This city has forests in the northwest big enough to get lost in. To the south black neighbourhoods, the size of Constantine that white people never enter. Convention centers with the look of fifties science-fiction space colonies. Warehouse districts full of resale contraband peppered with refrigerated corpses. Cemeteries a hundred times the length of a soccer pitch, with gravestones in forty-one languages. There's Chinatown, Greek Town, Bucktown, Boystown, Little Italy, Little Seoul, little Mexico, little Palestine, little Assyria...Two Arab neighbourhoods – the southwest Muslims and the northwest Christians – where people from a dozen countries congregate to eat, recite Arabic poetry, and mock one another's dialects.[4]

Prague is not as vast or as culturally diverse as Chicago. But the challenge it presents to anyone who would wish to encircle it with thought is as great. Its population of 1.3 million citizens (supplemented by an annual influx of 8,000,000 visitors) is no easier to imagine than Chicago's 2.8 million; its 10,000 streets than Chicago's 20,000; its 100,000 houses than the other's 200,000; its million rooms than Chicago's 2 million. Its 191 square miles are a challenge to a head – this head, any head - whose cross-sectional area is less than that of an average turnip.

Besides, anything Prague lacks in space, it makes up in time. It has had many more centuries, and more than enough history to furnish them, than *parvenu* Chicago which became a city nearly 1,000 years after Princess Libuse prophesied the glories of the future capital of Bohemia, none of which included the Easy-jetting crowd of which I am a part.

There are many ways of acknowledging its unimaginability. Here is one to which I shall return at intervals: thinking of what the citizens of Prague – asleep, stirring, awake – might get up to.

At a given time, indeterminate numbers of them are finishing dessert; rolling their eyes in frustration – with the referential objects of their eye-rolling encompassing (for example) a second cousin's current behaviour and track record of unreliability, recent government policies towards funding public services, or the inaccuracy of weather forecasts; dozing over a book or the TV; broadly welcoming a proposal; answering a questionnaire; composing, reading, 'liking', or retweeting tweets; wiping surfaces – kitchen units, windows, spectacles (rain, mist, grease), shoes, babies' bottoms, eyes; running to get fit, catch a tram, or a evade a pursuer; coming to a sexual climax; hunting for glasses, on their head or left behind at home, to unblur a Prague Wednesday...

We shall revisit those imagined citizens at intervals and think of them living the seconds and minutes of the multiple arcs of their daily rounds, engaging in actions that draw on an hour just past or on a yesterday present in patches; that continue or interrupt projects a month old, year-long, or the fruit of a lifetime; building on bitter experience, habits of expectation, intensive training. We shall do this chastened by the thought that the usually mute houses flanking our perambulations betray little of the animation within them, their silences revealing nothing of the voices, the bricks none of the thought and feeling, in their rooms.

The unimaginable present moment of the city, 'Now' unfolding in hundreds of thousands of minds for the most part sealed off from each other, is tracked by the contrails of recent and long-past events, recalled in happy, unhappy, or merely factual memories, usually fragmented, sometimes coherent. Their collective consequences are arranged by scholars in space-like calendrical and historical time, documented and archived. And they occasionally amount to, or deposit, a wonderful clutter of architectural treasures, populating the most casual glances – the 'Prague' sought, found, and lost by visitors from so many other cities.

This is a city like no other and yet like any other. While a citizen may see a 1000-year-old spire behind another citizen's left ear, she may also be puzzling over the irritated expression on his face.

Thus – or thus-ish – the hinterland of the city of individual and collective memory, of history and of recollection, resting on and slipping through the consciousness of those who live in it, visit it, anticipate or recollect it, of those minds harvesting the trillion smithereens of actuality or possibility into the stuff of an invented totality signified by the single word 'Prague', whose lack of boundaries is concealed by its being the subject of quite ordinary sentences. That puff of exhaled air again.

We who do not qualify as its citizens, like those who do, carry this portable Prague from moment to moment, from mouth to mouth, from person to person, from page to page, enacting the everyday cognitive *hubris* of talking about a city as if a tongue could pick it up or a pen inscribe it on a sheet of paper or a keyboard portray it on a screen. Visitors and citizens alike imagine that it is possible to harvest the ocean of a metropolis in the thimblefuls gathered by gazes supported on heads transported from the time-slice of one street to the time-slice of another, or zigzagging down a page; that it is possible to uncover Prague-in-itself – an eternal Prague seen from nowhere and nowhen – by means of our own and others' reports on experience.

I have drifted from the Anywhere, into which the falling toilet seat broadcast its touch-down on porcelain, towards the special Bohemian Somewhere, a city that for at least one author stole Paris' 19th century crown and became the capital of the 20th century.[5] The drift is of course inevitable; for, though Prague may be hidden behind the thick screen of a Wednesday in Tesco in Kodanska, there still remains, behind the Prague of Now, the Prague of Then; above all the 'magic' Prague of Emperor Rudolf and his court of alchemists and sky-watchers, of Giuseppe Arcimboldo whose portraits of faces constructed out of vegetables, fruit, trees, roots, sea creatures, anticipated the surrealism that reached the city centuries later; of streets at dusk bathed in lamplight as soft and as gold as candlelight; the 'hundred-spired' Prague culminating in St. Vitus' cathedral sitting like an ever-vigilant crow on the shoulder of the town; of Gothic towers, monasteries, Baroque churches, Renaissance palaces and elegant suburban streets where stone faces populate every nook and cranny, every exquisitely carved irregularity; of the Jewish Quarter where higgled gravestones, themselves half-buried, are maculate with grief and praise; of the broad Vltava ('wild water') represented by a short, dozen-bridged stretch of its 250 mile long journey connecting a spring in the Bohemian forest to the Elbe in another country whose place-names can be more easily pronounced; the Prague of the allegorical Castle, in whose

17

hidden corridors, even more hidden rooms, and yet more hidden bureaucratic minds, are unwound the sentences of documents pinning down its citizens in a realm where papers have rarely been entirely in order; the Prague or Pragues of Franz K. and the thousand literary critics who have adorned his every footprint and their own CVs with a thousand footnotes. There is the Prague of the three hundred year resentment that began after the humiliating defeat at the battle of Bilá Hora (White Mountain) ushering in a Catholic Rule and the Habsburg Monarchy, and triggered the Thirty Years' War that devastated Europe; the destination of Mozart's legendary journey to the world premiere of Don Giovanni in the then newly built Estates Theatre; the imagined Pragues constructed by 19th century patriotic historians and poets and language revivalists and politicians; the Pragues of the tragically brief years of the finally achieved Republic of Czechoslovakia, and of the brutal episodes that followed - the Nazi occupation, the Communist tyranny; and finally, after the Prague of Václav Havel and the Velvet Revolution, the Prague of Now. The Prague that intersects with us.

These are some of the many Pragues that lie beyond the reach of the scholarship and imagination of the author of this book; Pragues that will haunt its pages as an epistemic bad conscience. Against this, my Prague is, I hope, also sufficiently distant from the Prague of the Prague Piss-Up – where for a couple of decades after the Velvet Revolution, my countrymen Easy-Jetted into Bohemia, seeking the non-Euclidean geometry defining the shortest distance between two pints, and for whom the point of travel seemed to be to swap vomiting on flagstones at home for vomiting on cobbles abroad.

So many other writers have preceded me and their voices – more articulate, better informed, more carefully and knowledgeably observant, with a sharper ear for the music of the city and of the echoes of the voices of the past - drown out mine even in my own head.[6] If I bear my ignorance more lightly than I should, it is perhaps because as the philosopher JL Austin put it so perfectly, "One must be at least one sort of fool to rush in over ground so well-trodden by the angels".[7] At any rate, I am a latecomer, bringing to the table two sources of incompetence: experiences and memories that fall short of Prague; and a philosophical ache that too often reaches past the city to an anywhere that is close to being a nowhere. The city of so many articulate imaginations is as absent from this book as it is in Edward Morike's *Mozart's Journey to Prague*. We shall find ourselves still *en route* to Prague even when, having at last reached the Cathedral and the Castle, we are walking down Nerudova towards Malostranská Square, or waiting at Václav Havel airport for our plane back to the UK, trying to order our memories of the streets and cafés, the museums, and parks.

So many disclaimers! You may think I have taken legal advice, and no expense has been spared.

It is enough, for the present, to admit that *Prague 22* is born out of the anticipation and pre-emption of many kinds of defeat and to add that it embraces defeat as a liberation, an opening to another kind of possibility: yet another Prague to add to those created by novelists, poets, chroniclers, who have tried to capture its streets and their history in sentences, its districts in paragraphs, and its histories in chapters. The Prague of these pages is equidistant from the experiences on the one hand of those who travel in the hope of encountering the romantic city of the printed word and the illustrated page and of those on the other for whom Prague is the daily life of domestic bliss or grief, and the endless repetitions of professional or manual work; the Pragues of an imaginary Bohemia and that of shopping and childcare, of the Castle and of DIEM; the Pragues that meet and do not meet in suburban cafés. If the reader feels she has been offered a nightingale with laryngitis or a scentless jasmine, I will argue that my Prague, Wednesdays and all, is born at least as much out of honesty about my interactions with this city as of old-fashioned incompetence.

The device anchoring what follows is a much-loved journey, taken many times, on the 22 tram. The route provides a vertebral column for what would otherwise have been a shapeless account of the interaction between a 'nook-shotten city' of stone and cobbles and the imagination and cranny-shotten consciousness of an intermittent inhabitant of that city, trailing his head through streets and harvesting experiences that live on as memories recalled by the intermittent and random permission of days passed elsewhere and 'nows' competing for their share of attention. That interface between head and city is guided by the thick pencil of the moving viewpoint of the tram route and the panoramic windows of the carriages that permit eyes to sew together a Prague of sorts.

Though that route is the spine of the book, there is a good deal of 'Hop on and Hop Off' - as City Tours typically permit, with tours sprouting into detours, not the least into the deep, vast, and tumultuous past on which the city stands.

The resulting tenuous connections fall somewhere between the raw 'and' of the random wanderer and the 'therefore' of a pilgrim; between honest embrace of the accident of successive 'nows', with their nonetheless precious details, and a response to the ache for something that adds up or holds together. The tincture of any consistent *telos* is faint, particularly as the consciousness that samples Prague from the tram window is already clouded with recollections and is subject to distractions, often from random knowledge that diverts attention from no less random experiences. Even so, such parenthetical material sometimes opens vistas that, while they may interrupt the thread, allowing the beads to roll away from the string, make other perhaps equally valid connections. At other times it may be a case of hitting the nail on the thumb.

If there is alchemy in the Prague of *Prague 22* it is that of 'ordinary' consciousness and its capacity to make connections. For that reason, this very special Somewhere is not in the slightest bit diminished for sometimes being a bit like Anywhere and being experienced by Anyone.

# Preludes to Prague

Prague entered my consciousness, so far as I can recall, with my father's library. 'Library' is a grandiose term for a random accumulation of mainly second-hand items, packed in a tall glass-fronted bookcase in our lounge, with volumes such as *Houses for Persons of Moderate Means* (my father was a builder) sitting cover to cover with historical novels, thrillers, and Darwin's *The Origin of Species*.

Among them was *Prelude in Prague. A Story of the War of 1938* by S. Fowler Wright. The author was a prolific writer, an accountant and conservative political activist. He had a pronounced hostility to modern industrial civilization, expressed in a dislike of contraception and the motor car. The novel, published in 1934 proved to be prophetic. It imagined Hitler's invasion first of Austria and then of Czechoslovakia as the initial steps in his conquest of Europe. It was greeted with derision, though Wright's predictions were soon proved surprisingly accurate.

The novel implanted the idea of an exotic Prague in my 10-year-old mind. For reasons I cannot entirely explain, and I doubt whether any reader will regret a lack of explanation, I like to think that there was a circular mark left by a cup of hot tea on the covers, reasserting the dominance of Here over There. Or reminding me that here-most Here comes, with time, to be the remotest There. And so, I treasure the idea of the ring as a mark of past time – past even to my schoolboy past – a drawer with a false bottom. It was in keeping with the pre-decimal price tag according to which the book was sold at 1/6d 'cloth covers.' In short, the idea of the circle was an opening through which I might fall into that Land of Far Beyond that is the first decade of the life of one now in his 70s.

My father, as my mother said, was 'a great reader,' and a critic with strong views, able to sniff out writers whom he suspected of being paid by the word, padding out the plot with superfluous descriptions, interrupting incidents with incidental details: "And then he took a cigarette, tapped it on the packet to settle the tobacco, struck a match, applied the flame, drew on the cigarette, inhaled deeply, and stared into space, trying to gather his thoughts". Father would not have approved of *Prague 22*: "And then we boarded a tram".

I see him, in his chair reading – for we had no television until I had left home for university. (Nor indeed a phone because he believed we would have to pay for incoming calls, and thus incur expenditure over which he would have no control.) And he remained an avid reader until he went blind in his last few years. He switched to audio books over which he would fall asleep and wake up complaining that the plot did not make sense. Fed up with books, he would occasionally listen to music, repeatedly requesting the same pieces.

Among them there was what he called 'The River', the second of Smetana's sequence of symphonic poems, the one that traces the Vltava from its modest beginning to its broad flow through Prague before it joins the Elbe. My father never tired of 'The River' and he would whistle fragments of the melody for hours after hearing it, interspersed with snatches of 'I want to be Bobby's Girl'

– a song that had travelled covertly in his consciousness from the pre-Beatles 1960s to the 1990s where 30-year-old seeds became transient flowers.

\* \* \*

It is time to move on from the 10-year-old who would hardly imagine that his experiences would become the unreliable memories of an elderly man looking back over 60 or more intervening years. A dozen years later, I was a medical student at St Thomas' Hospital in London.

One consequence of the crushing of the Prague Spring in 1968 was a diaspora of young people fleeing Soviet invaders. The event was defined in the consciousness of the free world by the image of tanks with guns permanently pointed at hopeless resistance. Among the exiles was a scattering of to me exotic-looking young women who worked in the hospital canteen. After much hesitation fueled by fear of rejection, I invited to a party a girl whose name I won't invent to fill the gaps in memory. Those gaps also encompassed what happened as a result. Very little, I can safely guess, judging by the way things generally went in those days. The Czechoslovak beauties in the canteen remained in-mates of that Harem of Faint Hopes that populated my youth. I recall only their yellow uniforms, a permanently irritated senior person in the canteen who bullied these exiles, and high cheekbones.

As for the cheekbones, their altitude is almost certainly another artefact of memory but worthy of further exploration. It was probably an instance of the triumph of concept over percept. The elevation of the cheekbones had been secured by the descent of the Iron Curtain that had gathered the idea of their owners' native country – Czechoslovakia – into that of the Soviet Empire.

This in turn was an expression of another triumph of concept over percept: the displacement of the country in question, like a tectonic plate, from the *Mitteleuropa* to which Czechoslovakia rightly belonged, to something called 'Eastern Europe', notwithstanding that Prague is west of Vienna. Such alchemy of the mind exceeds anything achieved by Rudolf II's court alchemist John Dee and any of his other resident conmen. The Velvet Revolution in 1989, the shedding of Slovakia in 1993, and the rise of the 'Prague piss-up' through the 1990's, moved the country and its capital westwards, back to *Mitteleuropa*, though the Prague of the mind still tended to slide to the south and east of the Prague of the map.[8]

\* \* \*

Scroll forward to 1984.

"I have in my hand a piece of paper" - more precisely my author's copy of *Granta*, a literary magazine which contained a short autobiographical essay. 'Certain Thoughts Arising out of Being Pointed out by my 2-Year-Old Son'[9] was my first published piece of (non-medical) prose.

The cover of the issue titled 'Greetings from Prague' is filled with a magnified postage stamp. Most of the stamp is occupied by a wistful, gentle-looking Alexander Dubcek, the tragic leader of the Prague Spring. He is wearing a sky-blue jacket with one sky-blue button visible and a sky-blue tie and looks if he has just finished crying or is just about to cry. Behind him is St. Vitus' Cathedral set against a beautiful blue sky, enhanced rather than marred by a tousled archipelago of cirrus clouds. The Castle round the feet of the cathedral is punctuated with window-lights signifying the busy work of government, weaving its bureaucratic hold on the citizens of Prague. Below the Castle is the Vltava of Smetana's tune that gave my father so much pleasure in his blind last years. The river is divided by its rapids into a nearside blue-black ripplesome stretch of water and, on the far side, mirror-smooth water bearing a faithful image of the Cathedral, the Castle and the evening sky.

My little essay was in distinguished company. It was preceded by a bitterly satirical letter from the Polish writer Slawomir Mrozek arguing that competitive football, where one side could win and the other lose, was against the spirit of communism. The very idea that someone might be better than someone else was blasphemous. Only the Party, which transcended all individuals, was in any sense 'better'. The letter was signed off 'With sportive greetings.' I have only recently learned of Mrozek's fanatically loyal Stalinist early youth and still do not know how to pronounce his name.[10]

My own piece was followed by a long interview with Milan Kundera, author of *The Unbearable Lightness of Being*, by the novelist Ian McEwan, and a series of hefty excerpts from Kundera's novels in translation.

Nearly forty years on, I have proved to be the only one of the contributors to that issue of the magazine – they included Salman Rushdie, Martha Gellhorn, Gabriel Garcia Marquez, and Maria Vargas Llosa - to have kept their obscurity intact. (With exception of the LindonPrint Typesetters who are equally un-limelit.)

\*   \*   \*

Another two decades pass and we receive a phone call from our now 22-year-old son. He has arrived in Prague for the first time. For most of his twenties and thirties he is resident in the city and so we visit with increasing frequency what is now the capital not of Czechoslovakia but, following the Velvet Divorce, of the Czech Republic – also known as Czechia – though we find it difficult to shake off the habit of using the old name.

We get to know the city better, though familiarity and orientation come slowly for reasons that are retrospectively puzzling once the city becomes transparent to us, and what is out there, what is on paper, and what is in our heads, are more closely aligned. We learn to find our way around the streets unaided as a Prague of our own crystallizes out of the *urbs* and suburbs. It becomes (to vary the infamous observation of Mr. Chamberlain) the capital of a less distant country of which we know much, so much so that the reality of its various children's playgrounds is as familiar as the idea of the Castle.

Or think we do. Of which more, much more, presently.

\*   \*   \*

And so, to the final prelude. Visits to Prague are bracketed by airflights.

We lock the front door of our house, having checked that the burglar alarm has settled itself into a state of silent vigilance. We listen out for a sound signaling that it is set – it unconsciously mimics the opening motif from Mendelssohn's Italian symphony – as we sort out a minor confusion between the similar looking keys to Valley Road, Bramhall, and Norská, Vrsovice (no, I can't pronounce it, either – a portent of things to come). We take our usual taxi ride to Manchester Airport, often enduring a one-sided conversation with a driver whose unsolicited opinions we listen to in hopeless silence. He speaks at length and listens at shorth (*sic*), and I wonder out quiet whether he has read Nietzsche and come to the conclusion that the *Übermensch* the mustachioed philosopher prophesized was a taxi driver. His monologue is at least a distraction from the uneasy sense that perhaps, after all, we have failed to lock the front door. That action is so rational, so automatic, and fits so snugly into the process of leaving our dwelling, that it deposits no mark on our memory.

We arrive at least 2 hours earlier than necessary. After we have negotiated passport control and security and worried about leaving something behind in the trays into which we unpacked what had to be declared, we spend an hour or two at The Café of the Loudly Scraping Chairs, where once I left my passport on a table and regained it after a panic-stricken search. We savour the pleasure of having the entire trip ahead of us, which we declare as having begun once we have passed through security. Then there is a flight of about 2 hours – roughly the same as the train journey from Manchester to London – that gets shorter with repetition.

On our arrival in Prague, we are greeted by our first Czech word, our first linguistic tripwire: VYCHOD, meaning EXIT (though, for those of us arriving in Prague, it marks our ENTRANCE). The acute accent on the Y – which I cannot inscribe here because the computer insists that 'Y acute' is an instruction to do something I don't want it to do – is a harbinger of the linguistic scotomata, the scriptural opacities, to come.

I recently learned that these and other 'diacritical' marks – intended to save on consonants – were introduced by Jan Hus, the martyr, and a crucial figure in Czech history and indeed in this volume, when he was in hiding in South Bohemia, so we know whom to blame. Or we think we do. The Czech historian Josef Pekar gave the credit to Jan of Holesov (1366-1436) – a writer, theologian, linguist, and much besides. Since he was a theological opponent of Jan Hus – totemic hero of insurgent Czech nationalism – the matter of who invented diacritical marks was hotly debated in 19th century.[11]

Irrespective of who can be blamed for them, the additional barrier presented by the spattering of these marks on names and notices is the other side of the solidity of the presence of Czech culture. They create a pause before we can look through words for anything that might speak to us with sounds we can pronounce, even less meanings we can extract.

We follow a succession of familiar mid-blue signs flagging up Gates, Passports (alas, that circle of Euro-stars now shaved off), and Baggage Reclaim and pass certain all-too-familiar outlets (Paul's Patisserie, Costa Coffee, Relay Newsagents, Pizza Hut, Burger King) that attenuate our sense of being anywhere special.

A few familiar things make us smile a knowing smile, though precisely *what* that smile knows it knows not or knows only imperfectly. The first is the  advertisement on the luggage trolleys featuring bosomy barmaids, in low cut folkish dresses revealing generous helpings of mammary tissue being metaphorically milked for all they are worth. They welcome us with 4 litres of Prazacka lager, capped with inch-thick heads of foam, two glasses in each hand. The ladies have been flown in from the 1950s and suggest a good deal of uncorrected political incorrectness. The second is the machine dispensing coffee, water, and snacks – described as 'Very Goodies'. We encounter the third when we reach the luggage carousel.

As we await our bags, we are watched over by a lovely, warm wooden statue of a long-horned, goatee-bearded goat, with strikingly yellow irises encircling its pupils. Raised on its hind legs, it supports a pint of beer between its bent forelegs. On its face is a smile somewhere between smug and enigmatic. We have reached the home of Kozel (which means 'male goat'), the darkest of the popular beers and Mrs. T.'s favourite. The carving invokes places where the idea of beer is part of a mist of associations that hover round one concept of this city and indeed this country.

I have next to me, as I write, a Kozel beer mat whose *verso* portrays two vaulted characters – smiling brewers, draymen, or cellarmen with bottle-hardened faces. One of them holds two vast glasses of lager described as 'pay for honest work' clutched in his fist. His other hand is placed fraternally on the shoulder of his beer-mat mate. The warm brown ambience stands for the cellars and other dark beery places anticipated, remembered, and even experienced in the city. The little town of Velkopopovicky where the beer has been brewed since 1874 – continuing through the First World War, the Nazi invasion, and the endless 40 years of communism – is name-checked but there is no reference to the

Japanese business that now owns the brewery. All is not as it may appear. Perhaps that was the enigma infusing the goat's smile.

We have only a single road to cross to hook up with Prague's wonderful public transport system. The first leg of our journey from the airport to our flat is delivered by the 119 bus where we hold on to our wheelie cases which threaten to break loose as the vehicle weaves its way out of the airport. A mere 15 minutes takes us to Nádrazí Veloslavín – Veloslavín Metro Station. *En route* we sweep down a wide, arterial road, passing Bilá Hora (*vide* – much – *infra*) and The Cube – a large building which is what it says it is. We decant from the bus and descend to the Metro (Green) B Line on the first of many escalators where our failure to make progress with the Czech language is spelled out in the opacity of the text on advertisements we glide past. Even the pictures in the international code of iconic signs do not take us all the way from guesswork to comprehension.

There follows a smooth – super-smooth – tunneling through hyphens of darkness connecting the names of stations. Once we got to know the city, our recollections effortlessly penetrate the roof of the tunnel into the light outside and the names flower into places we can imagine, trips we recall, afternoons we remember. The station names inform us that we are deeply buried beneath the vast Dejvická square (Leninova Square under the communists), the Castle ('Hradcanská'), and Malostranská ('the Little Town'), before we pass under the Vltava River to Starometska ('the Old Town') close to Jan Palacha Square, named for the student who burned himself to death in protest at the crushing of the Prague Spring, and adorned with the gorgeous Rudolfinum, thence beneath Wenceslas Square where the Velvet Revolution came to its climax, and the magnificently domed Muzeum curating the nation's complex and often tragic history and its many cultures. Finally, we reach Náměstí Míru, the Square of Peace.

The sense that we are close to our destination hurries us out of the 'gleaming, futurist grotto'[12] of the station, and we do not return the gaze of 'the curving surfaces of the tunnel walls'[13] that greet us, or the coloured rows of anodized aluminium tiles – silver, aquamarine, royal blue, and amber-gold – that line the walls, with concave and convex indentations and protrusions that look like visual illusions, though they are real and designed to prevent heat warping. They are known locally as 'breasts' and 'anti-breasts'.

We ascend the longest and fastest escalator either of us has known. It has a claim to an even more impressive superlative: it may be the largest in Europe. After a challenging set of static steps, where the wheels on our wheelies offer us little help, we emerge into a vast space dominated by the magnificent basilica of St. Ludmila. Its twin spires will help to locate our district in the panorama spread out before us when, arrived at the Castle, we look back whence we came.

There comes a moment heavy with significance: we board the 22 tram for the first time. It takes us via *Jana Masaryka* and *Krymská to Ruská* – names that will mean more presently. At *Ruská* we dismount and walk the short distance to Norská.

The sound of our wheelies over cobbles prompts the reflection that, over an almost unprecedentedly long period of peace in Europe, this harmless sound has displaced the louder rumble of tank tracks advancing down the streets, spreading terror, impotent anger, and despair. At least until recently. Now, courtesy of V. Putin, we have been again afforded the spectacle of people fleeing from tanks with all their possessions gathered up into a wheelie, its small rumble fleeing from the greater one of tanks. Our reflections reach out in different directions. Thoughts about the improbability of European peace, made more probable by the European Union (one of the many reasons for our Grrrrs! at Brexiteers) compete for head-time with reflections on the principle, common to the tank and the wheelie, that may be the most profound of all the advances made by *homo faber.*

I am referring to the transformation, by the wheel teamed with the equally ingenious and often overlooked axle,[14] of movement in a circle into movement in a straight line. The topic touches tangentially (a straight line kissing a curved one) on a preoccupation that will haunt this visit: the principle of inertia, its origin in the framework of the totality of the stars and their planets, and the effort of walking uphill or keeping upright on a tram.

The ascent up the mild slope of Norská highlights the benefits that have accrued from the idea of attaching wheels to suitcases. We glance briefly at the long interval between the wheel (and the axle) ca. 3,500 B.C.E. and the wheelie ca 1972 A.D. It is striking how recent has been the foot traveller's liberation from the archetypal lugging that is the transport of suitcases stuffed with kit-and-caboodle, with a subset of our possessions, pruned by an exquisitely shaped but wavering sense of what a particular future might require of us, what we should select from the vast storehouse of our home with their over-filled drawers, wardrobes, shelves, cupboards and the rest - so that knickers are cheek-by-jowl with phone chargers, shoes with plastic dinosaurs (examples of T. Rex and some other -saurus), and Wittgenstein's *Philosophical Investigations* with toothpaste.

The nearly 6,000-year interval between wheel and wheelie illustrates how brilliant ideas which seem blindingly obvious in retrospect are invisible in prospect. The notion of a suitcase with wheels was patented in 1921 by Theophilus Hokkanen, a Finnish citizen living in Manhattan. It was not until 1970, however, that the first commercially successful design, invented by Bernard Sadow an employee of the US luggage Corp, went on sale.[15] Sadow had a 'eureka' moment when he saw a worker pulling a heavy machine on a wheeled skid. We are, or should be, grateful for that eureka moment as 30 or 40 years later we (relatively) effortlessly trundle our suitcases over the large-pixelated mosaic of the pavements of the city of Prague. Had that moment occurred earlier, my arrival as a student at Oxford, which involved a two mile walk from the station to my digs, where I was lodged with Boris Pasternak's sister as my landlady, would have been punctuated with fewer pit stops and my limb muscles would have been less bitterly seasoned with lactic acid.

And my father's youth would have been easier. One of his first jobs after leaving school at 14 was as a drug rep for a firm purveying what in those days passed for medicines. His case of samples was closer to the remedies offered by Emperor Rudolf's alchemists than anything corresponding to evidence-based medication. He had to 'hump his bag' (the phrase my father used in his frequent telling licensed a filial smirk shared with my brother at a *double* or 1.1 *entendre* – one for the sensitivity reader) from doctor's surgery to doctor's surgery. To build up his savings, he often travelled on foot so that he could save the fares that were allocated to him as part of his daily allowance. By this means he accrued enough to pay the deposit on the good will of a small firm of building contractors. This prospered modestly. Eventually he earned sufficient to fund the education of his 5 children such that one of them went to medical school where... Well you know the rest.

The last phase of the journey is a short, echoing stone staircase that takes us to the lift. Unlike many lifts, this one spares us a statement of the obvious: it does not inform us that the doors are closing, which would anyway be even less useful if it informed us in Czech. We are transported to the fourth floor whence we can descend by another short flight of steps to level 3.5, or *Patri 3*, thus honouring a principle that will influence the shape of the story that follows and which, as soon as we have put our bags down, I will introduce: CBA.

We pass through the tall wooden door with a carved polished frame – populated with, among other things, two mildly obese babies – and, well, here we are, greeted by the high ceilinged, large-windowed rooms of the apartment that we at first liked and have now come to love.

# CBA: A Statement of Principle

'CBA' stands for 'Couldn't be Arsed'. That I shall henceforth call it CBA is not only because that is shorter but also because the auto-correct function on this computer warns me repeatedly that 'this language may be offensive to your reader'. Dear reader, you will have the option to experience the mild thrill of offence if you wish. Otherwise, you may leave it as an abbreviation to be unpacked only by someone with a more robust psyche.

CBA warrants early discussion, because it accounts for some of the glow of approval and appreciation in which the eponymous 22 tram is bathed. It is also one key to the philosophical exploration that will from time to time gate-crash this cultural exploration of Prague.

Prague is a moderately hilly city, and its most prominent summit supports St. Vitus Cathedral and the Castle that encircles it. It is this arrangement that may have imbued its citizens with a sense of being observed, judged, and perhaps forever falling short of anything that can be approved of – a notion gathered up in the mind of Franz Kafka, or at least in how that mind is reflected in his works as refracted in turn in the minds of his far-too-numerous commentators.

I am already getting ahead of myself and, besides, the Castle in Kafka's The Castle is not the *Castle* in Prague. Nevertheless, those charged with maximizing footfall and shifting merchandise have seen no harm in conflating the one with the other. The spiritual gaze of the cathedral perched on the shoulder of the city is invisible though it is signified through the multiple spires that point to the heavens where God's strangely absent presence is rumoured to be found, underpinning the ever-present but usually disappointed possibility of violent or peaceful intervention from the inhabitant of Eternity. The secular gaze of the Castle – the largest castle complex in the world, as we are told at the beginning of every tour or guidebook entry – is materialized in windows that are as numerous as the ommatidia of a cockroach's eye or of the StB, the secret police who enabled the Party to invade every aspect of citizens' lives before the Velvet Revolution.

Happily – for this visitor and this book - it is possible to complete the ascent to the summit in the sitting position in a tram. For the inhabitants of Norská there is a further piece of luck. The nearest tram stop (Ruská) is a short *downhill* walk and there is a continuous tramline to Pohorelec – the tram stop above the cathedral and the Castle. All journeys from Pohorelec are downhill.

A defence is needed perhaps of CBA – which might be more politely unpacked as The Principle of Least Effort – though I will later provide a correction to, even a retraction of, this principle. I am, after all, a retired physician and loyal to the ends and aims of my late profession.

The starting point is this: we are embodied subjects.[16] This seemingly simple, some may say blindingly obvious, truth lies at the heart of many of the knots philosophers (including the ghost behind this page) have spent a lifetime trying to unpick. There are many positive aspects of embodiment for anyone seeking to experience Prague. Enjoying the food, the beer, the ambience of the places in which they are delivered, feeling the warm or cold air on one's cheeks and other exposed parts: these are hardly disembodied experiences though what they mean, or might come to mean, is a different matter.

Nor are the hands-off encounters permitted by vision entirely ethereal though they may seem so compared with the grope, and even the grunt and groan, of touch, or the invasion of smell. For there are no views without viewpoints; no viewpoints (ultimately) without eyes; there are no eyes without heads to give them their location; and there are no heads without torsos to elevate and nourish them and legs to propel them through space. To experience the city, from a viewpoint within the city, we need to transport ourselves around it; and in order to transport ourselves around it we need to transport our bodies or more precisely arrange for our bodies to be transported. The preference for the latter, when the gradients are uphill, should require little explanation.

Ocular heaven or cultural bliss is difficult to square with physiological Hell or even mere discomfort. There are disinclinations built into upward inclines. The incipient ache of muscles and the fully-developed ache of joints, experienced to a background music of one's own puffing sometimes scaling up to panting, are all too familiar to elders losing their battle against that law – the Second Law of Thermodynamics- that waves all organized structures (including human bodies) towards chaos and dissipation. More to the point, the sensations of effortful walking belong to Nowhere – geographically or culturally – and hence they curdle, or in the most extreme instances occlude, the special thisness of a city such as Prague. When I am short of breath, it matters little whether the air I am sucking in and blowing out is Bohemian or Mancunian.

For our physiology has no sense of place: it deploys the same repertoire of responses and delivers the same general experiences in a street in Paris in the Spring as in Manchester in the Winter; or, to bring things nearer home, whether the relevant body is ascending a staircase in Norská or performing the same act in Valley Road. My body, with its organs, their functions, the processes that sustain them, is a citizen of nowhere. Consequently, it is scarcely surprising that the list of the authors of articles in a leading medical journal such as *The Lancet* is like a League of Nations. And, as we shall discover, many parts of our bodies are named after a Czech genius who spent much of his extraordinary life in this city.

While a circular journey from home back to home must have as much downhill as uphill, the difference between going up and going down is analogous to that between earning (always difficult) and spending (always too easy): descent seems to squander hard-earned altitude. Hence the preference for the unearned ascent that is enjoyed by passengers on public transport, physiological free-riders watching Prague slide past as they travel from the beautiful and fascinating but relatively obscure suburbs to the iconic centre.

Hence CBA: fundamentally an affirmative action for the narratives of place over those obtrusive anti-narratives of the body that get one to the place. Or, to echo and contradict the famous preoccupation of Milan Kundera, a commitment to marginalizing The Unbearable Heaviness of Bodily Being, oppressing those of us who are on the home straight to ontological demotion.

Which is not, of course, to deride the human body, this state-of-the-art product of several billion years of competition between organisms, beginning with anaerobic microbes. It is absurd to overlook the astonishing evolutionary journey whose successive landmarks are: first, the acquisition of the capacity to reproduce, to move, to set itself off from its surroundings; next the ability to suss out and illuminate what comes to count as an environment; and, finally, to think about itself and what it experiences as its world – a realm constructed in conjunction with fellow humans past and present. This is the journey that ends with tourism, the search for knowledge, understanding and fun, assisted by guides and armed with cameras to capture what has not been experienced.

It is not, in short, to dismiss incarnation as a matter of regret, as a blunder.

THE ASCENT

# Hop-On:

# To Ruská or the Interval
# Between Two Sneezes

My last act before departure from our apartment is to adjust the Velcro fasteners of my shoes. The sneeze as the straps are lifted in order to be adjusted highlights the quiet of the stairwell. We close the door behind us, perhaps taking the opportunity again to note the obese babies carved on the wooden door frame, a detail that seems to remind us that we are far from home, even that we are 'On the Continent'.

We descend the stairs, noting the shoes that flat dwellers leave outside their doors – a Czech courtesy we now emulate back in England. Listening to our echoes in the unquilted stonework of the steps is another reminder of our being a long way from home. Even the Art Deco banister – pale green wrought iron that looks like a musical score awaiting notes – adds to the sense of being far from Valley Road, Bramhall. We inhale the smell of cooking: a stew that tells us that we are in Eastern Europe, though I suspect that I could not distinguish it from Lancashire hotpot in a blind tasting. There is a little struggle with the outer door whose default position is to be closed, thereby ensuring that forgetfulness will not deliver an open invitation to those whose ingress is illegitimate.

We are out.

In the street.

On our way to the Castle.

There are two routes to the 22 tram stop on Ruská.

The first takes us (strictly, we take it) to the right. We pass the Buddha restaurant and a community centre of uncertain purpose till we reach the top of Norská. We turn left down Ruská, using a zebra crossing whose rules of engagement are different from those in the UK. As we have discovered over the years, the crossing is not a place of safety, whatever the green man says: the rights of zebra crossers are not clearly defined or universally respected. We are therefore tempted to signal our presence on the crossing by waving a white handkerchief. More precisely, one of us succumbs to the temptation to do this and the other would rather he didn't. The reader may already be able to guess who's who in this micro-drama.

Our descent takes us past several cafés. On the first corner is Neklid (trans. 'unrest', 'anxiety', 'alarm', 'restlessness', 'disquiet', 'fidgetiness' – don't ask!). It is dark and snug in winter and spills out on to the pavement in Spring, where it remains until Autumn, with tables and chairs elevated on decking framed with a low wooden fence. We have had several memorable drinks in Neklid. One occasion we could not take our eyes off two stout, bearded yeomen whose grog-blossomed faces looked as if they had jumped out of a beer mat. Then there is the self-styled 'Design Friendly' café at the junction of Ruská and Estonská, the latter a lovely broad street where the grand turn-of-the-20th century houses look across at each other from a respectful distance. A few yards further down, we pass Café Bike, which promises coffee and 'waffle' – food not speech, notwithstanding the singular – and then a little 'Vinotek', a cosy hole in the wall with a handful of tables where wine is tasted, and adjectives of praise are generated, simultaneously broadcasting the good taste of the wine and the good taste of the tasters. Across the road, watching our descent, is a succession of mighty mansions built in the late 19th century as textile, sugar, and iron industries boomed. Behind them, courtesy of the roads ascending from Ruská up to Korunní, a majestic main road through Vinorhady – the most elegant suburb of Prague – we are afforded our first glimpse of the Zizkov TV tower.

It is perhaps wise to deal at once with this architectural poke in the eye. It is more than 700 feet tall - over twice the height of the highest tower of St. Vitus Cathedral. A slim silver steel three-legged structure with silver boxes attached to it, it seems from some angles to be the result of an unhappy marriage between a slim-line rocket, a pack of garden sheds, and a TV aerial in Gulliver's Brobdingnag. It terminates in a red-and-white striped fat pole whose purpose is not certain, though it is certainly not intended to suggest a barber surgeon at work. At times, the tower gives the impression of a hypodermic syringe, though its purpose is to harvest signals from the ether rather than to inject substances into the sky. While it can be surprisingly invisible from some nearby streets, it is unavoidable from pretty well everywhere else in the city, because its height is supplemented by that of its location – one of Prague's highest bumps. It wasn't finished until 1992, after the Velvet revolution, but its construction was started in 1985 and its jet-age ugliness and all-seeing gaze makes it look like the monument of Communism that it is.

There is a good reason for visiting it, and taking the lift to the public observation deck, most obviously because it offers a spectacular view of Prague but also because it is one of the few places in the city from which it cannot be seen. (The reason is the same as that which Guy de Maupassant gave for dining in the Eiffel Tower.) An additional reward is a close-up view of sculptures by David Cerny an artist and prankster who has done so much to put the Ha-Ha into Praha and whom we shall meet at intervals during our journey. The sculptures fastened to the tower are 2-metre-long fibre-glass infants with bar-codes for faces. From a distance they look like slugs, thus constituting a characteristic Czech two-fingered salute to this one-fingered up-yours left by the Soviet oppressors who built this monstrosity in the teeth of the muted protest of the citizenry.[17]

Our descent offers enough to distract us from the Zizkov Tower. Just down from the Vinotek is Studio Tiare offering manikur-pedikur-kosmetika-kadeniktu-masáze. Occupying pole position in the window is a poster showing an extraordinarily beautiful young woman with huge eyes, full lips bracketing large white teeth, and a torrent of liquorice black hair. She has a severe glare – the standard facial expression of the professional model – though this may also be a consequence of her being fixed in the squatting position for the many years we have passed the time of day with her.

Just before Ruská joins Moskevská, where we shall find the first 22 tram stop of our journey, there is what we have come to believe is a music school, though we have never seen anyone enter it armed with instruments or heard it emitting notes. It occupies a slice of a long stretch of beautiful neo-Renaissance style houses. We often pause to contemplate its entrance; more particularly the stone statues either side of the ornate door. On the left is a young man translocated from the depths of rural Czechia playing the violin, his intensity expressed in his tilting over his instrument. He is, we suspect, assisting peasants to merrymake. On the right is a maiden, whose closed eyes and flung back head testify to the passion of her singing. Her long folded skirt and a strikingly prominent stone nipple asserting itself through her blouse distracts from her bare feet that are as large-toed as those of Aristotle's sandalled feet in the giant statue we contemplated in the main square of Thessaloniki. Unlike Aristotle's, her feet have doubtless squidged through a good deal of mud and excrement as they have stamped their native grounds or tapped out the rhythm of the music played by the handsome violinist.

We pass on, renewing for the nth time our intention to look up the meaning of the beautiful ceramic title, terminating in a question mark, between the violinist and the singer. Just next door is something we acknowledge each time we pass it: an obese frog-like creature with protruding eyes and clawed hands on his belly, smiling with a complacency, undiminished by its having to support part of a balcony. It is the spitting, or secreting, image of a British political rabble-rouser, whose capacity to articulate ignorant grudges made him the main driver of Brexit. But don't get me, indeed us, started.

The alternative route to the tram begins with a left turn out of our flat. We descend past a little sunken 'Potraviny' or convenience store which a Vietnamese family keeps open all hours. The street ends on an especially high note: a handsome seven-storied 19th century apartment block, 'like an opened book'[18] with one half in Norská and the other in Kodanska. Its pink-stuccoed sides are embossed with rectangular bays and balconies. The cylindrical spine, punctured with numerous windows, gives way to a spire topped with a dark green onion dome above a balustrade which we envy for the spire-and-dome-and-finial populated views it must have of Prague. The building on the opposite side of the road is an equally impressive escapee from the Land of Far Beyond. We could be forgiven for expecting, when a window is opened near the top, to see a chocolate or a pixie rather than a plump, middle-aged, bearded man looking out. His returning downward and outward gaze turns our upward and inward one into that of two Toms a-peeping.

We therefore look away. Which is a good thing since we must now risk our lives on a zebra crossing *(vide supra)*. It is here that the 135 bus seems to lie in wait for us. Though its forehead announces its intention of heading to Chodov (rhyming slang perhaps for its attitude to us), it seems bent on swinging into our path.

Survivors of yet another road crossing, we proceed along Kodanska past the shell of a high-ceilinged Vietnamese restaurant that was a year in the decorating and ornamenting, and remained open only a few months, and thence to the other end of Estonská where the 135 threatens us from the opposite direction. This prevents us from the giving the attention they deserve to the cobbles, the majestic (a word I see I will have used nine times by the time you reach the end of this text) houses, and Haraldova Sady, a park donated by an Italian businessman. He planted mulberry orchards there and founded the Prague silk industry – something we could not tell by looking.

It is only if we cross the road to the park that we can see the magnificence of the buildings we normally hurry past *en route* to the tram. At the centre point of a street-long row of gorgeous buildings, three storeys up, is a cloaked man with a lance, riding a fine brown horse, and sporting a halo. Our safe assumption is that the canonized horseman is Good King Wenceslas. Three storeys down there is a modest patinated bronze plaque, inscribed in raised capital letters with a name and some text we cannot read. The date 1942 told us, at our first reading, all we need to know – although a subsequent inspection reveals the date to be 1946.

After we have crossed the elegant Estonská, we pass on our right a Pensioner's Centre unnervingly titled SENIOR BOX. It is rather firmly sealed off, with the only hint of what is going on within being given by a picture of half a dozen elders round a laden wooden table. We get a better view in dark evenings when we see much autumnal beer-fueled animation. Next to Senior Box there is the picture-framing shop where we arranged for our map of Prague to be captured for our lounge. It is also an outlet for live art, including one or two eye-popping nudes, notwithstanding that on the opposite side of the road is a school. The beautiful turn of the century building must look less charmingly antique to the children entering it with varying degrees of disinclination, boredom, and perhaps fear.

We reach Moskevská and pass a mere four cafés on the final hundred yards to the 22 stop. The little field opposite the tram stop – filling in an area of irregularity where cobbled streets settle their differences with steps – seems to specialize in virtuoso black-bird songs in the spring, though they have a touch of a Moravian accent – or so I joked, I thought at the time successfully, with my Czech daughter-in-law.

During the journey, my body has been unpacking its own narrative. A trio of co-codamol tablets, taken to ward off neck pain during our expedition, has been absorbed via the intelligent wall of my gut, entered my blood stream, and been delivered to the relevant tracts of the nervous system. By this means it has been transformed from chemicals into optimism or, if that is a little too propositional, into well-being and free-floating good cheer.

This may be why I have reflected that it is never necessary to run after a tram, even when a possible candidate creams past before we reach the stop. Thanks to Prague's wonderful transport system, there is no such thing as missing a tram: we are simply early for the next one. Indeed, we might even pass up the next one because it does not have the wide windows of the latest model. Our wait at the stop is scarcely long enough for us to fail to make sense of the adverts on the shelter.

The 22 that arrives is an example of the most recent variant. Its face is almost entirely given over to a square cyclopean eye and the windscreen wipers are like oars. We climb aboard, thus commencing two out of 373,434,000 passenger journeys on the Prague trams in 2018, the only year for which I have figures, though these may be updated in a subsequent edition of this book if it sells sufficiently well to warrant reissue.

The tram door sneezes closed – unconsciously referring to the Velcro sneeze of my shoes – and the driver peeps a warning of impending departure.

# Ruská - Krymská

We are treated to a third instance of mechanized sternutation as a fellow passenger inserts her ticket into the machine that registers it with a sneeze.

We have scarcely started searching for a seat before we have become the beneficiaries of youthful courtesy: two citizens of Prague jump up. We assume this is prompted by an instantaneous ocular carbon dating of our ageing flesh and the appearance we may give that we are, or may be, embarked on the descent from up-and-about to down-and-out. It is this, too, that enables us lawfully to ride ticketless: the cumulation of time in our faces counts as our ticket.

We accept the vacated seats with mixed feelings. We are of course grateful that we can stare at Prague without strap-hanging for dear life. And we are relieved that the world is less relentlessly selfish or self-absorbed than it sometimes seems. But there is a tinge of sadness, prompted by reflection on how rarely this courtesy is evident in our native country, once famous for its (admittedly often-hypocritical) politeness. If I am offered a seat in the London tube it is almost invariably by a foreign visitor. I am also anxious that my words of gratitude in Czech should sound like a fulsome 'Thank you very much' rather than a perfunctory or entitled 'Ta'. I therefore italicize my *Dekují* with the carnal Esperanto of a warm smile.

We have window seats. Yippee! As we swerve round the corner from Moskevská into Ruská, we enter a steep ascent towards Krymská. I have – or rather labour at – a flashback to the time when we first came here on an early visit to Prague. On that occasion, this stretch of road seemed remote beyond imagination: a foreign part of a foreign city. The sense, a decade or more ago, of the doubly far-flung applying to a place that is now, after many visits, neither far nor flung, is as elusive as it is complex. It is as if the remoteness of the self that first came down this slope – being guided to the once-famous Shakespeare Café and bookshop – has cancelled out the remoteness of the slope.

*Krymská* ('Crimea') is said to be 'the hippest' area of Prague. Seen from this tram, it looks a bit tatty, even grubby. Which brings me to something I want to deal with early to get it out of the way.

No city is perfect. Indeed, imperfections are inescapable. Utilities cannot be readily or routinely delivered in neo-classical structures. Drainpipes, litter baskets, waste land or building sites to populate or correct it, elephantine bin lorries panting up the road, rows of utilitarian mineral orange sodium lights elevated on plain concrete stems revealing wide streets as collocations of accidents, are inescapable urban universals. All cities are maculated with un-intentional spaces where instruments of labour are de-animated to clutter by the pause in agency. And ordinary citizens must live in ordinary houses -as indeed does your interlocutor. No-one will cross Europe to visit his low-rise, English vernacular detached house in Stockport, much though he loves it. Even less will social, afford-able, housing – one of the great achievements of decency scaled up to an urban level – attract pilgrims feverishly turning pages of guidebooks as they try to connect what they see with what they read and unpack the promise of the latter from the experience of the former. And the lower floors of even the most magnificent buildings in Prague are often occupied by shops. With shops come shop fronts bearing plastic names, and windows whose contents often add up less to a display than to bricolage.

In Prague, there is much mitigation of such necessary banalities. Many utilities are indeed ornate. A couple of examples will have to stand for thousands: the wonderful *trompe d'oeil* wall in the Metro below Námesti miru which I have already mentioned; and the angels, with clock faces between them, on the beautiful Vinorhady Water Tower used to pump water from an underground reservoir. And I cannot resist a third: the manhole covers that look like giant coins.

There is another approach to mitigation. Much social housing has been exiled to the edges of the city in so-called *paneláky*: multi-storey apartments built out of prefabricated panels. They look positively romantic on distant hills and their reputation has risen since they were built to house the rising urban population in the 1950s.[19] The hostility to these "undignified rabbit pens, slated for liquidation" imposed on the people of Prague by the "unwelcome intruders and occupiers" of the communist era has in recent years been challenged.[20]

Even so, there is much that is ordinary in Prague as there is in every city, much that will inevitably fall short of anything a tourist may have paid good money to see. There will be necessary disappointments. But there are also unnecessary ones. I want to dwell briefly on a class of these for a short while. I am talking about graffiti or grrraffiti or graffaeces.

On one side of the road, and to a lesser extent on the other, the buildings between the Ruská and Krymská tram stops are smeared with them. The road consequently looks unwashed. That is why, when we have friends to stay in our flat in Norská, we warn them in advance: we do not want their first impression of the city, and of our quarter of it, to be too influenced by this visual litter – this litter-you-can't-pick-up – and Prague to be judged accordingly.

Too much of the face of Prague is defaced in this way. Less, it must be said, than parts of other European capitals but not much less. The arrival to Paris by train is sleeved in graffiti. Some quarters of Berlin are especially afflicted with this malign rash, though the perpetrators seem to be more talented with their spray guns than those in Prague. The graffiti are, for obvious reasons, concentrated on the ground floor and, being at eye-level, can sour one's impression of even the most beautiful buildings. What effect this disfigurement has on the residents it is easy to imagine: it must be like encountering the same dollop of dog dirt on the door step or a drunk's vomit on the wall each time you return home; or being faced with the mockery of a malicious, smirking face.

Graffiti are puzzling at many levels. They are clearly not explained, as litter can be, by mere idleness or thoughtlessness. In his quietly impassioned lamentation on ordinary litter, Theodore Dalrymple – who described the United Kingdom as 'the litter capital of Europe' – notes that it seemed as if people "dropped the packaging of what they ate as a cow defaecates in a field without awareness of an alternative."[21] Litter is a symptom that the second person plural has grown so numerous as to have become an impersonal collective that couldn't care a damn about the collective.

Posting graffiti, by contrast, requires positive effort and some outlay on equipment. Devices for spraying paint and the paint to spray with them cost money. And the defacement of buildings must be done out of sight – under the cover of darkness: the hours of the house-spoiler are as inconvenient as those kept by the housebreaker. What, then, motivates these 'artists'? The desire to spoil things is often as strong as the impulse to build them. It may be fueled by a resentment at living in a city where there is so much beauty, grandeur, and history, and which people cross the world to admire.

The question brings me to Adolf Loos – a Czech architect 'who became more famous for his ideas and writings than for his buildings'. [22] Loos has been most celebrated and reviled for his declaration that 'All ornament is crime'. By this criterion, Prague is a vast crime scene: every wall, window, roof, door, banister, is an opportunity for ornamentation. Loos was of course wrong. On the other hand, graffiti – incompetent and unwanted – are most certainly a crime.

There may be some paint-spaffers who, believing that they are indeed artists without inverted commas, wish to exhibit their talents, notwithstanding that their work has necessarily to be anonymous. The frequently expressed idea of graffiti as 'the art of the people', a democratic public art, is difficult to uphold. It privileges the producer over any consumer. Even if the artists are talented, their emissions remain uninvited invasions of everyone's visual field. Uninvited guests who are witty are no less uninvited and not necessarily welcome, especially if they demand attention. Anyway, the vast majority of 'street art' in Krymská and elsewhere in Prague – and indeed the world – is little more than random streaks and stains and ill-executed letters of the alphabet adding up to nothing. It has no justification to be classified as art, not even when that term has been widened to encompass any item that lays claim to this status.

Even if the stuff were talented, this would not mitigate their status as litter. After all, discarded packages looked at closely are often quite beautiful. I have before me a tin that once contained Nescafé Gold – Barista Style, rich and full-bodied, finely ground, coffee- so I know that of which I speak. Its visual echo of the warm darkness of the Kozel beer mat adds to its connotative glow. But I would not enjoy it if it were replicated on the side of my house or indeed the house across the road.

There have been times when graffiti have served a political purpose, expressing views that lacked another platform. The best-known example in Prague is the John Lennon Wall in The Little Quarter. In the 1970s and 1980s poems, messages, and drawings could be inscribed on the Wall by students and other brave, disaffected citizens, to protest against the regime. They were described in the newspapers as 'alcoholics, mentally deranged, sociopathic, and agents of Western capitalism' – quite a lot to live up to.[23] Their work was regularly white-washed by the authorities who painted THE WALL IS OVER! to press their point home. But the wall was not over and the 'Lennonists' (sic) continued to make their subversive points. After the Velvet Revolution, the Wall lost much, most, perhaps all, of its subversive force: it is now a place of pilgrimage for tourists, a palimpsest on which anyone can write, draw, or paint anything. The graffiti here, as elsewhere in Prague, are unwelcome gatecrashers in the cityscape and as far from the romance of rebellion as the dog dirt on the pavement, which certainly awakens citizens to a higher level of alertness but does little to advance the well-being of mankind or the cause of justice. I was a Liverpudlian whose adolescence coincided with the rise of the Beatles – yes, they were the greatest songwriters since Schubert, as the music critic William Mann claimed.[24] Even so, I do not regard the Lennon wall as a destination worthy of a 743-mile flight.

The idea of graffiti as art and as protest, as giving voice to the voiceless, was something I once explored in a story that seems unlikely to be published so I may as well tell it now. Its protagonist was 'Midge' a short, square, permanently angry, young woman in a state of endless protest against the *status quo*. She wore Mao-ist garments barnacled with vast numbers of badges proclaiming the many causes to which she lent her support. She embraced the idea of graffiti as giving a voice to those who are usually 'silenced'. On one occasion she worked with her 'community' – a handful of equally enraged *enragés* – to cover the entire end wall of a terrace with an uncommissioned mural. It took a weekend of labour where energy was as plentiful as talent was scarce. It was titled 'The Art of the People' lest this should not be understood. The morning after it was completed, Midge went to inspect the masterpiece. It had been thoroughly trashed by other anonymous graffiti artists, with the inscription 'The Art of Other People'.

Such a mean-spirited tale of comeuppance is a marker of the intensity of my loathing of graffiti – especially those that pretend to be politically significant. There are, of course, occasions where otherwise suppressed voices in brutal regimes can speak, as in the case of the Lennon wall. This is territory that the reader does not require me as a guide. I mention it, however, to justify reference to the Prague artist David Cerny who has already appeared in these pages and will pop up, cocking snooks at intervals.

Cerny came to fame as an art student in 1991, not long after the Velvet Revolution. Working with his friends, he covered with pink paint the monumental tank that had been installed in July 1945 to commemorate the liberation of Prague by the Red Army, a liberation that subsequent decades had shown to be less liberating. He placed a large erect middle finger on the turret. The outraged authorities re-painted the tank green and Cerny was arrested. In protest at his arrest, some members of the parliament, who were immune from prosecution, re-painted it pink. After several cycles of green-to-pink-and-pink-to-green it lost its status as a national monument and was eventually put somewhere where it could cause little offence in either of its (Soviet) Green or (Velvet Revolution) Pink iterations.

Leaving aside such rare exceptions, graffiti must be con-demned for, at the very least, making everywhere an any-old-where – rather as tattoos disfigure beautiful flesh with an unhappy fusion between a bruise and a cliché. Or as torn fly-posters for a show that has long been discontinued remind us that the past leaves a trail that is not always beautiful, not always tinged with melancholy, and that it does not tidy up as it goes along.

I wish to distance myself from Adolf Loos who claimed that "The modern man who tattoos himself is either a criminal or a degenerate… The tattooed who are not in prison are latent crimi-nals or degenerate aristocrats".[25] Loos' reference to 'degenerates' makes uncomfortable reading, given the use to which the term was shortly to be put in German-speaking countries; and even more so in the light of the fact that Loos was a paedophile who may have continued his predatory activities even when he knew he was dying of syphilis. For this reason alone, I would not, however, go so far as to condemn the street-stainers as 'degenerates'. Rather, I would, on behalf of all the beautiful cities of Europe, beseech ye graffiti artists, in the bowels of Christ, or the passenger-laden bowels of trams, to desist.

Hence my anxiety to pre-empt any impression of sordidness that guests at our flat might derive from looking out of the window of the tram as it ascends along Ruská through Krymská. I try to re-direct their attention from what is immediately before them with descriptions of the near reaches of the absent: the wonderful broad streets of Vinorhady on one side and the hippest Krymská street hidden away, leading to a beautifully landscaped park to which it invisibly points.

The temptation to hop off the tram at this point – at the very least to wash out the taste of tetchiness – is strong but not overwhelming. Let us remain in our precious seats until the next stop.

# Krymská to Jana Masaryka

The tram continues uphill and Ruská gives way to Francouszká until the slope flattens and we reach *Jana Masaryka*.

On the way we have passed Machova – a street named for Karel Hynek Mácha ¬ a poet who died at the Keatsian age of 25, the day before he was due to be married to the mother of his child, and not long after his lyrical epic poem 'May' was published. More precisely it was self-published as no respectable publisher would take it. Posterity, as is its wont, has judged otherwise: 'May' is considered one of the greatest Czech poems and the poet has had, though not of course enjoyed, an extraordinary posthumous existence. He has more than once found himself portrayed on postage stamps and in this form, hitching a ride on envelopes, flown around and beyond "well-beloved earth, beautiful earth,/ my cradle and grave, the womb that gave me birth".[26]

In his philatelic after-life, he is often represented by a representation: his monument in Petrina. Petrina is a beautiful, wooded hill, adjacent to the rise that elevates the Castle and St. Vitus cathedral to their position above Prague. User-friendly paths wind through Petrina, each twist and turn offering new revelations of the city and of the river whose hairpin loop, enclosing a peninsula called Holesovice, blunts delight with slight confusion.

The Mácha monument – which always takes us by surprise - is something to behold. The poet's presence is italicized by the sculptor's fidelity to the creases in his waistcoat and the furrows of his luxuriant cymotrichous hair where, in winter, snow collects. He is elevated on an elaborate, two-levelled plinth. In his right hand he carries an open notebook, laid lightly on a low wall, while in his left hand there is a bouquet of lilacs. He looks at the flowers with adoring blind metal eyes and inhales their scent with the anosmic rapture of metal nostrils. Love, youth, spring, and poetry are all gathered up in this site of pilgrimage.

The correct term for the light green garment coating the monument is 'verdigris' but it seems wrong, as it connotes scrap yards and the wrong kind of decay: of rot and rubbish, rather than poetic mutability. Better to speak of a patina, a marriage between metal and oxygen, conveying a poignantly ambiguous message in which the loss and preservation of past time are plaited together. The green carries a hint of Mácha's spring month – a strange alloy of bronze irony – brought about by his statue's mating with the air, egged on by the wind and rain. The life of statues is as precarious as the posthumous fame of those whom they commemorate.

The heavy burden of significance carried by Mácha in his afterlife was signalled by an event of great poignancy in May 1939.[27] Two months earlier the forces of evil had completed the appropriation of the Republic of Czechoslovakia. Slovakia had allied itself with the Axis and retained some independence while the remainder of the country had become the Protectorate of Bohemia and Moravia, under the 'protection' of the Nazi government. On this May Day, Mácha was exhumed from his resting place in Literomice, a little town forty or so miles outside of Prague. The grave was described as 'a pauper's grave', though the absolute impoverishment of non-existence makes this distinction of little concern to the dead. He was taken to the Pantheon of the National Museum in Prague where he lay in state. His coffin was then transported on a hearse, drawn by two white horses, and chaperoned by mounted guards, to the National Cemetery next to Vysehrad, the 1,000-year castle. There he joined eminent compatriots such as Jan Evangelista Purkinje, Antonin Dvorak, Bedrich Smetana, Karel Capek, and Alphonse Mucha. When we visited the cemetery, we were struck by the competitiveness in the housing of the dead: 'keeping up with the boneses' one might say. Or one of us, whose mind is a pundemic, will.

Mácha's re-interment took place on the next day:

"Perhaps half Prague" made its way to Vysehrad,
and those who were able brought with them a bouquet
of spring flowers. The grave was strewn with white narcissi,
red carnations, and blue lilac – the national colours of
the defunct Czechoslovak Republic.[28]

Along with the body of Mácha – the poet of spring, youth, love, and hope – was buried the 20-year-old Republic, which had been the fulfilment of a dream that had occupied the minds of those whose lives allowed space for such dreams in the 300 years since the defeat at the battle of Bilá Hora in 1620, whose name was imprinted on the forehead of the 22 tram, as its final destination. It would be half a century before the Republic was resurrected, after the collapse of the Nazi regime and the end of the 40-year Soviet occupation exercised through a succession of puppet governments, when the jackboots of the right had been defeated and the jackboots of the left had retreated.

For a citizen of the United Kingdom, born after the Second World War and too late even for peacetime National Service, any visit to Prague prompts thoughts about moral luck; more precisely, historical luck as a result of which it has not been necessary to risk one's life, to go into hiding or exile, or to comply with things that disgust me with myself, and to bite my tongue while ignorant bullies lay down the law, if I am to go about my daily business relatively unhindered or to protect my children from the obliteration of their life chances.

Because we accept this as normal, I cannot resist quoting the opening of John Maynard Keynes' prophetic *The Economic Consequences of the Peace:*

> The power to become habituated to his surroundings is a marked characteristic of mankind. Very few of us realize with conviction the intensely unusual, unstable, complicated, unreliable, temporary nature of the economic organisation with which western Europe has lived for the last half-century. We assume some of the most peculiar and temporary of our late advantages as natural, permanent, and to be depended upon, and we lay our plans accordingly. On this sandy and false foundation, we scheme for social improvement and dress our political platforms, pursue our animosities and particular ambitions, and feel ourselves with enough margin in hand to foster, not assuage, civil conflict in the European family.[29]

# Hop-Off: A Visit to Grébovka

Such thoughts would have been appropriate had they come to us as we dismounted at *Jana Masaryka* tram stop and walked down the road named after Thomas Masaryk's son. Masaryk senior – philosopher, visionary, and statesman – fathered, if anyone did, Czechoslovakia and was its first president. Perhaps such thoughts did occur to us – directed as a rebuke to Brexiteers (don't get me started) rather than to myself. The reader is promised that this will be my last reference to that act of national self-harm made possible as a triumph of simple falsehoods over complex truths. Whether I will keep that promise remains to be seen.

Jan Masaryk. How does one do justice to the story of this mercurial, courageous, complex, witty, tragic man? Suffice to note that Jan, after ten years as a drop-out in USA (his mother's native country), working among other things as a pianist in a cinema and a labourer in a brass foundry (where he ran English literacy classes for his co-workers) and spending his limited earnings on gambling and attractive women, returned to his homeland in 1913. He was shortly afterwards conscripted into the Austro-Hungarian army to fight in the First World War. After Czechoslovakia was created in 1919, he became a diplomat, ultimately representing his country as Ambassador to the UK. In 1938, he resigned in protest at the German appropriation of Sudetenland and went into exile in London. For the duration of The Second World war, he was the Foreign Minister of the Czechoslovak government-in-exile.

After the defeat of the Axis, he returned to Czechoslovakia as Foreign Secretary. The government, however, was increasingly dominated by the communist party, taking its orders from the Soviet Union. Eventually, he was the only non-communist minister in the cabinet. He was alone in supporting the Marshall Plan of which Stalin disapproved. "I left for Moscow as the minister for foreign affairs of a sovereign state. I am returning as Stalin's stooge".

In March 1948, a month after the formation of a Communist government (so-called "Victorious February"), he was found dead, in his pyjamas, in the courtyard of the Foreign Ministry beneath his bathroom window. His death has been attributed variously to suicide, accident, and murder in a series of cold case inquiries. The most recent, in 2021, concluded that suicide, accident, or murder were all possible causes of those few moments of terror and a shriek like an acoustic flame in the Bohemian air, separating a rich and conflicted life from a dead body.

Whatever its cause, the tragedy was immensely convenient for the Czech Communist Party which had assumed a Soviet-controlled mixture of power and impotence that it would retain until 1989. On Masaryk's memorial plaque there is a quote: 'Truth will prevail' (the Czech national motto derived from Jan Hus and adopted by his father) to which he had added 'but it will be a chore' giving the final word to his inner Good Soldier Schweik, to the self who fled from his perhaps oppressively serious academic, public-spirited family, to drop out in USA, before he returned to serve his country. He shares with Mácha a philatelic after-life on envelopes, as a detached head, looking rather too serious, even wistful, for such a wonderfully humorous man, next to his initials and his enviably calligraphic signature.

It would be wrong to overlook Jan Masaryk's support for the Benes decree which ordered the expulsion of 3,000,000 ethnic Germans from the Sudetenland, a northwestern area of the Czech Republic bordering on Germany, after the end of the war. Yes, the Sudetenland Germans had welcomed the invading forces, but many of them had been reluctant, and often second class, citizens in the newly created Czechoslovakia after the First World War. The expulsion, with the loss of everything they possessed, and the extreme cruelty with which they were treated – rape, intentional starvation, robbery, slave labour, incarceration, internment in concentration camps, murder – were legitimated by the Benes decree as "justified acts of retribution". Between 20,000 and 270,000 deaths were associated with this act of revenge, often forgotten by Czechs. As for Jan Masaryk, he "boasted that the Czech nation was finally 'over with the Germans of Czechoslovakia... There is no possible way to get us to live under the same umbrella again'". Thus, the voice of ethnic cleansing.[30] And of revenge against the Nazi rapists of the young country his father had done so much to bring into being.

At the entrance to the street named after him – chosen because it had included his family home – is a conspicuous sign composed of large red plastic letters on a larger yellow plastic background: DROGERIE. After this wobbly start, Jana Masaryka settles down to 19th century elegance, its buildings beautifully maintained, their majestic (that word again!) stone facades painted in soft pinks and yellows and browns. As with many streets in Vinorhady, the wide pavements are planted with trees, so the sun of hot afternoons is filtered, and the quiet, broken by intermittent traffic, seems particularly special – a positive hush. The pavements are checkerboards of squares, big pixels inside bigger pixels.

There is a network of such roads, many named, as is often the case in Prague, after other countries or cities: Belgická, Lucemburská, Americká, Holandská, Madridská, Záhrebská, to name a few. They have a natural point of convergence in an hexagonal piazza whose sides accommodate five cafés with a fountain in the centre. Or rather they converge in my mind. The uncooperative map does not, however, corroborate this. Private spaces constructed by strolls, or hurries, or something in between, and printed on a confused tapestry woven out of tangled threads of other strolls and hurries in this street, city, country and other streets, cities, and countries, are not registered on the maps any more than the creases, deepened by endless folding and unfolding, are matched by scars across the terrain abstractly portrayed in the map.

We are eventually led – by a zig-zag route where the zigs correct the zags, and the zags correct the zigs, and neither is the fault either of the roads or the maps in our hands – to the beautiful Havlickova sady (park) with the majestic (I know) Villa Grébovka overlooking its slopes. Among the latter are the remains of the 14th century vineyards built by Charles IV that gave Vinorhady its name. They afford a compendious view of southern and eastern Prague.

The Villa Grébovka is modelled on the Italian Renaissance suburban villas favoured by the Austro-Hungarian aristocracy as their summer homes. It was built in 1870 and its subsequent history has mirrored that of the insurgent (the First Republic liberated from the Austro-Hungarian Empire after the First World War), crushed (by the Third Reich), crushed again (by Communism), and resurrected (Velvet Revolution) nation.[31] That history gives a certain urgency to the Villa's present role as the headquarters of the Central and Eastern European Law Institute whose mission is to 'advance the rule of law locally and globally'. The tragic history of Czechoslovakia, perhaps encapsulated in the image of Jan Masaryk, propelled to his death from the Foreign Ministry where he stood increasingly alone in his defence of liberal democracy between the tyranny of Nazism and the tyranny of Communism, adds poignancy to the nobility of this aspiration.

The grounds of the Villa have delivered many sunlit dawn walks when the dew on the grass polishes the dust off our shoes; dawns so peaceful that in Summer the fizzing of the insects in the flowering trees – only slightly louder than the buzzing, like thought dust, that has enclosed my head for the last decade – is the nearest there is to noise. You can almost hear the leaves, detached singly by the gentlest of forces from the Rapunzel tresses of the willow trees, pirouetting to the ground. Red squirrels, hooded crows, jays, and doves add to the quiet animation of the early hour. The doves weave a crochet of sound-smoke connecting trees whose shadows on the grass create the most beautiful natural artwork. Even the carping of the crows speaking their seasonless charcoal seems to add to, rather than detract from, the peace. As for the air, the slightest of breezes, doubled by our walking, just makes the transition from stuff to process, from being to becoming. The sound of distant trains is replicated in the occasional gust harvested by pine trees.

Thus, the mornings. When we return in the afternoon, the park is more populated but, surprisingly for a public space, nobody seems bent on annoying anyone else. We neglect the grotto, the fountain, the pavilion, the café, the gazebo, the sloping vineyards, the view of Prague, and find shelter in the shadows cast by the trees, settling down to a book that has nothing to do with Prague.

To stretch out on the grass is momentarily to embrace the condition of being embodied subjects: the whole-body delicious-ness of the relaxation of limbs, and living the distances between an itch in the ear, the soft rain of acoustic filings not quite gathered up to tinnitus, the slight upwelling of saliva, fingers touching each other, pressure on the buttocks, legs made to know their length by the feet italicizing themselves in the after-touch of their journeying over the surfaces of the city. Our viewpoints on Prague acknowledge themselves as what they are: viewblobs.

The ache of a fixed yawn, unrelieved by yawning, is the inheritance of one of many early risings. Somnolence overtakes us, spreading like sun-warmed mist, igniting a whole-body smile. The relaxation of the *levator palpebrae superioris* (the smaller the muscle, the bigger the name) permits the descent of a curtain cut-ting off the viewblob from any view and interrupting an afternoon in Prague with a private stretch of night. Drowsiness is at one with the doves' coo-ing that seems like fur-lined fingers-stalls of smoke, gossipy comments, oohing-oohing asides. The sleep of a dozy afternoon connects me with nearby Petrin, with distant Cheshire countryside where we have taken so many walks, our garden at home in Stockport, a square in Edinburgh, a pine forest in Samos, and...and...and...

And thence to sleep. The city dreamt of by Libuse half a million afternoons ago is displaced by a sequence of inconsequential dreams. I will not share them: you did not open these pages for a stranger to bore you with his dreams. They are not only implausible – which is what we might expect in dreams – but also insultingly banal and poorly constructed, with neither sex nor violence to enhance their box office attraction. Nor are they funny or clever or informative or in any other way illuminating. Enough said.

"Dreams are notably means of discovering our own inclinations. The wise man learns to know himself by the night's black mantle, as by the searching beams of day. In sleep we have the naked and natural thoughts of our souls…"[32] Thus the essayist Owen Feltham in 1628, nearly three hundred years before Moravian Uncle Sigmund made the same mistake. Contrary to what in many quarters counts as received wisdom, we do not in our dreams communicate in symbols, presenting ourselves to ourselves as an inkblot to be interpreted. Or not usefully or helpfully or illuminatingly, anyway. Owen and Sigmund are mistaken equally regarding the light hauntings of a shallow afternoon doze on the grass and the full-blown narratives of the four-postered time-tabled slumber of the night.

It is not what dreams signify but what they are that is mysterious. And at least as magical as any dream is the fact that Mr. Feltham's thoughts, given wings with a feather pen, have Easy jetted to this place 700 miles and 400 years distant, to be read in his bed by one whose unsuccessful attempt to defeat insomnia resulted in this afternoon moment when he is gathered up in his own arms and laid gently down to earth, and the soft, silent shutters replace the prospect of Prague with a micro-night tingling with light-echoes of day, starred with the circulation's murmur to itself, as the smoke of thought dissolves into a nap half way in duration between a blink and a night.

The mystery of the dissociation between our bodies dropped in the park and our minds in an elsewhere that is a nowhere remains untouched by the 24 volumes of the Collected Works of the Moravian Magus described by Vladimir Nabokov less charitably as "the Viennese Witch Doctor" as "a great comic writer", and "the Austrian crank with a shabby umbrella" who had a "a vulgar, shabby, fundamentally mediaeval world picture".[33]

Nevertheless, Moravian Freud earns a place in this chronicle because he justifies a sideways glance at another work of David Cerny. This time it is a sculpture of a besuited Herr Professor Freud. He is to be found in Husova, one of the busiest streets in the Old Quarter of Prague, hanging by his right hand from a pole projecting from a building. His left hand remains nonchalantly in his trouser pocket.

We are woken by an inquisitive dog following a trail of Arsebook messages. This simple stimulus reverses the earlier mysterious dissolution into sleep with the greater mystery of our instantly reassembling ourselves and a district of Prague defined by a gaze tinted with a little knowledge. The two-way alchemy between being wide-awake and deeply asleep and back again does not impress us as much as it should; indeed, we feel slightly deflated like a teddy bear that has leaked sawdust. The metaphysical wonder that we are rarely wonders at the metaphysical wonder that we are.

We retrace steps that, in this sunny day, have left only prints in our memory, and unreliable ones at that. We exit the park, journey along Rybalkova, and, more surprised than we ought to be, find ourselves back in Machova.

During the latter part of our return to the tram, the theme of historic luck returns to preoccupy us. Unlike some of our fellow passengers on the tram, we have never had our courage tested by the minions of a totalitarian state, with their fists, weapons, edicts, and the million-tentacled agents of their power. It is, however, a kind of indulgence to claim vicarious guilt. Dostoyevsky's assertion[34] – which we once saw inscribed on a memorial to the Berlin Wall – that we are all responsible for everything in this world is a dangerous sentiment to which we can assent only insincerely. It seems perverse, licensing a moral levelling up that can slide into blaming victims for their plight and the opponents of evil for the evil which they oppose.

What is true, we might think, as we return along Jana Masaryka Street is that those of us who have had the luck – extraordinary by historical standards – of being born in a country not yet ruled by tyrants, having access to adequate food and dental anaesthesia, being treated with respect by the police, enjoying a long life expectancy, do not deserve our luck. How could we? If we are guilty, it is of taking our luck for granted as the natural state of things and of doing less than we might towards transforming the lives of those who are less lucky than we are, or keeping silent when the rights and protections we take for granted are abused. Or when we forget what our luck has cost those who are not so lucky. On these counts largely guilty as charged.

We are not, however, alone in forgetting what has happened, and the courage of those who made it possible to unhappen, the price they paid, never to be reimbursed. This is mourned by the Czech writer Ivan Klima. He spent four years of his childhood with his parents in Theresienstadt concentration camp. After the war, he saw Communism as a source of hope. This did not last. His father was arrested again, this time by the communists. He was subjected to a show trial because, as an engineer running a factory, he had failed to meet its production quota. Ivan himself was expelled from the communist party for a speech criticizing censorship. After the Prague Spring his books were banned in his native country. Now he regrets how, in the years after the Velvet revolution, totalitarianism has been replaced by 'total entertainment'.[35] The courage of those who lost everything in opposing iniquity is rewarded with the ultimate ingratitude of amnesia.

It is reflected in the sad note to the Exhibition in 2019 to commemorate the 30th anniversary of the Velvet Revolution:

---

Because the ethos and ideals of the November legacy have not yet been fulfilled and, to this day, remain a vivid challenge for us.

This awakens an uneasiness that suspects that there might after all be some truth in what Father Zossima said about the universality of guilt. We elders have not worked hard enough at turning our own extraordinary luck into improving the luck of others.

Fortunately, we have a tram to catch.

# Jana Masaryka to Náměstí míru

Normally, we would return to Norská after our visit to Havlickova sady and Grébovka. The fore-ordained structure of this text is, however, too precious to sacrifice on the altar of a realism that feels bound by fidelity to small truths. Instead, we shall re-set the clock, re-start the afternoon, and resume our journey to the Castle.

And so, this paragraph, which breaches the boundary between autobiography and fiction, boards the tram. Not for the first time, I relish the recorded female voice announcing the next stop: *"Pristi zastavká* ('next stop') Náměstí míru". It is a voice 'redolent of Bohemian summer evenings'. Or so I say and perhaps think.

Before us – only two stops on from the graffiti-stained walls of Krymská – lies the first spectacular example of Pragitecture. The twin spires of St Ludmila's church are perfectly placed to be seen at the end of Francouszká and, more distantly, we glimpse our ultimate destination represented by the three spires of the Cathedral encircled by the Castle. In addition to numerous cafés, we note a flower shop, an outlet for electronic goods, a mini-market, DIEM, and an 'Antikvariat' whose window looks like a car boot sale, selling stuff ranging from bric-a-brac to serious, that is to say expensive, antiques. We look out for the bust of Lenin in the window. Its pure white marble makes his baldness twice as bald and the sunglasses on his nose twice as funny. This might have been an opportunity to reflect on the idea of the knick-knack – a word meaning 'a pleasing

trifle' created by a reduplication of 'knack' meaning 'a small ornament of minor value' – and to trace the borders between antiques,
knick-knacks, and junk. Lenin, however, is the signal for us to stand
up to prepare to disembark if – as is often the case – we want to
again break our journey to the Castle.

For a septuagenarian on a tram, the decision when to
stand up is explicit because it is hedged about with uncertainty. He
or she does not merely stand up: he or she *does* 'standing up'. The
challenge is to remain upright while the tram decelerates and, as
is the way with moving vehicles, jerks to its halt, as if each section
of the journey were a sentence requiring a fat full stop. This brings
hazards – most obviously that of falling over, or of banging into a
sharp or unyielding surface. But there is an additional danger at-
tending the small Bayesian error of being surprised by the tram:
being flung against another passenger who may not appreciate
this unwanted carnal intimacy. The latter is of particular concern
to a male antiquity in the era of 'Hashtag[36] Me Too'.

---

This is not a grumble about being embodied. Of course, it
means that, unlike angels, we are subjected to the many humiliations
that come with incarnation; for example, the cognitive limitations
resulting from being located and 'low-cated', having one's view
blocked. But there is the rich compensation of hugs and smiles and
the many modes of calorific and perhaps more intimate exchange.
Indeed, it goes deeper: incarnation is a necessary condition of being

anywhere in particular, anyone in particular, and having anything in particular to do, say, or think. The lives of the *dis*embodied after all are pretty empty. A day in eternity must seem – well, eternity.

I mention this to highlight a theme haunting these pages: that the person seeking to know the city is also an organism who has to be transported through it and, as such, subject to what we call 'the laws of nature' though – as has been argued by a contemporary thinker – they are strictly 'the habits of nature' translated into 'the laws of science'. [37] The ontological democracy between persons and things is signified in the co-swaying of the strap that is hung on to and of the one hanging on to it to maintain rectitude, dignity, and propriety.

The vehicle has oozed to a halt – no jerk after all - and it is time for another hop off.

# Hop-off: Námestí míru

We might begin by noting the irony of the conflict over its name: Námestí míru meaning 'Peace Square'.

The square was founded in 1884. The beautiful suburb of Vinorhady had now developed to the point where such an honour was justified. It was first christened Purkinje Square, memorializing someone whom we shall meet in due course. Between 1926 and 1933, it became 'Peace Square' – in part to commemorate a visit to the local town hall by Rabindranath Tagore to give a lecture on the path to world peace.[38] It was re-named Vinorhady Square in 1933, perhaps in response to the fear that embracing peace may not be the best preparation for dealing with the poison brewing beyond the borders of the young Republic. In 1940, it was called 'Reich Square', and retained this name until 1945 when it was once more Vinorhady Square. In Spring 1948, a communist government – 'peaceful, joyful, and healthy' like its Soviet masters – finally crushed any opposition and renamed the square 'Peace Square'.

It retained this name after the (largely) peaceful Velvet Revolution. Notwithstanding his allergy to the word 'peace', in the light of its use by tyrannical governments and totalitarian dictatorships, Václav Havel argued for a 'semantic *perestroika*' that would rehabilitate the word, and honour those 'quixotic' opponents to the tyranny that followed Prague Spring. And so, it is into Peace Square – Námestí míru – that we descend from the tram.

For a square so named it is far from peaceful: it has a buzz most hours of the day, and most of the days of the week. Trams, buses, and Metro trains disgorge large helpings of folk who, if they are not simply changing trams, buses, and trains, spread out into the square. Its vast central space is often occupied by the market named after St. Ludmilla (of whom more presently); and winter days are perfumed with the scent of Glühwein and cinnamon tredelniks. Beautiful roads fanning out in all directions – Francouszká, Americká, Jugoslávská, Slezská, Anglická, Rumunská, and Italská – make its hubbub a true hub.

It is dominated – so long as you are not busy looking at your phone or responding to the unrelenting demands of a two-year old – by a twin-spired neo-gothic basilica. Built at the end of the 19th century, it is named after St. Ludmila of Bohemia. Her giant portrait – commissioned to celebrate the 1100th anniversary of her death in 921 – is hung above the entrance. Her massive halo, competing with a crown for space on her holy head, looks as if it would obstruct her passage through doorways and if not sustainably energized would have left a hefty carbon head-print over the centuries. One can only imagine the trouble it must have caused her as she navigated it through any interiors she might encounter in eternity and the bother of keeping its battery charged, even if it were as economical with power as an LED bulb.

It may seem inappropriate to think about halos in this way but there are so many of them in this ex-communist, atheist city, it is difficult not to give them the attention they seem to demand. Besides, when a metaphor becomes headgear, a literal-minded pondering on the relevant physics and reflecting the halo in one's thoughts about the intersection between the temporal head and the discoid sliver of eternity surrounding it, are irresistible. It would be interesting to know whether the saints were informed of their canonization and whether, along with the arrival of the much-coveted cephalic aura (and the instructions for maintaining it), there was a job description – such as looking after firefighters, soap makers, or artillerymen and being available to be celebrated on a particular day of the year – that came with the list of duties to which they were assigned. For many, there might be a tinge of disappointment at the juniority of the ministries assigned to them.

Ludmilla is (or was, depending on your beliefs regarding her present state) one of the few saints to be the grandmother of another saint: none other than the familiar St. Wenceslas. Wenceslas has a vast square of his own a little more than a mile away in the centre of Prague, where he is known as Václav. In England, he is represented by his full name when, as Christmas approaches, the tongues of millions of carolers rehearse his heroic deeds in various modes of candlelit darkness – yet another reminder of the bizarre ways in which the world holds together in the collective consciousness of humanity.

As is customary with saints, Ludmila's story is not a happy one, though we are to believe that it had a happy ending given that for good people rotten time opens on to blissful eternity. She was murdered by contract killers hired by her daughter-in-law Drahomíra the wife of Duke Vratislav I of Bohemia. (Many have imagined murdering their mother-in-law, but few have translated dreams into action.) Drahomíra was jealous of Ludmila's hold over her son Wenceslas; in particular, she disapproved of the Christian education their grandmother was inflicting on her boys, taking them away from their mother's 'pagan ways'.

When Ludmila had been disposed of in 921 – by strangulation with her veil, a hazard the manufacturers doubtless flagged up in warnings on the label – Drahomíra, honouring a pact with the Devil, did her best to stamp out Christianity. This aim was frustrated by Wenceslas when he came of age and ascended the throne. She therefore suggested to her other son Boleslaw that he might oblige her by doing the necessary. He did indeed oblige her – and then spoiled everything by repenting of his crime and converting to Christianity. Drahomíra went into exile and was later repossessed by the Devil. Her mother-in-law Ludmilla and her dead son were both fast-tracked to canonization.

As few readers will need reminding, Wenceslas is *the* national hero, and the Patron saint, of the Czech Republic. Ludmila is the Patroness of Bohemia. Despite hailing from a country of whom England knew little, Wenceslas was also embraced by the English Catholic church; which is why – with the assistance of a 13th century Finnish spring carol composed by the head of Turku cathedral school and words supplied by a 19th century English hymn writer – his charitable work is, as already noted, celebrated every Christmas by Brits, some in advanced degrees of alcoholic intoxication. And why his name has been uttered in all the houses I have lived in during my decades of extra-uterine existence.

When I was a child, I always mis-heard the opening line of the hymn celebrating his St Stephen's Day journey through the snow to deliver Christmas goodies to a poor peasant as 'Good King Wenses last looked out'. Such are the hazards of posthumous being and the chaos that results when it is curated in the imperfect minds of one's conspecifics, something that may prove to be a preoccupation of the present author. The posthumous presence of the French historian and man of letters Hippolyte Taine in my consciousness has usually taken the form of a disappointment: his name is the next-door neighbour of the absence of my own name (Tallis) in the Indices of many books I have read, consulted, or flipped through.

It is not impossible, however, that Drahomíra may have had the last laugh. Even after the fall of the communist regime, the Czech Republic remains one of the most atheistic countries in the world.[39] To add insult to injury, actual paganism is on the increase – admittedly from a low baseline. And during the time of the Nazi occupation, Wenceslas was appropriated by the Nazis: the St. Wenceslaus Eagle was the greatest honour the Protectorate could give to a Czech who had collaborated with the occupying force. And, less seriously, David Cerny has him astride the belly of an upside-down horse, with its tongue lolling, hanging from the ceiling of Lucerna Palace built by Václav Havel's grandfather – just round the corner from the great Wenceslas Square.

Notwithstanding the awe-inviting hush of the high-shouldered space within St Ludmilla's church, and the nave, side-aisles, transept, and apse culminating in stained-glass windows transforming Vinorhady light into the radiance of portraits and stories that are really an excuse to celebrate the colours that adorn our sublunary existence, we rarely visit it. The view from the broad, steep steps in front of the basilica is panoramic and the vision of (say) Wednesday is more enticing than glimpses of eternity; the sight of humanity than opaque rumours of God. Or that, at least, is how we excuse our philistine neglect of the church.

The crowd in the square is doing, or would shortly be doing, or has come from doing, what citizens do: tasking and multitasking;

talking while yawning; contributing to a great cheer that troubles the rafters on a roof; walking, or crying; making pastry while looking forward to a holiday; rocking a baby to sleep; examining a scar while listening out for the doorbell and revising a report...struggling with a button with mounting impatience...getting annoyed with a can opener, a wasp, a child repeatedly asking the same question about the possibility of an ice cream, their country's foreign policy, the representation of an historical event, the result of a football match, or the timbre of someone's voice...impatiently waiting for a payment to be authorized...racking brains to remember this, that or the other: for example, the opening line of 'May', an aunt's maiden name, the date of the battle of Bilá Hora, the name of the successor to Charles IV, of a flower, or of a mountain...rummaging in a handbag, a little basket, the body of a lover...making jokes about Skegness (improbable in a Prague citizen but not to be ruled out)...wondering whether to wear shorts...controlling their temper...drinking someone's health...ransacking the adjective box to articulate admiration of the bouquet of a wine...waiting for a door to slam or for someone to sneeze...fidgeting, fretting, and fidgeting as a sign of fretting...struggling with a shoe-lace or exams leading up to a medical degree...washing a lettuce in a colander...judging someone to be a moaning Maria...using alliteration...imagining a prank or disapproving of one...resisting scratching an itch...thinking to themselves in Czech...

All relentlessly secular. So, although the market is named after her, something she might not altogether have welcomed, St. Ludmilla gets hardly a look in. There is so much to do to be an average citizen, an ordinary human being, a statistic in a census, a pixel in a scene gathered up on the retina of one who casts a casual glance. The claim of the notoriously thunderous Thomas Carlyle "It is well said, in every sense, that a man's religion is the chief fact with regard to him. A man's or a nation of men"[40] seems far from empirical reality. But then the dyspeptic Scot was not big on data.

For the present, and from the double distance of the church steps and of present memory, the crowd is just milling, as crowds do, and not obviously madding. This tenuous ever-changing 'we' shares flickers of narratives through facial expressions, habitus, clothes, and adornments...

I am distracted by the thought that the time might be right for a little refreshment and a subsequent shared thought confirms that it is. Visits to other highlights of the Square – worthy destinations in themselves – are therefore postponed to another day, another trip, another life. This need not prevent our visiting the remainder of the square in our minds, courtesy of the written word.

Foremost among the buildings brushed aside by my indecent eagerness for food and drink is the Vinorhady Theatre, usually described as 'one of the cornerstones of Prague theatrical life'. It was opened in 1907 and is a spectacularly beautiful Art Nouveau building climaxing in two angels at either side of the roof of the central block. One of the winged creatures is holding a sword, the other a mirror – make of which what you will.

The involuntary and tragic dramas in the building since it opened its doors – with the surprising choice of a play about the beautiful Lady Godiva of Coventry who rode through the city clothed only in her beautiful, thigh-length hair in protest at the oppressive taxation her husband was imposing on his tenants – have often been at least as compelling as the events on the stage.[41] The execution of the cloakroom attendant Marie Spilková, accused by the Nazis of underground activities, and the decade or so when the theatre was re-designated the Central Theatre of the Czechoslovak Army, charged with educating the young in socialist ideas, gives something of the flavour of its life under successive totalitarian regimes.

Perhaps the most shocking story was the treatment of the great actress Jirina Stepnickova.[42] After a gilded start to her career at Národní Divadlo (the prestigious National Theatre), she chose at the age of 24 to transfer to Vinorhady theatre. She remained loyal to the company despite a stellar career in Czech films. When the Nazis invaded, she was in her late twenties. At great personal cost, she refused to star in German films. After the war, she went to London to study, and returned to Prague as a single mother. By this time the Communist takeover was complete. She refused to appear in Communist films. To add insult to injury, she said a prayer for Czechoslovakia during one of her theatre performances.

This was a step too far. The Secret Service set a trap for her. In 1951 she received a fake letter from a producer with whom she had worked, and whom she greatly trusted, offering her an escape to West Germany where she would work with him. She was arrested at the border, along with her 4-year-old son. A two-day trial was sufficient to find her guilty of treason and in 1951 she was sentenced to 15 years in gaol. Her little boy was sent to an orphanage where he was stigmatized as the son of a traitor. At the time of her trial, many of her colleagues at Vinorhady theatre signed a petition requesting that she should be put to death for treason. Of all those colleagues only one had the courage to face her and apologize when she was released ten years later in a general amnesty.

Where shall we eat? There are at least twenty cafés and related establishments to choose from, not to speak of a scattering of pop-up outlets on the square, seducing us with a multitude of scents. The most obvious choice among the standing invitations to sit down is the Czech Beer Museum. It has no less than 30 craft beers whose hue is echoed in dark paneling and brown chairs, sympathetic wooden floors and tables, and all-day dusk. Instead, however, we choose Grosseto – a Pizzeria ristorante, a lovely spacious restaurant, serving reliably delicious pizzas and other Italian food, imposing no piped music, and having a name that can be pronounced without effort. (This accolade is confidential, by the way. I don't want the place to be crowded out when we next visit. And, no, I don't have shares in the company.) It is for these reasons - and not because (as erroneously claimed in a guide that shall remain anonymous) Czech food is German cuisine that has been regurgitated - that Grosseto is our usual first port of gustatory call when we arrive in Prague from an evening flight and our last when we depart for the airport after lunch.

To compound what may seem like the perversity of our choice, one of us drinks not beer but his usual Pinot to accompany the invariable Four Seasons Pizza that spatializes time in quadrants of dough. (I recently learned that each quarter of the pizza has a topping that stands for a season: artichokes for Spring, olives for Summer, mushrooms for Autumn, and ham for Winter.) I sometimes defend my fidelity to habit by quoting the philosopher Ludwig Wittgenstein who said that he did not care what he had to eat so long as it was always the same.

Wittgenstein was connected with Prague through his mother Leopoldine (abbreviated, either by hurry or affection, to

'Poldy') who was from the city. The career of so many academic philosophers who have spent their lives studying a philosopher who was dubious about the very idea of philosophy and hostile to academic philosophers is, in addition, a tenuous connection between Vienna, where Wittgenstein passed his childhood, and Prague – itself a theme that hangs like a mist in the margins of these pages and will assert itself courtesy of a light rain by a bridge over the Vltava.

Most importantly (perhaps) the restaurant has a privileged view of the square. St Ludmila's church looks particularly arresting when, at night, it is illuminated. To eat a pizza in Prague is therefore less philistine or culturally insensitive than it may seem; for Grosseto is a standpoint from which it is possible further to reflect on the reflections that the church – and the square in which it is located – have prompted.

How does the classroom or guidebook information I have just shared with you about Czech history live in anyone's mind? What does it mean to the people pouring off and on to the trams, buses, and into and out of the stairs leading to the Metro? We may assume that Prague citizens, like this visitor, have their Pragues of the mind. It may be expected that the national narrative can eke out only a precarious existence among their million occupations and preoccupations; that this story of coastless Bohemia is as important and unimportant as is 'our island story', the tale of 'a sceptred isle', of a 'precious stone set in the silver sea' to busy Brits on a busy Wednesday.

In its typical telling, the tale that attaches Ludmila's name to the twin-spired basilica that we glance at between mouthfuls of

*Four Seasons* begins several hundred years before she became a grandmother. It starts with the leader 'Cech' who – in that special twilight zone between myth and history – led the Slavonic tribes into the Czech lands. (Where that 'z' came from, who knows.) It unfolds, precariously in the memory of ordinary citizens, to embrace the beautiful Princess Libuse who chose a ploughman Premsyl as her spouse. Perhaps the luckiest ploughman in history, he ploughed, and she cropped.

Thus was the Premslid dynasty established. One mild summer night, when she, her husband, and a quorum of elders, looked from a cliff above the Vltava, she declared: "I see a great city whose fame will touch the stars". She ordered a castle to be built, thus giving our journey its destination or its pretext, a consequence we may be sure she did not anticipate. She called the Castle and the city Praha, meaning 'threshold' a place where you bow your head as you enter.

Things did not go smoothly. We have already mentioned that unpleasant business which led to two posthumously canonized dead bodies – St. Ludmila and her grandson St. Wenceslas. And there was plenty more bloodshed. Nevertheless, the dynasty lasted for four centuries – as great a span as that between the Battle of Bilá Hora (whose location is signalled on the forehead of our 22 tram as its terminal stop) and the appearance of its name on my computer screen.

After the male line died out, a Premslid daughter married a prince of the house of Luxembourg. This was a spectacularly good choice; for he turned out to be none other than Charles IV of the Bridge, of the re-built Castle, of the University, and of the eponymous Square three tram stops away from our pizzas. He subsequently acquired the double accolade of being 'the father of the homeland' and the one and only Czech to be elected Holy Roman Emperor. No wonder he was voted in a survey in 2019 as the most influential person in Czech history – ahead of Thomas Masaryk, Václav Havel, and even the crooner Karel Gott (celebrated in Germany as the Golden Nightingale of Prague) who prospered mightily during the period of normalization between the Prague Spring and the Velvet Revolution, thanks in part to his self-serving opposition to the dissidents' Charter '77.[43]

Charles had to assert his claim to Czechness rather strenuously as he had spent most of his childhood elsewhere. By the time he returned to Prague to take the throne he had forgotten the language of his subjects. He crash-coursed himself to fluency, something for which your interlocutor, stuck for over a decade on *dobry den* and *Pristi zastavká* and a handful of other phrases, can feel only admiration mixed with shame. Perhaps as a protestation of his Czechness, Charles fostered the cult of St. Wenceslas and provided the saint with luxurious accommodation – a tomb and chapel in the re-built St. Vitus cathedral – and splendid headwear for his skull. The pure gold crown was studded with the most precious of precious stones. Charles' successors were allowed to borrow the crown only for their coronation.

What St Vitus, the Cathedral's saint, thought of this arrangement we cannot tell. His assigned roles in protecting individuals against a) lightning strikes, b) animal attacks, and c) oversleeping, may not have compensated for this posthumous, politically inspired snub. And it seems unlikely that his association with frenzied dancing and with the choreiform movement disorder triggered by rheumatic fever (St. Vitus' Dance – which I learned about roughly the time I was smitten by the lady refugees from the Prague Spring) would have pleased him.

And so there we have it: Charles IV's extraordinary 32-year reign, that brought Bohemia out of the penumbra and established Prague as its chief city such that "it blossomed into one of medieval Europe's foremost commercial and cultural capitals".[44] Alas, after Charles' death, things started to disintegrate. Though the confessional wars associated with Jan Hus – whose sermons in Czech and denunciations of the venality of the church provoked much resentment – did not break out until 40 years later, Charles had sown the seeds for them by encouraging evangelical preachers to thunder against the corrupt clergy.

Thus, the sum of a trillion consequential and inconsequential accidents of overwhelmingly forgotten lives ordered into a story, even a pattern or a destiny – revealed by the guttering mind-light of the retrospective, usually bespectacled, gaze of scholars, poets, dreamers, patriots, teachers, trying to overlook the multi-dimensional darkness into which they peer – and here recollected between the Four Seasons of a pizza.

It is time to set aside history for the present since we have a tram to catch. As we pay the bill, tip the waiter, and on our way out compliment the row of chefs dexterously juggling uncooked pizzas, and tending them with large shovels, we might reflect on the precarious existence of the past in a present that once was its remote, unimaginable future. The fate of the Seven Cities of Ur is to be scattered into multiple repetitions of 'Er…': a fate replicated in microcosm in our minds as the Pragues of our successive visits are buried by their successors and memories are inhumed beyond the reach of the racked brain by the amnesia necessary to unclutter our minds.

We reflect, as we await the next instance of the 22 tram, how little our fellow passengers – like us – are aware of the history that has shaped them. The hopes and fears, and lusts and disgusts, and must do's and I-wonder-whats, of the immediate present dominate their thoughts. Consider the present concern of your interlocutor who is getting irritated with the auto-correct function on his computer that keeps on challenging 'tram' in '22 tram' with a wriggly red line pointing out that it should be 'trams' (which you and I know it shouldn't as it is the tram's number not the number of trams). This distraction while I am trying to reflect on how my childhood – in which, after all, there was created the conscious subject capable of putting together experience into a world that is and is not his world – is conserved with a similar lack of care.

For the present, we hand over the posthumous existence of Libuse, Charles IV, Jan Hus, and many others competing for our attention, to others' fallible memories.

# Námestí míru to I.P. Pavlova

We are part of a 'pouring into the tram', bubbles in a seething mass. For this stage of our journey, we decline courteous offers of a seat – delivered at the speed of conditional reflexes – because we intend to dismount at the next stop.  Remaining upright is at first something of a challenge as we smoothly swing to the right and then to the left before we enter Jugoslávská and then cross Londynská – an acknowledgement of one capital city to another that is particularly generous considering the events of 1938 of which, perhaps, the less said the better. Two minutes are sufficient to take us to the next stop: I.P. (pronounced 'Ee Pay') Pavlova. We do not always resist the temptation to say that 'the name rings a bell', though we do not salivate when the tram signals our impending arrival with the ringing of a bell.

# Hop-Off to the Café Mistral

Resisting the Farmer's Market offering honey, fruit and fruit juices, vegetables, flowers, dairy, and meat products ('including sausages'), we descend into the busiest of the Metro stations. In 2008, the daily passenger count was 118,000.[45] (I am afraid I do not have more up to date figures and gladly accept criticism on this account.) The station was opened in 1974 when the Soviet Union ruled the nation through a puppet government headed by Gustav Husak, whose many medals (including that of the Hero of Czechoslovak Socialist Republic awarded three times) amounted to sufficient ironmongery to sink a ship. This may explain the name of the station: Pavlov was seen as one of the jewels of Soviet Russia. The fact that he despised and hated the Bolsheviks and made no secret of it – saying that the regime's treatment of intellectuals made him ashamed to be a Russian – did not prevent the communists exploiting the propaganda value of this great scientist. They gave him a grand funeral, having surprisingly refrained from bringing about the event that made it necessary. His survival until 1936 to die of natural causes in his late 80s was a miracle.[46]

And in case you think we have the wrong Pavlov, there is, just before we reach the escalator, a large picture, painted in 2011, depicting the commuters as anthropomorphic dogs. In the foreground there is an individual holding a hamburger and a copy of Pavlov's *The Experimental Physiology and Psychology of Animals*.

I ought to declare an interest. I yield to no-one in my admiration for Pavlov as the physiologist of the digestive pathways, and for his Nobel Prize-winning contribution to explaining what is happening in the darkness of my body to the Grossetto pizza ingested a few minutes ago. And his work on conditional (this is not a misprint) reflexes – and on deconditioning (pulling the habit out of the rat) – was pathbreaking in a terrain that scarcely existed before he set foot on it. Where we part company is in the philosophical claims he made on the basis of his scientific research. Here is a particularly eye-poking example:

> Our belief in our freedom of the will will fade and, more-over, our mastery of ourselves will gain much from a greater and greater understanding of the   physiological mechanisms of our brain activity.[47]

As I have asserted, more than once during a descent of the escalator, to Mrs. T. who is the most patient recipient of my philosophical grumps, the claim is self-contradictory. I will not insult anyone's intelligence by spelling out why. More irritating still, Pavlovian behaviourism is the ancestor of the neurodeterminism (the belief that brain science has shown that we lack free will) that has caused me so much theoretical grief over the years. The very fact that we have intellectual disciplines revealing the habits of nature as the laws of science and our capacity to use said laws of science to enhance our power to exploit the natural world to serve our unnatural ends highlights the distance from which we interact with the world.[48] In short, I.P., to exercise our free will.

But we are getting distracted from our surroundings, whose most salient feature is the escalator down which we are descending or, with our consent, being descended. There is already a distraction nearer to hand: escalators make some of us think of other escalators. The handiest of those recollected escalators, tirelessly decanting bodies from the surface to the depths and vice versa, is one we have already met: the moving staircase in Námestí míru Metro station. I forgot to mention that the latter station is the deepest in the European Union and that its escalators are the longest. (Did I?) They have 533 steps, and it takes 2 minutes 20 seconds to descend and three seconds more than that to ascend. There is plenty of time therefore to converse, to puzzle fruitlessly at the adverts, to note how the passengers on the opposite side always look as if they are tilted by a strong wind, to comment wryly on Heraclitus' famous claim that 'the way up and the way down are the same' and yet again to plan an article called 'Heraclitus on an escalator', and to think about other similar structures, notably the long escalator in the Highbury and Islington Tube station.

The latter qualifies for mention not because it is the thirteenth busiest station in our country of origin – the first twelve would have had as strong or even stronger a claim on our attention. Nor because, with three consonants in 'Highbury' in a row and 'bury' pronounced 'berry', it demonstrates that the Czech language does not have the monopoly on names unpronounceable to non-natives, though in a typical English fashion we are inclined to blame the difficulty we experience in acquiring languages other than our native tongue on the acquired language and not on ourselves. No, it is because we have often travelled on that London *escalier mécanique* on our journey to see our younger son and his family.

In Islington we would sometimes remind each other of Námestí míru and in Námestí míru of Islington, enjoying small-change world-sharing, sometimes relishing the strangeness of our capacity mentally to fly 700 or so miles and land on a precise target while we are standing still, though being moved by the escalator like items on a production line. And we would reflect on the wonder of shared episodic, autobiographical, even autonoetic, memory where with the aid of a few words we can direct each other to converge on the same spot, selected out of many billions of spots of space-time that we have journeyed through together and apart. It is no less a miracle than the ability of a swallow returning from Egypt to arrive at the same eaves of the same house in the same village in a country a thousand miles from its winter residence. In the back of our minds is the thought that there is something about those very minds that is not of space and time, though at least one of us shrinks from the faintest hint of Cartesian dualism.

According to JM Barrie's lecture on Courage, "Someone said that God gave us memory so that we might have roses in December".[49] This captures only a little of the joyful astonishment at how memory permits us to connect two capital cities (London and Prague for those of you who are not paying attention) and the ground for such astonishment is in no wise diminished by the non-existence of God or of any kind of Cartesian ghost in the machinery of our bodies. If we do not always appreciate the everyday fulfilment of the dream of mental teleportation – of instantaneous transportation across space and time – it may be because it is so commonplace: that which occurs every day comes to seem, well, everyday. And we often forget how much is packed into the interval between that which we remember and the moment of remembering. Memory would not be possible at all were not so many of our experiences buried in so many layers of forgetfulness, so that we can see through the immediate past to the many strata of the medium and distant past. Even when memories are recalled, the present is too absorbing, too busy pointing to its small and large futures, to hover over the miracle of excavating the past.

And so, here we are, in Escalator 3 (I.P. Pavlova), marveling at our ability to connect Escalator 2 (Náměstí míru) with Escalator 1 (Highbury & Islington), trying not to take this for granted.

It is too easy to take escalators themselves for granted, until that is they break down, when the stress of commuting is compounded by that of urban fell-walking and the principle of CBA is trashed. The Dutch architect, architectural theorist and city planner Rem Koolhaas has just tapped me on the shoulder:

> Two simple, almost primitive, inventions have driven
> modernization towards mass occupancy of previously
> unattainable heights: the elevator and the escalator.[50]

The escalator is an almost comical reminder of our hybrid nature. We see our fellow humans as packages on a conveyor belt, clothed, talkative flesh, outsourcing effort to machinery – yes – but embracing their status as material objects, democratically aligned with suitcases, push-chairs, and discarded packaging lurking as a fire hazard. And this sentence from Koolhaas immediately preceding the one just quoted is worthy of a pause:

> As more and more architecture is finally unmasked as the
> mere organisation of flow – shopping centres, airports – it
> is evident that circulation is what makes or breaks public
> architecture.[51]

Quite so. We continue circulating. Or – where circulation thickens and coagulates – start milling, or even flocking, this being the existential price we pay for the convenience of using public transport that takes us to our destination: being reduced to one body in a crowd of bodies.

The purpose of our digression from the 22 tram route is not simply to taste the joys of automated, effortless escalation. We are headed to Charles University, established six hundred and seventy years earlier, where I have been hired to give a series of lectures on Humanism in the philosophy department. You are loyally accompanying me to ensure that there is an audience.

Much work has gone into the lectures, and they eventually turned into a fat book.[52] The enthusiasm of the attendees is not overwhelming. Some hover in the borders of sleep, knowing that they will be rewarded with a 'credit' for attendance, irrespective of their level of consciousness while they attend.

This is not my most dispiriting experience as a lecturer. When I taught medical students, I became an expert observer of the staging posts on the slide down the Glasgow coma scale: drooping eyelids; wilting of postural tone; draining of expression from the face; a three-note yawn like a lost fragment of Palestrina; slackening of the jaw with a trickle of saliva poised on the edge of the mouth. Everything, that is, short of a full slump and loss of sphincter control. And I have given talks to philosophy groups where some people have come, or so it seems, because the park benches are full, or in pursuit of free heating, or by the rumour of strong drink available *gratis* after the talk was over.

The lack of enthusiasm evinced by some of my students was perhaps consistent with the spirit of Charles IV when he established the university in 1348. He did so

> in order that faithful subjects of our kingdom, who ceaselessly hunger for the fruits of knowledge, should not be forced to beg for foreign help...[and] seek out alien nations to plead for the satisfaction of their longings in unknown lands.[53]

Least of all beg for cognitive assistance from alien nationals arriving by EasyJet.

Any dream that this bringer of 'foreign help' might have entertained of being carried round Jan Palacha square on the shoulders of gratefully enlightened students – past the Faculty of Arts of Charles University, the beautiful Rudolfinum, a smiling statue of Antonin Dvorak, the Academy of Arts Architecture and Design, completing the circuit on the open side that offers the most perfect view of the Castle, Petrina Hill, and Charles Bridge – was not realized. A good thing then that it was not seriously entertained. All, however, was not in vain. To understand how the endeavour to inspire the students at the venerable university was not entirely without fruit, it is necessary to return to the escalator, alight on the significance of a slight jolt as we embarked on our descent, and to connect this with the pulls and pushes that mark our tram journeys.

We are (again) talking about embodiment and the principle of inertia. We arrive, without too much contrivance, at that extraordinary polymathic genius Ernst Mach. He was a son of Brno (not, *pace* Autocorrect Function, a misprint for Bruno), alumnus of Charles University, and occupant for nearly 30 years of its chair of experimental physics. It was in this city that Mach wrote the majority of his 150 publications. His bronze head protrudes from the lovely warm yellow wall of the building that had been the Department of Physics of Charles University in the Old Town not far from the Estates Theatre where Don Giovanni had its world premiere. His achievements in physics, in physiology, and philosophy would each have been sufficient for an illustrious career and a place in the pantheon.

If Mach's name is familiar, it may be because he is associated with the idea of the sound barrier which is breached when a jet plane exceeds the speed of sound (called Mach 1) and a sonic boom is generated. His bearded bronze head, looking at a world brought into focus by Chekhovian spectacles, is enclosed in an early image of such a shock wave.

Before we discuss the physics, a sideways glance at one of his many fundamental contributions to physiology is justified. It was he who discovered (independently of Josef Breuer) that balance was mediated by the movement of fluid in the semi-circular canals of the ears. The importance of this mechanism in securing a septuagenarian's control of his body as he rises in preparation for leaving the tram cannot be exaggerated and no attempt will be made to do so.

Mach's most profound achievement was the principle named after him. 'Mach's principle' is concerned with the origin of inertia – the tendency of a body to remain either in uniform motion or at rest unless acted upon by a force. The explanation for this takes us far beyond the tram and its passengers or the line of commuters being decanted from overground to the underground.

But the connection is undeniable. Mach is reported to have said, in a popularization of his Principle, that, "when the subway jerks, it is the fixed stars that throw you down".[54] Local physical laws – including their expression in the form of threats to the reputation of your author as an upright individual on a tram – are determined by the large-scale structure of the universe from whose influence even a deep tunnel offers no insulation.

It is such a lovely thought that I want to let Mach repeat it in other words:

> When…we say that a body preserves its direction and velocity *in space*, our assertion is nothing more or less than an abbreviated reference to *the entire universe*.[55]

Or, as the physicist John Wheeler expressed it: "Inertia here arises from mass there".[56]

What on earth (or indeed elsewhere) could this mean? The story begins with Isaac Newton and the Second Law of Motion: everybody (including the body typing this sentence and everybody using public transport) will continue in uniform motion in a straight line or at rest unless acted on by a force. This seemingly unproblematic statement is riddled with problems. At the heart of these problems is that of distinguishing between uniform and changing velocity and between the state of motion and the state of rest. Newton solved that problem by asserting that motion is relative, yes; but relative to something that provides an absolute frame of reference: space itself.

Mach rejected the notion of absolute space as providing the necessary reference point, for reasons that went very deep. All experienced and, more importantly, experien*cable* space was, he said, a network of relations and not some kind of invisible stuff. Behind this claim was Mach's conviction that only that which is or could be experienced was real. To propose that there are stuffs such as absolute space that lie beyond possible experience is not only philosophical but scientific nonsense: it is "an arbitrary fiction of the imagination".[57]

What is it that provides the distinction between a body – including a strap-hanging tram-riding philosophizing body – in uniform motion between stops and one that is jerked forward as the tram decelerates? It is, according to Mach's visionary idea, the total mass of the rest of the universe, providing the reference point which insists that there is a difference between a tram and its contents travelling at a uniform velocity and a tram slowing down such that its human contents are at risk of outpacing the slowing tram and falling flat on their humiliated faces.

This principle is at work when (to look ahead) the 22 tram moves round the sharp bend between (say) Malostranská and Královsky letohrádek: you are pressed to the side of the tram because you are accelerating with respect to the matter in the universe. Thus, the force we encounter in our endeavour to evade the labour of ascent (remember CBA and the disinclination associated with upward inclination): we trade off gravitational force for inertial forces, though resisting them is less effortful than the alternating leadership of our left and right feet in panting ascent.

The trade-off brings us to one of the most profound moments in physical science, indeed in all science, nay, in human cognition. We come, that is, to the connection between Mach and

Albert Einstein and our promised return to the escalator. Einstein at first embraced Mach's relativization of space and all motion and his embrace encompassed gravitational forces. This was based on the thought that there was nothing ultimately to distinguish gravitational from inertial forces: to distinguish the attraction of one body to another from the resistance of any given body to being accelerated or slowed down.

To demonstrate this, Einstein imagined individuals in a free-falling elevator in outer space where there are no outward cues as to motion or the absence of it. The passengers would not perceive masses underlying a gravitational field. Other individuals in an ascending elevator would not be able to ascribe the pressure under their feet to either inertial or gravitational forces. Objects in free fall, including the body of your author, do not feel their own weight. There is no perceptible difference between the manifestations of a gravitational field and that of inertial resistance to a change in velocity.

This ignorance – famously the subject of what Einstein described as "the happiest thought of my life"[58] – was a darkness through which light came. The ignorance of the lift-dweller was a consequence of the equivalence of gravitational mass – the weight an object has in a gravitational field – and inertial mass – its resistance to being accelerated or slowed down. The Einsteinian light began to glow in that bronze head of Mach attached to the wall of the institute where he discovered so much on behalf of humanity – its bald, bearded, seriousness italicized by pince-nez glasses reminding us of the images of so many others of his generation – but otherwise unique.[59]

Just before Einstein was appointed to a chair in theoretical physics in Charles University, he visited a now ailing and ageing Mach who had long since moved to Vienna.

> "Please speak loudly to me" he barked when Einstein entered his room. "In addition to my other unpleasant characteristics, I am also almost stone deaf".[60]

Einstein gently suggested that atoms might be real entities rather than mere theoretical constructs. Surprisingly, Mach conceded that, if this explained otherwise inexplicable observations, then it would be reasonable to accept their reality. Though neither party knew it, this was a prelude to a much greater dissent on Einstein's part. His journey from special to general relativity led him to suspect that, after all, there *was* such thing as space that was more than the mere relationship between entities; and that inertial forces were not entirely the product of the interaction between entities and a frame of reference created by the sum total of other entities.

The reader will by now be impatient to know where we are going and why. I need to come clean. Let us deal with some background facts.

The first is that this book is about a body in Prague as well as a conscious mind. The body in question weighs about 80 kg or about $1/10^{23}$ of the weight of the oblate orange of the planet (Earth) out of which he has grown and on or close to the surface of which he has passed his life and will pass what years remain to him. The second is that the relationship between the mind feasting on the sensibilia served up by the city and the body self-propelled through it is a profound mystery. There are many ways of coming upon this mystery. One is to remind ourselves that our human bodies are the only material objects that know – measure, record, and fret over – their own weight. Which is why the philosopher Dr. Jan Halák and I are converging towards a conversation we shall have in a café just off Jan Palacha Square and round the corner from Charles University. Among the things we want to discuss is a paper by Jan entitled "Embodied Higher Cognition".

I dismount at Starometska and walk the short distance to Café Mistral. As always, I am early, because I hate being in the wrong, however small the wrong is, and to be late is to be in the wrong unless there is a compelling reason. Elderly retirees do not have such reasons to hand.

I stir my coffee while waiting for Jan and, watching the beverage mounting the sides of the cup, reflect on Mach's Principle, and the way the distant stars transform the rotational movement into centrifugal force. I momentarily lose a sense of my immediate surroundings, notwithstanding that my bent head acts and reacts equally and oppositely to the arm that is supporting it and that that arm is in a similar dialogue with the table. The equality of the dialogue does not extend to the person whose arm it is. Inasmuch as I am a person, my material being is privileged, so that it is the stars, not I, who are distant. I am always the centre of the world lit up by my own attention boosted by that of my fellows and I cannot be conscious of my absence from those places where I am absent. Embarrassment, for example, nails me to the mid-point of all existence. Thus thinking, I register a cardiac ectopic beat mediated doubtless by the Purkinje bundle whose discoverer we shall meet presently.

And suddenly Jan is here, with a nice smile that does not in any way diminish my initial and lasting impression of him as a classic intellectual with, to steal Isaac Babel's lovely characterization of his bookish narrator, "spectacles on his nose and Autumn in his heart"[61] – the zeugma beautifully mirroring the hybridity of the embodied subject. Jan's genuine courtesy introduces an element of formality each time we resume relations that falls just short of the traditional shaking of those prehensile items, our hands, that would have linked the primordial and primary mediators of our bodily agency.

We are soon entering the territory that brought us together: what another Jan – the brave, dissident philosopher Jan Patocka who died following protracted interrogation by the Secret Police – called 'the lived corporeity of being a situated bodily agent'[62]; or, more briefly, the embodiment of embodied subjects here exemplified by two individuals discussing this issue over coffee in a sunny afternoon whose sunlight is harvested by the large-windowed café and played with by its many shiny surfaces.

At the heart of the discussion is something that arrested me when I first encountered Jan in a wonderful paper tucked away in an obscure journal, his insights a precious signal lost in the murmuration of academic noise.[63] It cut to the heart of the mystery of the relationship between the first-person being who I *am* and the third-person or no-person being of the body, the mere *it* that is; between a meeting such as the present one, seen as either the intersection of the trajectories of material objects or as an appointment that has been honoured by two subjects. The 'I' and the 'it' are at the same time distinct and profoundly unalike and yet as inseparable as the *recto* and *verso* of a sheet of paper. Our bodies are at once closest to ourselves and remote from them. The story of my life, after all, is and is not the story of my body.

In the academic paper where I first encountered him, Jan introduced me to the thought that the very idea of a material object – as something out there existing in itself independently of anyone's experience of it – takes its rise from our experience of our own body as something that we both are and are not, that is colonized only patchily by our own sensations. Most of our body, whose 'is' supplies the necessary condition of our 'am', is hidden from us for the entirety of our lives. It is this characteristic that makes our body the prototype and ever-present example of an object; of a material object that is more than whatever it is that we experience of it; of an entity that has a being-in-itself that is not entirely cashed out as experiences.

We return to this topic today. I notice my hands on the table and see a handy example to illustrate Jan's fundamental point. I can look at my hand and I know that there is more to it than I can see. I can feel the afterglow of warmth in my palm as I lay down my cup of hot coffee. I offer him the notion of 'experiential stereopsis' – where we experience something simultaneously from within and from without - and it is accepted. What is felt from within is put into italics when I *use* a hand to pick up my coffee cup. The controlled movement of my hand as I apply the cup to my lips is possible only by virtue of its being part of a greater whole – hand, arm, shoulder, trunk – that provides the movement with its platform. We agree that our experience of that greater whole is partial: my consciousness incompletely penetrates the flesh of which it is made, though I cannot doubt that it exists. The boundaries between the 'I' that I *am* and the body that merely *is* are multiple and shifting.

Jan orders another coffee and I steer our conversation towards a thought originating from the American philosopher Willard van Ormand Quine. Quine, too, had argued that our intuition that there are objects out there is rooted in our sense of our own body; that the experience of the flesh of which we are made is the prototypical experience of an object that is more than what we are experiencing of it. We share astonishment that someone as hard-nosed or tough-minded as the naturalistic, materialistic, Quine should not only argue that our experience of our own bodies is the basis of our sense of material objects but that even regular objects such as glasses and rocks and trees may be 'cultural posits' fashioned out of 'irritations on our sensory surfaces' and on a comparable 'epistemological footing' as Homer's Gods.[64]

This is heady stuff. Or out-of-head stuff. We suspect that we are entering a realm of ideas we cannot get our heads round. We therefore return to firmer ground, supported on a concept, a technical phrase, that is familiar to both of us, though Jan has greater mastery of the terrain in which it sits – more specifically of the philosophical literature that has grown like a coral reef around it. The phrase is 'body schema' and it refers to something that haunts the bodies Jan and I have brought to the table and that Mrs. T. and I have arranged to be transported around Prague.

It is central to the thoughts of Maurice Merleau-Ponty, the great philosopher to whom Jan has devoted much of his academic life. It tries to capture some of the distance between our bodies as material objects – which they most certainly are – and our bodies as that in virtue of which we are in a world, engaging with that world as the source of our endlessly changing and evolving situations. This far we agree. The body schema is our inner sense of the spatiality of our body, a largely unconscious "persistent and enduring sense of the body's ability to act in a particular situation, and the means by which particular habits can be acquired".[65] This is not to be confused with, or reduced to, an *image* of our body such as that which is made available to us through our senses, as when I catch sight of, hear, touch, smell, taste, experience the aches and pleasures of, and otherwise register, my own body.

So far, so good. The very idea of a body schema re-locates our agency in our body and narrows any separation between a supposed mind that brought me to Jan and a body that was brought thither. But then Jan wants to take the idea of the schema to places where I feel that it has no clear foothold. I fish out his latest paper and he smiles at the dense underlining and annotations of his reprinted thoughts.[66]

It concerns Jan's attempt to apply the body schema to 'higher cognition' – the mode of consciousness that operates in the realm of facts and arguments, and even mathematics. It is Jan's attempt to disinfect the human agent of the last whiff of a Cartesian ghost. He quotes Merleau-Ponty's claim that "thoughts come into being via bodily accomplishment"[67]. And – even more boldly – "while we do not think 'with' specific parts of our body, or by simply moving them", Merleau-Ponty argues that "we don't think without the transfigured body, [the] bearer of significations"[68]

At my insistence, we get down to cases. I offer a simple example: my reminding myself that the Czech Republic is no longer 'Czechoslovakia'. After the Velvet Divorce it has become 'Czechia'. What bodily accomplishment, what posture, what inflection of the body schema, does this correspond to, I ask. Consistent with the 'myside bias'[69] of the polemicist, I cannot remember Jan's answer and so, in this text, my challenge remains unmet. I suspect that his answer dealt defly with my objection to his position.

We somehow get to talking about breathing as an event that is situated between an activity and a passivity, something we do and something that happens, indeed continues happening even when we are in coma, and of the expropriation of breathing in speech and song. Eventually I share some of the thoughts that have preoccupied me on the way to our meeting regarding our bodies as entities subject to the laws of physics and in the grip of inertial and gravitational forces; and the ontological democracy in which people and pushchairs, children and suitcases, youths and discarded cigarette packets are equal grist to the escalator's mill.

By a route I cannot recall, we arrive at our most visited question. What is, or would be, the status of the material world and of nature in the absence of subjects such as he and I who import viewpoints into an inanimate universe and gather some parts of it together as 'here' or 'relevant' and set aside other parts as 'elsewhere' and 'irrelevant' – as entities pulled together during the several billion-year interval between the Big Bang and the first conscious subjects. We circle gingerly around the idea that something as solid and ancient as the solar system may not be as independent of conscious subjects as it is respectable to think. The very idea of the universe in the absence of conscious beings to experience it, to gather it together or to pull it apart, is dizzying. How would it appear in the absence of appearances?

We are unable to stand still long enough to remain in the vicinity of this elusive question. Instead, we relax into scholarship. I revert to Quine and his puzzling over the question as to

> how we, physical denizens of the physical world, can have projected our scientific theory of [the] whole world from our meagre contacts with it: from the mere impacts of rays and particles on our surfaces and a few odds and ends such as the strain of walking uphill.[70]

Jan and I endeavour to bring into focus the strange relationship between the little 'here' of where we are, with the inertial forces that act upon us, and the vast 'there 'of the frame of reference of the universe. Quine's talk 'of the strain of walking uphill' reminds us of the embodiment that, while it brings us under the habits of nature, confers upon us the capacity – unavailable to the coffee in our cups or to the Vltava flowing a hundred or so yards away– to exploit those habits of nature, exposed as 'the way things go' or (when humanity becomes more sophisticated) as the laws of science, so that we can carve out a life of doings in a universe of happenings, including such quietly spectacular doings as this meeting, where the sum total of things is gathered up into a topic of conversation and 'the universe' becomes the subject of a sentence, something that is even more epistemically cheeky than making Prague the subject of a sentence.

We talk a little bit more about 'the strain of walking uphill', though I do not banter until later about the principle of CBA. I guide the conversation in the direction of Ernst Mach and Einstein's 'happiest thought'. We do not ascend above the elementary physics that we both remember from our high school years several hundred miles and several decades apart. But the interesting question relates to the sense of our own mass or weight. I revisit the thought that we alone, of all the material objects in the world, measure our weight. Indeed 'my weight' is the first possessive we carry after our sex and our cardiorespiratory status as judged by the midwife.

Thus, the strangeness of our status as material beings that in different ways possess themselves. The feeling of being heavy, the strain of walking uphill, bring together our subjectivity and our objectivity, an objectivity that Jan highlights when he pats his stomach to indicate that he is full and does not wish to add to his calorific intake because he is concerned with his own outline.

When our two hours is almost up, I suggest a glass of wine. I crack my worn-out joke (but perhaps new to the reader of these pages so I will repeat it – if you cannot change your material, change your audience) that 'Getpistemology' is my favourite branch of philosophy. Jan nods and smiles understandingly. Puns, like fart jokes, may not have the same place in Czech life and culture as they do in my life and in what passes for culture in my country which I like to describe as 'increasingly barbaric'. Courtesy of a glass of Moravian white wine, our talk of embodiment is lit with a blush of well-being – in my case spreading out through the solar plexus. I even feel relaxed enough to connect our discussion of the embodied subject with the CBA principle and the jerk of the tram.

We bid each other farewell and look forward to our next meeting. Our alternating footsteps drawing different trajectories take us out of sight and sound of each other. We acquire membership of different Prague crowds, milling, thronging, flocking, queueing, filing, and sitting in different places. I note again how surprising it is that I do not feel diminished by these reminders of being such a small numerator – the smallest possible numerator - perched on such a large denominator: that I am $1/X^{th}$ of the random groups I join and part company from. Perhaps it is because I am preoccupied with the strangeness of what I have been up to: talking about the body that is talking, about the mind that it embodies, and referring with absurd ease, between sips of coffee, to the universe, making it, like Prague, the subject of a sentence. It is not just a question of Jan and I travelling towards each other or even of being directed towards an invisible purpose, but that of moving by prior agreement from appointment to appointment, between locations in space and time that we are able to specify in a future that is not yet part of the universe (and may never be) and a past that is no longer within it.

One such appointment is our next meeting, noted down in our diaries. By this means we project ourselves out of our bodies to a future location in space-time where those bodies might meet and resume their discussion. On the Metro I try to focus on a passage from Jan's paper

> [O]ur mobility extends far beyond the mere capacity for a change in location in objective space: it is "a means of articulation of a universe".[71]

"A means of articulation of a universe"! I am suddenly struck by the asymmetry between the small item that I am and the boundless 'where' into which I am cast, and by my own capacity to enclose this boundless 'where' in my thoughts. A strange, entirely justified, joy overwhelms me for a moment or two. It is in such moments that philosophy finds its purpose.

As I leave the station I look up and see a generic old man walking towards me. It is, so it transpires, my own reflection and I narrowly avoid walking into a shop window next to where Herr Professor Pavlov greets my return. Given that I am the centre of the RT-known universe, it is surprising to see how ordinary I look and so representative of general fogey-dom (or -ness or -hood).

# I.P Pavlova to Stepánská

But that Hop Off to Café Mistral was another day and today we are still *en route* to The Castle.

We therefore remain on the tram while it is others who descend to the Metro. From the comfort of our seats, we watch a great exchange of folk. Our tram is a vast windowed gut, stuffed with clothed meat populating its hollowness, so that the armpits of strap-hangers threaten the well-being of the owners of nearby nostrils, bringing the whiff of Axilla Number 5 within nose-shot, and elbows fall just short of being pushed against ribs or, more compromisingly, thoracic hemispheres.

There is, in truth, not much to say about this stretch of the journey. Continua of majestic (I know!) buildings either side of the wide road face each other across layered traffic with crowds on and spilling off the pavement, on to tram-routes and bus routes, and cars corralled into their prescribed lanes. The 'ordinary' shop fronts (to lapse for a moment into the discourse of a consciousness patinated by too many Wednesdays) conceal much that is beautiful in many of the buildings. And, by the way, one or two the buildings are far from beautiful.

Somewhere along Jecná is the Pivovarsky Dum ('brewery house'), whose outward appearance is perhaps the least attractive of any building on the entire journey to the Castle (with the exception of the Zizkov Tower whose glimpses generated an earlier rant). The impression given by its square blocks of stone is of a prison and the disheartening impact is exacerbated by the blackness of the rough surface that reminds me of the dark, not-as-exciting-as-Satanic mills, of my 1950s' Northern youth. But appearances are deceptive. A glance within reveals shining pipes transporting vehicles of pleasure from vats to barrels to glasses en route to bellies and thence to brains. The imagined aroma of the constituents of beer and animated voices in the echoing spaces makes my passing glance from the tram seem designed to demonstrate the falsity of first impressions.

Rounding off a junction at which Jecná sprouts a fork at least as grand as itself – Katerinská, whose name I welcome because I can pronounce, or only mildly mispronounce, it – is the Cross Café. The reader may note that I have not described either Jecná or Katerinská as a 'street', a 'road', an 'avenue', or indeed by any other similar descriptor. The truth is that none of these terms seems to capture these – what shall I call them – urbanities? Yet another reminder of the wider failure of the connection between the words in my head and the city my head is passing through. The bridge between two languages and two cultures has unpaired piers.

I am prompted to cite Rabindranath Tagore, whom we met two stops back in Námestí míru. As a poet and self-translator of genius (from Bengali into English) he once said that a poem in translation is like an embroidery seen from the back. The failure of translation neither begins nor ends with poetry, though I am one whose linguistic limitation means a lifelong debt to translators. And as the author of monographs on philosophers – Parmenides and

Heidegger – whose language of which I know little, my debt (and *chutzpah*) is even greater.[72]

I almost forgot the Cross Cafe. I patronized it once out of curiosity, was intrigued by its multi-partitioned spaces, enjoyed a perfectly adequate cup of coffee, and by this means unwittingly entered a long one-sided correspondence. Last week (years later) there appeared on my screen yet another email from the establishment. It began with something that looked rather urgent:

### OSCHUTNE NOVÉ JARNÍ MNAMK!

Or did until it was translated: "Taste the new spring cakes!" And yesterday my in-tray carried the question "How is our honest ice cream?" and I was invited to view a video answering the question. "You will definitely have saliva!" I was promised. And the distinctly Pavlovian promise was kept, as the one-minute action film of the act of creation of the ice cream, set to excited music, gripped the attention of my salivary glands.

In this stretch of the journey, we are often preoccupied by looking out for the green flashing cross of a *Lekarná* or pharmacy, below which the date, the time. and the temperature are reported. It is the temperature that concerns us as time is available on our wrists, gripping our pulses, and we usually know which day of the week it is. Why we are concerned with knowing the temperature in degrees Celsius rather than simply enjoying it is not clear. Admittedly, if it is very hot (over 30) or very cold (minus something or other), it seems to make the day an adventure; and while the broken temperature records are not a personal achievement, our being present where they are broken may seem so. Which is why we find the obstructions created by other traffic and other passengers blocking our view of the green cross frustrating.

We make connections in our thoughts with other much-consulted thermometers. The most evoked is the thermometer in a café in a little village called Psilli Ammos, at the foot of pine covered hills, on the island of Samos. The island has already figured in this text as the location of a delinquent toilet seat that gave rise to the pistol shot twinned by memory with the one that provided the starting signal for our pilgrimage through Prague. The café is called 'Paris' and its sparkling water refreshes the thirsts of two people who, in defiance of the principle of CBA, have walked several miles in the August heat that the thermometer reports as being in the mid- to upper thirties. And the name of the Café illustrates how proper names can be scattered at random through the world, seeded by dreams and visions, and mere accidents of association.

'Paris' is a ubiquitous presence in the Bohemian capital. Its most notable manifestations include the supremely elegant Paríszká Street (ouch!) that goes from the Jewish Quarter (much of which was flattened to permits its construction) to the Old Town Square. In its shops, greed is distilled into elegant consumption and well-known luxury brands are elevated to icons in the hushed, near-sacred spaces. Getting serious shoppers to keep a certain mini-mum velocity along this road is as difficult as rolling a burr along Velcro. A few hundred yards away is the spectacular Art Nouveau 'Hotel Paris', near the Municipal Building. And there is the small replica of the Eiffel Tower at the top of Petrina whence 'eyeful' is more than a pun. Which is a good thing, as you live only once, and you have misused too much of the gift of breath – generated by the long agony of evolution – in enjoying playing with the sounds and senses of the spoken word.

# Stepánská to Karlovo Námesti

The next leg of our journey is more, much more, than mere continuation. The side-roads to our right give glimpses of the dome of the neo-renaissance National Museum, the greatest frozen cry of national consciousness in a city full of such consciousness, where joy, anger, hunger, anguish, grief, delight, the bored sense of being in the thin of it, are gathered up into documents, glass cases, diagrams, asking to be remembered by those who are hurrying to the end of their own lives.

Previous visits to the city have furnished us with memories we can draw upon so that we can construct in our imagination the, as yet unvisited, museum and the long Wenceslas square upon which it looks from its elevation. At the museum end of the square, the eponymous king sits bronzily and mightily on his bronze and mighty horse. We can mind-walk the length of the square and wander off in many directions into the Old Town, pausing at the Estates theatre, or Old Town Square, with statues (a massive Jan Hus and a modest Franz Kafka), spires and clocks, and shops and pop-up stalls, and crowds, crowds, crowds – all the while remaining seated on the 22 tram, "What extraordinary creatures we are to unpack so much from glimpses" I confide to my tram-mate, impersonally proud on behalf of my species.

Closer to our tram than the Museum there is the vast early Baroque Jesuit St. Ignaz church, at the junction of Jecná and Karlovo náměstí. It attracts particular attention on account of the statue of St. Ignatius of Loyola, the founder of the Jesuit Order, placed atop the façade. The soldier-turned-mystic has been there for 350 years, and yet his halo is undimmed. It encircles his entire body, making him look as if he had dined on a three-course meal of the KGB's best weapons-grade polonium.

Of less universal interest is a shop we had once entered in search of reading lamps for our flat in Norská. The wattage of our indignation at the asking prices for the most ordinary sources of illumination outshone that of any of the products on sale. We naturally wondered who could possibly afford items that lay so far beyond *our* means. Absurdly, we were soon speculating about the Czech economy and coming to no informed conclusion but needless to say populating our ignorance with oligarchs and even the return of the Soviet Union in the form of Russian oligarchs of unimaginable wealth, exercising power through their wallets rather than tanks.

Such are the ways of thought, of mundane mind-light between lamp-light and Jesuitical divine light. Instant cognitive hyphae connect this with that and that with the other and the other with something else, and so we reach beyond a retail outlet selling over-priced lights into a boundless elsewhere of semi-organized sense, and we alight on a financial re-colonization of the Czech Republic by Russians. Such is the nimbleness of the provoked mind. The age of miracles is not past: it is present in the connectedness and continuity of free-wheeling consciousness, wheeling all the more freely for being evidence-lean.

# Karlovo Námesti to Neomeste Radnice

> [Charles IV] founded Prague's New Town…a masterpiece
> of rational planning with its spacious boulevards and
> square.[73]

And so, we arrive at Karlovo Námestí (Charles Square), once the largest square in Europe and still a front-runner for that title. Our tram route divides two halves of what is, as with Wenceslas Square, an oblong. But this scarcely matters, given that the geometry of a city bears little resemblance to the structure of the experiences and memories we have of it. Its lived geometry has an only tenuous connection with the lines on the architect's parchment and those on the tourist map.

Karlovo Námestí was a cattle market until 1848 when, a mere 500 years after Charles caused it to be built as the heart of his New Town, it was named after him. Upgraded from a space filled with beasts emitting moos at one end and pungent flop at the other as their torsos in between grew into main courses, it is beautifully laid out – like a park or, indeed, two parks, so rewarding that even on the cold, snowy winter afternoon when we first circumnavigated it, 'retreat' would be entirely the wrong word for our subsequent decamping into the lamplit dusk of a café.

As our tram swings into the square, we look down Resslova and catch a glimpse of the so-called Dancing House and, beyond it, The River. The Dancing House consists of twisted twin 10 storey towers, nick-named Fred and Ginger. Seen closer, one building, presumably Ginger, looks as if she is shrinking from a rather aggressive pass. The building provokes a smile rather than a shiver of delight. Its triumph of glass sits ill with the surrounding Baroque, Gothic, and Art Nouveau buildings, though it seems unembarrassed by its failure to read the dress code. There is an implicit pressure to admire this construction which looks as if it has been warped by intense heat – appropriate perhaps, given that its predecessor on this site was destroyed by American bombs in 1945. After its erection in the 1990s it was deemed to be an 'instant classic' of post-modernism: a listing building classified at once as a listed monument.

If truth be told (and there is no high barrier to telling this truth), I do not have strong feelings about Fred and Ginger so long as: a) it doesn't seem likely to fall over me when I pass it; b) there is no law regulating the direction of my gaze – I can look away from the buildings at any time; and c) I am not obliged to take seriously the idea that the two buildings are *yin* and *yang* or 'static' and 'dynamic' "which…symbolize the transition from a communist regime to a parliamentary democracy".[74]

In Resslova, between the Dancing House and Charles Square are a church and a pub, both associated with the unimaginably brave Czech parachutists who in 1942 assassinated the Reich Protector Reinhold Heydrich, the most enthusiastic advocate of the Holocaust. Operation Anthropoid did not go entirely according to plan. After they had succeeded in shooting their hideous prey, the assassins went into hiding. Unfortunately, they were betrayed. St. Cyril and Methodius Church, where they were concealed in the crypt with the collusion of an heroic priest, was surrounded by hundreds of German troops. The assassins committed suicide to avoid being captured. The occupying forces subsequently murdered 1,300 Czech citizens as a reprisal for the killing of a man who never shrank from wickedness when the opportunity arose, or from creating such opportunities when they did not. He was possibly the most devotedly evil major figure in the Nazi regime – an accolade for which the competition was indeed fierce.

The day before he died 'The Hangman of the Third Reich' recited a couple of lines from one of his father's operas to his hospital visitor – none other than Heinrich Himmler:

> The world is just a barrel organ which the Lord God turns Himself. We all have to dance to the tune which is already on the drum.[75]

Such self-forgiveness for a life devoted to almost unparalleled cruelty did not seem entirely wise given that, if he really believed in God, he would expect shortly to meet him face-to-face, be judged, and one hopes sentenced accordingly.

There is a museum in the church where the story of Operation Anthropoid is told. A little way down Resslova, there is the aforementioned pub. In Krcma U Parasutistu – the Parachutists' Tavern – are numerous artefacts preserving the memory of the assassins of 'The Butcher of Prague'. TripAdvisor has many positive reviews:

> I visited here with my partner, after stumbling across it whilst en route to the horror bar[76].... It's a cozy place full of WW2 memorabilia. The manager was very pleasant, and we ordered one starter between us which was huge.

I would go as far as to say it's the best sausage I've ever ate, we had two traditional Czech meals which were both fantastic. Portion sizes were huge also. Good food, good beer, and good service. All for very cheap! Highly recommend.[77]

Thus history, seen through the lens of TripAdvisor. *Sic transit gloria mundi.*

To our right, as we enter Charles Square, there is a statue. It is of Elishka Krásnohorská (1847-1926)[78] enjoying her posthumous glory as little as her granite arms, exposed by her short cape, are relishing the sunlight: her I-less, she-less bones are unaware of being anyone anywhere.

It is sad that she cannot savour her well-deserved fame. She was a poet (publishing verse in a leading poetry journal as a 16-year-old); a librettist (for Smetana no less, composer of 'The River' whistled by my father as – so the reader will recall – part of the miscellany that included 'I want to be Bobby's girl'); a literary and music critic; and a feminist theorist and activist, who found time, energy, and generosity for, among other things, promoting educational opportunities for destitute women. All of this was achieved despite being a lifelong martyr to arthritis.

She certainly deserves something better than the use I made of her in the final lecture of my series at Charles University. Looking beyond life to the question of posthumous existence, I projected a picture of her statue and remarked that granite does not enjoy the rainbow of thought and there is no blush of awareness in stone cheeks – in short that posthumous celebration is for the benefit of the living.

Observing the diagnostic signs of advancing coma in my student audience, I did not elaborate. I refrained, for example, from observing that there is no sparkle in her eyes reciprocating the gaze of those who stare at her idly, or very idly, wondering who she is or was, or looking past her to a café that plants a welcome idea in their heads. She cannot feel the falling snow that erminizes the hedges, mobcaps the gate piers, applies fingerstalls to wooden posts, myelinates bare twigs. Nor is she humiliated by the fascinator adorning her concrete waves of hair, carelessly donated by a passing pigeon heading to an unimaginable elsewhere, too busy to pause in its flight. Her many sorrows – from aches in her joints to aches in her heart – are as lost to her as the tears on a farewell handkerchief washed, ironed, and put away ("Neatly, please!") in a drawer. Her stone torso still, however, casts a shadow like the one once cast by her living body. And more surreal than any surrealism is the scroll in her right hand, that she cannot read.

The scroll is a reminder of one of the other modes of her posthumous life: the voice in the writing she left behind; joy and fear, imagination and frustration, anger, and hope, teased out into a trail of ink, frozen breath made to breathe again in carefully or carelessly read pages competing for attention with so many other pages. She wished, she said, that her 'ponderings' might be 'transformed'

And soar unto the ends of the earth

Upon their dusky raven wings!

On Cheskian hills amid their flight,

They would perforce awhile descend,

And with a rainbow-radiant smile

E'en 'mid their tears a greeting send.[79]


*Pace* Tagore, a tapestry seen from the back may still be beautiful. My smile through the window of the tram as we drift past the statue, the fusion of a body and a gravestone, may not be rainbow-radiant but it is sincere. Though – to be honest – the smile is divided in its reference because it prompts me to think about the caprice and accident that governs the afterlife of the great.

The other day (I am not an entirely reliable historian of The Life of Raymond Tallis – hence the '-ishy' temporal indicator) I was reading a 'Style Guide for MA students'. I wanted to check the advice I was giving to my supervisees about how to reference their texts. A sample reference was to a book about the Elizabethan poet and dramatist Thomas Nashe (yes, bossy auto-correct, he *does* have an 'e' so withhold your wobbly red line, miracle of technology though it is). It piqued my curiosity, and I pursued him through Wikipedia and beyond: his life, his works, his reputation. Thus did an idea of him develop in an additional mind, though it faded – but not entirely, as these sentences demonstrate – when the doorbell rang. Thus 'Brightness falls from the air'.[80]

And I find myself thinking about a passage in James Joyce's *Ulysses*. Leopold Bloom, leaving a bar after he had consumed a bottle of cider, passes a picture of one of the legendary heroes of the Irish Independence movement: Robert Emmet. This young rebel was executed at the age of 25. Bloom remembers his famous last words: "When my country takes its place among the nations of the earth, then and not till then, let my epitaph be written, I have done". The words are interrupted by a succession of Bloom's farts ["This language may be offensive to your reader"], his thoughts as to their cause, and his relief that they are not overheard or oversmelt by a lady who is passing by. Thus, a moment in a legendary hero's posthumous life and a post-mortem reminder of our pre-mortem helplessness as to the place we occupy in the minds and memories and lives of others.

As for Elishka, she is soon erased by my consciousness of the impossibility of taking in the cornucopia of majestic (at least the sixth use of this adjective) history-steeped buildings around the oblong square.

The Baroque-Gothic Mladot Palace or 'Faust House' where the English alchemist and in-house mystic for Rudolf II lived is a reminder of how inescapable 'magic Prague' is. There is the New Town Hall which, according to *Prague.org* offers "stunning views of Prague with tons of history behind it". Views that 'stun' and history ladled out in 'tons' – so much space, thus much time – served up by a Gothic building modified in the renaissance with a 70-metre tower to be ascended in 221 steps would normally present a serious temptation to disrespect the principle of CBA. Unfortunately, for reasons that are not entirely clear, we have on several occasions failed to find a way into the building.

There are others, some six centuries ago who might have wished for such a failure.

Let me explain.

The tower of the New Town Hall was the site of The First Defenestration of Prague. The story, as is so often the case in this city, is Jan-packed. On 30th July 1419, a crowd of Czech Hussites (followers of Jan Hus), led by a 'charismatic' priest Jan Zelivsky, marched from the church of the Virgin Mary of the Snows a mile or so away, to the Town Hall.[81] They had been incensed by the refusal of the town councillors to exchange their Hussite prisoners.

Someone rather ill-advisedly hurled a stone at Zelivsky from the window of the Town Hall and hit the target. The mob was, as mobs often are, collectively incensed and, turning from a mass noun to a verb, they mobbed, as mobs often do, the tower. Once inside, they got to work and defenestrated the judge, the burgomaster, and a quintet of lesser members of the town council – a more efficient way of removing officeholders than defeating them at an election. (All that leafletting, all that door knocking!). The seven dignitaries suffered the ultimate, indeed ontological, indignity of being transformed from embodied subjects to subjectless bodies. What the Virgin Mary of the Snows would have thought of that, one can only speculate. Clearly, the mob thought she would have been delighted, though the scars on the face of the Black Madonna (a story for another day) suggest that the relationship between the mother of God and the Hussites might have been rather complex.

Defenestration, with the terrifying descent marked perhaps by a shriek falling with the fall it traces, is a reminder of the strange status of embodied subjects instantiated by your author on the tram, sipping a city with his mind, trying from the standpoint of one particular day to engage with a vast quantity of yesterdays. The defenestrated councillors would have had no time to sing the psalms that Hus is said to have sung as he was eaten by the fire to which he had been committed.

Bodies are smaller than minds judged by what the latter open up – 'stunning views and tons of history' – and yet minds are dependent on bodies. The body may outlive the mind and certainly – as a councillor on a pavement – outlast the mind. That bodies can say 'body' and 'body image' and 'body schema' – as did Jan and I in Mistral – is a measure of our transcendence of our bodies.

The horror of the descent, the few seconds it took to transform the councillor from a being-in-the-world that cares for itself and its family and its office and its God and (for example) its rank in the quoits championship, to a piece of meat might have served as a reminder that incarnation is not an unmixed blessing. A reminder, too – as Hus unfolds to Hussites and Hussites engaged in eponymous wars – how visions of the next world license thuggery in this one and how competing versions of the nature of the Creator and what we owe to Him result in bloodbaths between the favourites of his Creation.

As for Jan Zelivsky, the priest who instigated the defenestration, his triumph, as is the way with earthly triumphs, was short-lived. He was promoted to general of the Hussite army and led his forces to defeat at the Battle of Brux in 1421. Based on this performance, he was sacked. Less than 2 years after he had presided over the First Defenestration, and because of his involvement in civil wars between various Hussite factions, he was arrested by the Prague Town Council and was decapitated, a blow from which he did not recover.

Revenge may or may not have been sweet. Zelivsky was buried in the graveyard of the Virgin Mary of the Snows where, two hundred years later, he was joined by one Marshall Russworm, a major donor of the fund established to restore the church, who was executed on a charge of murder.

The reader might be puzzled as to why the Virgin of the Snows should have been given this meteorological soubriquet. There is no record of her passion for skiing or sleigh-riding, or other pastimes that might anyway have been difficult to pursue in Nazareth or Bethlehem. No; the story is even stranger. On the basis of it, she should strictly have been called The Virgin of the Freak Weather.[82]

It begins in the Eternal City Rome with a childless man, John, wishing to make the Virgin Mary heir to his vast fortune. There was, however, a problem: how to do it? More precisely, what do you give to someone who wants for nothing? The problem was solved when the Virgin appeared to John and his wife – and to Liberius, the then current Pope – in a shared dream. She directed them to build a church in her honour on the crown of the highest hill in Rome. She would give the benefactors a sign as to what she wanted.

And she did. On August 5th 352 A.D. snow fell on the chosen hill. This was clearly a miracle since snowfall was unheard of at the height of Summer in Rome and the day was recorded as being otherwise hot and sultry – which was good, as Gortex had not yet been invented. The snowfall indicated not only the preferred loca-tion of the church but also its outline. Hence the soubriquet 'of the

Snows'- which had the incidental virtue of highlighting the Virgin's purity.

Somewhere between the glance down Resslova towards the Parachutist's Pub and the first sight of the New Town Hall, it is evident that The Angel of History, ticketless but smuggled in through the mind of this passenger, has boarded the tram. By which I mean that now seems as good a moment as any to reflect on this imaginary creature – borrowed by the thinker Walter Benjamin from a painting by Paul Klee which he owned, and counted as his most precious possession –before we further embroil ourselves in the vast tapestry of rumours and records on which the national consciousness of the citizens of this city stands or with which they are entangled.

Let Walter Benjamin speak:

A Klee painting named 'Angelus Novus' shows an angel looking as though he is about to move away from some thing he is fixedly contemplating. His eyes are staring, his mouth is open, his wings are spread. This is how one pictures the angel of history. His face is turned towards the past. Where we perceive a chain of events, he sees one single catastrophe which keeps piling wreckage upon wreckage and hurls it in front of his feet. The angel would like to stay, awaken the dead, and make whole what has been smashed. But a storm is blowing from Paradise; it has got  caught in his wings with such violence that the angel can no longer close them. This storm irresistibly propels him into the future to which his back is turned, while the pile of debris before him grows skyward. This storm is what we call progress.[83]

The last sentence is the killer, but it should come as no surprise. It was written shortly before Benjamin took his own life. He was fleeing from Nazi Germany and the Fascist police in Spain were closing in. He had witnessed the catastrophe of the First World War, the collapse of the Weimer republic and of progressive political parties in the face of the rise of Nazism, and the outbreak of The Second World War. How we should judge his despairing conclusion is unclear. The belief in the reality of progress I have defended in many books [84] and so have others[85] but here may not be the place to engage with this argument but rather change the subject to something closer to a central preoccupation of this book.

The idea of the Angel of History presupposes a consciousness in which the past can be gathered up. This consciousness knows the life and fate of hundreds of millions of citizens over thousands of years better than each one of them knows their neighbours or remembers their own childhood. It is a dramatic illustration of how the habit of abstraction makes the afterimage of epochs seem more solid than the events that make them up. Of course, there is no single angel, possessor of an all-encompassing backward glance; rather, there are countless tiny angels for whom the head of a pin is a more than sufficient dance floor, and they harvest a scatter of pixels hoovered up from different pictures. The dark night of the Done and Dusted is illuminated by guttering pinpoints of a million first-order memories or fallible second-order recollections of chronicles. This is the afterlife of what once was real in teeming crowds of distracted, busy minds, making what will become The

Future, leaving their tiny footprints in the parish in which they spent their lives, that are now located in The Past.

It is not clear what Klee would have thought of Benjamin's appropriation of his rather innocent-looking, even gormless, Angelus Novus as the Angel of History and the interpretation he placed on the painting. The artist might have been astonished – perhaps outraged. And might have shared our scepticism about a backward glance of humanity trained on its own collective past as being anything more than a dust-storm of mind-sparks.

I stumble on this again and again. The other day, back in Stockport, I was listening to a radio programme about a once-hot-button issue, the Arian heresy. Roughly a third of the way through the programme, two things came to compete for my attention: fiercely disputed views regarding the divinity of Christ; and a succession of pans that refused to fit neatly into the dishwasher. My thoughts spread outwards into the horrors of the conflicts that Arianism provoked and a wider judgement on a dishwasher which seemed to regard any item I attempted to fit into it as an intruder. It brought home how my consciousness of our collective past was not even an undivided tingle of light in boundless darkness.

While, as Ernest Renan said, "forgetting is as important to a nation as remembering"[86] – at the very least to reduce the torrent of individual and collective experiences, of events, facts, movements to something mind-portable – it is possible to overdo the forgetting. The Angel, as will now be evident, is an inadvertent analogue of a mind supposedly getting to know a city; of a man on a tram enclosing Prague in his thoughts.

Even so, it is difficult, as we travel down Charles Square to resist connecting the tragic Parachutists with the defenestrates. The First Defenestration triggered the Hussite Wars. Historians have traced the path from these wars to the Battle of Bilá Hora 200 years later, which the locals lost. This was the starting gun for the pan-European confessional wars of the 17th century. Czech-speaking Protestant Bohemia was brought under the rule of the Catholic Habsburg empire for 300 years. The smoldering resentment of the Czechs and their patriotic dreams of a resurgent nation were impotent until the establishment of the Czechoslovak Republic after the First World War as part of the Treaty of Versailles. The imposition of the Czech language in schools, the economic hardships in the 1920s and 30s that fell disproportionately on ethnic Germans, provided Hitler with a pretext for repossessing Sudetenland in 1938 as part of Greater Germany. He wanted, he claimed, to prevent Czechoslovakia from descending into a chaos resulting from the internecine strife between Sudetenland Germans and the ethnic Czechs. The remainder of Czechoslovakia was invaded in March 1939 and designated by the bitterly ironical term of the 'Protectorate' of Bohemia and Moravia. From this it was but a short step to Heydrich, his assassination, and the horrors that followed. Thus, the connection between July 30th, 1419, and 27th May 1942 and the Town Hall of Charles IV's New Town and the Parachutist's Church.

One could almost believe that this narrative of causes and effects entertained by two passengers in the tram successfully stitches together centuries of experience of tens of millions of people.

But, of course, it doesn't.

# Novomeská Radnice (New Town Hall) to Národní trídá

This section of our journey begins and ends with Jan Evangelista Purkyne. Though he is less well-known than Charles IV, Jan Hus, Franz Kafka, Václav Havel, or Karel Gott (the Prague Nightingale), he has a fair claim to being Prague's most remarkable citizen.

We have just passed his monument as we left Charles Square. He is seated on a bronze chair, itself seated on a plinth. He is wearing a fine frock coat and sporting an even finer head of hair than his square-mate Elishka. He has an intense look on his face. To judge by this expression and his extended hand put in italics by his index finger, he is explaining something to someone. Unlike most explainers he has much to explain, as we shall discover. Just before our next tram stop is the street named after him – Purkynova – which provides a further pretext for talking about him.

I first came across Purkinje (as he is spelt in the English-spelling world) when I studied physiology at Oxford, perhaps two years before I encountered the Czech ladies working in the canteen at St. Thomas' hospital.  There is hardly a part of my body that Purkinje did not illuminate with his brilliant gaze.[87] The surname of this Bohemian genius is sprinkled over many locations between my bald head and my toenails.

That name is most famously attached to the highly special-ized cardiac fibres that conduct electrical impulses at high speed from the atrioventricular node, strategically located near the centre of the heart, to the cardiac ventricles – its main pumps, the dray-horses – thus ensuring the four-chambered organ fills and empties, guzzles and regurgitates, in a coordinated and efficient way. Purkinje concluded that these fibres were "an independent locomotive ap-paratus". They would have had a role in the tachycardia prompted in my frame by the ladies of the diaspora of Prague Spring.

In the cerebellum, which regulates the movement of our limbs, enabling us to walk without staggering despite the intrinsic improbability of the upright position, there are Purkinje neurons. Of enormous complexity as regards both their intrinsic structure and connections, they are among the most intriguing cells in the body. They have a key role in sculpting purposive locomotion out of what would be otherwise random movements. In this they are assisted by Purkinje axis cylinders enclosing them. Beyond this, there is mystery.

And then there are Purkinje bone corpuscles, Purkinje spaces in tooth enamel, Purkinje images in the eye. Purkinje's fingerprints, in short, are all over us – including, incidentally, our fingerprints.

Yes. He invented the science of dermatoglyphics long before Francis Galton publicized this central tool of Crime Scene Investigation:

> After innumerable observations I found nine important
> varieties of patterns of rugae and sulci serving for touch

on the palmar surface of the terminal phalanges of the fingers.[88]

Thus, the fathering of fingerprint ID. And he was the first to describe the 2-4,000,0000 sweat glands, those nano-pipettes contributing their nano-squirts to the drops and rivulets that trickle down our skin as the ambient temperature rises. They are small enough to be planted in neat rows even on the furrows of the fingerprints.

Having so many of the parts of my body identified by and named after a 19th century *Mitteleuropa* genius underlines the impersonality of the item to which I owe my existence and which I (and others) identify as me. My body is a citizen of nowhere, something of which I have been constantly reminded in my decades as a doctor. The truth is that I could not pick out my own heart from a line up. In such a line-up, it would be anyone's heart, an impersonal machine for securing the circulation that supported the other impersonal machinery. My brain would be equally, or even more, a stranger. I might find that I did not know the back of my hand 'like the back of my hand'. Indeed, at a certain level of attention I could not recognize the elements of my own face.

Thus, the thoughts of a man whose face is currently invisible to him because it is that from which, rather than at which, he is looking. Or a man whose self-presence is being returned to him as a faint image in a tram window as he strains to catch hold of himself. Of an embodied subject trying to wrap his arms round the mystery of his own embodiment – or 'ambodiment'.[89]

In addition to Purkinje's many discoveries there were his contributions to how discoveries might be made: the techniques and methods of physiology and the other biological sciences. He devised the microtome that divides tissues into minute slices and he invented ways of mounting them on slides – both processes essential to understanding how they work alone and together. As a spin off from his life-long interest in the eye and in subjective visual experiences and illusions, he invented the predecessor of the ophthalmoscope. And he came close to understanding living tissue as being composed of cells, something that is usually associated with Theodore Schwann, an idea that is the equivalent in biology of the atomic theory in the physical sciences. It was he who invented the term 'protoplasm' for the colourless material that composed the living part of the cell.

Perhaps the most striking, if not the most fertile, of his experimental innovations was his habit of using himself as an experimental subject in studies of drugs. He discovered some spectacularly ghastly consequences of overdoses of the likes of digoxin and nutmeg. Fortunately for the future of biological science he retired from the role of experimental animal after he had married.

No-one, in short, did more to put fizz into physiology. Against opposition from many of his colleagues, he transformed the teaching of the subject, jazzing up his lectures with demonstrations. In his first chair in Breslau, he had to overcome hostility from the establishment who were appalled that a foreigner should teach in a German university and who, what is more, wanted to establish an independent department of physiology. It was only when he became Professor at Charles University, where he remained for the last 19 years of his life, that he was allowed to create a department that did justice to his vision of physiology as an independent biological science devoted to identifying and investigating the distinctive functions of living organisms such as this organism RT admiring the genius whose name is celebrated in the street – Purkynova – we are now passing.

His achievements look even more impressive when they are placed in the context of his life. Academic hostility was not the only obstacle to his progress. His father had died when he was young and his only way out of an impoverished childhood was the priesthood which gave him access to an education in a monastery. The deaths of two of his children from cholera and his wife two years later from typhus were terrible early tragedies and he remained a widower for the rest of his life.

> I have been afflicted by many unfortunate bereavements and my living quarters thus became half empty, but physiology entered to glorify these empty rooms.[90]

He was saved from despair by an insatiable curiosity, boundless energy – and an unimaginable talent which he bore with an astonishing modesty.

They converged in an ambition that overlaps with the preoccupations that haunt this visitor to his native city:

> [t]o learn to know man as an embodied spirit above all the creatures on earth, endowed with excellent bodily and spiritual strength, in order to investigate all of nature, to recognize its sublimity.[91]

He then talks about 'the Godly origin' of this sublimity and God's will, which is where the tram-rider and this extraordinary man part company, though it is difficult not to believe that his vision was to all intents and purposes a secular humanist one. As he famously said, "the longing for a higher-grade education took me into the monastery and the same longing took me out of the monastery".[92]

Purkinje was also a poet – having been inspired by a friendship with Goethe and a love of his and Novalis' writings – and a tireless Czech patriot who actively contributed to the movement leading to the re-birth (or perhaps conception, even invention) of a national Czech identity that resulted in the independence of the Czech nation 50 years after his death. His patriotic decision to write (as well as teach and examine) in Czech slowed the spread of his reputation which explained why he did not receive credit for many of his discoveries. He showed a deep respect for young investigators and was allergic to talking about himself. Science, he said, is not about names but about discoveries. This from a man whose fame towards the end of his life was so great that letters from people outside of Europe addressed to 'Purkinje, Europe' arrived at their destination.

A good place to end is with something he said a few months before his death:

> I have indeed discovered various things but, as for the immortality of my name, this should not be taken literally. A hundred years hence perhaps only a few will know who Purkinje was. But that makes no difference. For, indeed, we do not know who discovered the plough, and it serves all humanity. The cause remains the same, but not the name and that is the important thing.[93]

Well, a hundred and fifty years later, we can say that this was one of the few things he got wrong. But such modesty cannot be regarded as a failing. If it is, it should be more widespread. He most certainly earned his place on the 50n and 1kc and 7kc stamps, where we see his benign, wise, bodiless head floating above JAN EVANG PURKYNÉ. And his place in the bodies of the billions of his fellow humans who do not know his name.

We wake out of our thoughts about Purkinje to discover that we have travelled down Spálená past the Four-wing building of the Municipal Court. I am not entirely sure that I would know how to notice the force of 'four-wing' without the assistance of words written in one place, printed in another, and read in a third. But I shall not allow this to obstruct our re-tracing of the route taken by mob-handed Hussite evangelicals bent on defenestration.

That route is now better groomed and more impressively enclosed than the 15th century track, doubtless metaled with cow flop, that connected the outraged priest Zelivsky with the object of his rage. We wonder what passed through the mob's mind as they returned along Spálená to the church of the Virgin of the Snows in the afterglow of their bloodbath? Did they slap each other on the back and exchange high fives – "Well done, lads, you played a blinder". "Did you see how his fat belly burst open and his guts spilled over his bloody chain?" Or did they feel guilt, even horror, at the reduction of eminent fellow citizens to long pork wrapped in blood-stained clothes? Did they have any inkling as to what they might have started? Did they experience terror and wonder at this dramatic demonstration of the tragic intersection in the embodied subject between lived time and an idea of eternity?

As we have seen, the retrospectroscope makes it too easy to connect the defenestration with the horrors of the Parachutist's Church as we did when we shared the tram with the Angel of History. Time therefore to change the subject from this ghastly Hussy fit, though not perhaps before reminding ourselves of another portentous outbreak of violence just round the corner in Národní trídá (National Street). It took place at a time when cobbles-and-excrement had been replaced by asphalt, and the city of Prague had been transformed into something unimaginable to the Hussite mob inflamed by indignation 570 years earlier.

On 17th November 1989, a demonstration was convened to commemorate International Students' Day. This was also the 50th anniversary of a demonstration against the Nazi occupiers that resulted in the murder of 9 students and the internment of 1,200 others in a concentration camp. The 1989 demonstrators marched to Mácha's grave in Vysehrad and then returned by the same route as had been taken by the students half a century before. As they entered Národní trídá, the riot police blocked off the streets and attacked and savagely beat the demonstrators. This brutal and primitive response – and a (happily false) rumour that a student had been killed by the police – triggered increasingly massive demonstrations and other acts of defiance in Prague and elsewhere in Czechoslovakia. Eleven days later the Communist Party relinquished power and on 29th December 1989 Václav Havel was installed as president.

Purkynova branches off from Spálená just before we reach Národní trídá. A little earlier we experienced our usual surprise at the suddenness of our graduation from the suburbs to the urbs. Charles IV might have taken exception to the description of his New Town as 'suburban' but there is no denying the feeling that we are now entering a city centre.

The moment of transition is marked by 'Gentleman Brothers', an establishment – self-described as 'exclusive' though whom it excludes is not clear – where masters of cranio-facial topiary practise their art. Its livery matches its, perhaps ironic, perhaps twee, name. On the dark brown paneled exterior there is a motif of the outline of a gentlemen with white hair, bow tie, and a jacket represented by its lapels. For reasons that are lost in the mists of Tallis, the shop gives me a little fizz of mnestic pleasure. I have on recent visits to Prague been inclined, without the support of additional evidence, to connect it with some cigarette packet of my childhood. I try not to spoil the moment by an nth recitation of my joke about my baldness: 'I made a hair appointment, but my hair didn't turn up'.

There is a bit of unfinished business left over from Purkinje's description of human beings as 'embodied spirits'. It hinges on a happy coincidence. Ostrovsky street, the home of the Václav Havel Library, is directly opposite Purkinjova, a left turn to the latter's right. By an even happier coincidence I share an English publisher with the Director of the Library: Michael Zantovsky, brilliant biographer of Václav Havel[94] (and journalist, prolific translator, diplomat, and many other things, not the least a man of considerable courage). And so, on one of our many visits to Prague, we enjoyed the privilege of being taken on a personal tour of the Library by the genial Director.

During our conversation, I mentioned to Dr. Zantovsky that I had been struck by a homely detail in his biography of Havel, embedded in the dark story of the years of 'normalization' after the Prague Spring, of how Havel kept himself prepared for sudden arrest. Prominent among his stand-by kit were aperients and toilet paper.[95] Dr. Zantovsky responded with a tale of another dissident in China who prepared himself even more thoroughly with a kit bag laden with a long list of items which I need not share with you. More relevant is what lies in the hinterland of this story: my own variation on the Riddle of the Sphinx.

I am tempted further to justify the direction things will take in the next few pages by claiming that it was in Spálená that I called in at a Drogerie to purchase aperients (sharing ingredients and warnings with their English counterparts) to stimulate the peristalsis necessary to separate me from the most alien contents of my body, entities that all too irregularly provide the most striking evidence that that body is not identical with me, that it has its own work to do, business to conduct that is remote from the curriculum vitae that I regard as the real story of Raymond Tallis.

I resist the temptation and confess that the chemist in question was in 'Národní' not far from the National Theatre, and just down from a favourite café of the Czech surrealist Viteslav Nezval who was said (and the rumour has not been denied) as a teenager to have played the accordion while studying the stars – which sounds harmless enough, compared with what teenagers often get up to – and a couple of hundred yards from Café Slavia, of which more presently. I should not, however, allow myself, or the reader's journey, to be dictated to by contingent facts of no significance. I say this in full awareness that it may have been through the recalcitrant gut of one Martin Luther, that the history of Europe – embracing this country and the far-away island that once took fatal pride in knowing little of this country – was utterly changed.

Time, that is, for another Hop-off.

# Hop-Off. The Riddle of the Sphincter(s)

We are all familiar with 'The Riddle of the Sphinx'. Or think we are. But the preoccupation that has permeated this journey encourages me to focus on something more mysterious than that riddle. It is the riddle of the *sphincter* – rather of two sphincters. At the heart of that riddle is our hybrid nature as embodied subjects – people who are inseparable from our bodies and yet not defined by them in the sense of being identical with their physical or even physiological properties.

My preoccupation with this topic – Agenda Item Number 1 in the conversation with Jan Halák – is not terribly surprising, given that I spent several decades as a physician intervening in the complex partnership between the 'I' of the person and the 'it' of the body, trying, with varying degrees of success, to load the dice in favour of the former when the latter strayed off the straight and narrow path of 'dynamic equilibrium in a polyphasic system'[96] and started to drift towards the unregulated chaos of the rest of the universe. Day in and day out, Tallis-the-Physician had to confront the hybrid nature of his patients.[97]

Readers truly familiar with the traditional Riddle of the Sphinx will know it is rather disappointing. It could have come out of a Christmas cracker:

Question: What moves on four legs in the morning, two legs at noon, and three legs in the evening?

Answer: A human being, who begins by crawling on all fours, proceeds to walk on two legs, and ends by leaning on a third leg that is a stick.

But there is a deeper riddle manifest in the Sphinx itself: the creature has a human headquarters and animal hindquarters. This is a compelling image of our fundamental ambiguity. It justifies the pun (if *anything* can justify a pun) that names this hop-off.

The two sphincters are the mouth and the anus – the former described with characteristic charm by Samuel Beckett in *Murphy* as 'the anus of the face'[98] They mark the beginning and the end of the alimentary tract. One sphincter emits an estimated lifetime total of between 100 and 800 million words and the other approximately 11,000 kgs of material in about 27,000 sittings. The difference in outputs could not be more profound. It goes even deeper than the contrast between the personal, cultural, accented emissions of the upper sphincter and the impersonal, Esperanto of the emissions of the lower sphincter that require no translation for foreigners, though the jokes they have attracted may. The asymmetry is in sharp contrast to what is seen in, for example, the symmetrical worm where input at one end and output out the other are merely different kinds of matter.

The distance between the sphincters can be measured in feet and inches. It is a surprising 30 feet long in the post mortem room but shorter in the living body when it is in a variable state of contraction, busy chivvying things forward from the entrance to the exit. But the distance between the headquarters of the subject and the hindquarters of the body cannot be measured by feet and inches. It is not a simple one of spatial separation; nor is it captured by (to echo philosopher Gilbert Ryle's famous phrase) the contrast between a ghost and a machine. The semantic output from the front and the material output from the rear belong to different orders of being, more disparate even than the nightingale's song and its droppings. How is this difference possible?

I am not persuaded by the standard story that electrochemical activity in the brain explains how flesh gives rise to the conscious subjects experiencing that flesh as their very being and discussing things with the flesh of others.[99] Nothing in the body as revealed to us through natural science explains the transformation of exhaled air into an account of the world in which embodied subjects find themselves; nothing that explains how The Stinker is also The Thinker who not only wraps faeces in paper purchased for that purpose but also encloses them in inverted commas. And it justifies a retort to those who, wishing to humble us, quote St. Augustine's anatomically correct observation that *Inter faeces et urinam nascimur* [100] ('We are born between faeces and urine'). Sure, it's true; but we are the only living creatures who articulate and reflect on this fact – and take pride in being able to do so *in Latin*. More broadly, we should not overlook the distance between faeces and 'faeces'; between eliminated material and verbal reference to that material; between what-is and that-it-is; between corporeality and cognition. It is in this difference that the ever-widening gap between animal nature and human culture, between faeces and theses *(vide infra)*, history-less biology and historically consequential theology, arises.

Humour draws on our ambiguous status as persons and as organisms. In his essay "On Laughter"[101] the French philosopher

Henri Bergson identified one of the key elements of comedy as the obtrusion of mechanism into the flow of our lives. Raymond Tallis slipping on a frozen puddle in Národní trídá and thus becoming a lump of stuff subject to gravitational forces would be such an instance, though he might not enjoy the slapstick so wholeheartedly as passers-by. More to our present point is the familiar joke that has Rodin's Thinker enthroned on the toilet. It seems unlikely that the sculptor would have laughed along with us. He might, however, have been interested in a recent article, in that must-read journal *Techniques in Coloproctology* published by Cleveland Clinic in Florida. Its authors argue that The Thinker's posture assists defaecation by improving the anorectal angle.[102]

Anatomical considerations apart, it is possible that the protracted endeavour to defaecate may be good for thought. The toilet is typically sealed off from the flow of quotidian events. Like abstract thought, the windowless smallest room is seasonless; and your train of thought in the lavatory is less likely to be derailed by others seeking your attention. Besides, there is something about the effort of concentration that overlaps with that of defaecation, as Rodin acknowledged:

> What makes my Thinker think is that he thinks not only
> with his brain, his knitted brow, his distended nostril,
> and his compressed lips, but with every muscle of his
> arms, back and legs, with his clenched fist and his
> gripping toes.[103]

Which brings me naturally to the hero of this hop-off, the most famous of all constipated thinkers. He was a man of extraordinary strength of conviction and unimaginable courage. His influence on the history of the world, for good or ill, has been greater perhaps than that of any other individual in the last 500 years. I am speaking of Martin Luther, with whom I have in common a preoccupation with philosophical thought and with the bowels.[104]

As no-one needs reminding, Luther's actions resulted in a profound split in the Christian Church that precipitated many bloody conflicts and ultimately triggered the Thirty Years' War which directly or indirectly killed about a third of the population of Europe. Offset against this, we have The Peace of Westphalia ending the war which established some of the principles are still implicit in modern international relations – not that they did much to prevent the horrors of 20th century Europe. The protestant tradition of thinking for one's self without being told what to do by priests ventriloquizing on behalf of God may have had a crucial role in the Enlightenment from which the tram-riders have by the grace of chance benefitted. Protestantism may also have been behind the rise of capitalism whose continuing ascent has had consequences that continue, for good or ill, to engulf the globe. Whether or not this latter is true – establishing causation in history is a difficult business as we have reminded ourselves in our thoughts about Walter Benjamin's Angel of History – there can be no doubt that Luther deflected the course of European, and hence world, history. For good or for ill.

According to the *Sydney Morning Herald* Luther's fulminations against the Catholic Church "changed not just the way Europeans lived, fought, worshipped, worked and created art but also how they ate and drank".[105] *How they ate and drank?* Yes. Luther was an advocate of hops in the production of beer as opposed to gruit which the Catholic church promoted for at least two reasons: it had a monopoly on its production (money, money, money makes the world go round); and it was recommended by the 12th century German mystic and abbess Hildegard of Bingen. She claimed that hops "make the soul of man sad and weigh down his inner organs". [106] It seems unlikely that she was speaking from first-hand or first-head experience but her word commanded obedience: evidence-based authority was as always marginalized by authority-based evidence. For Luther, siding with hops against *gruit* may have been just another way to raise two fingers against the Catholic church. But there was something else at stake.

Hildegard may have been a first-class mystic and a terrific composer, but Luther thought that she was an unreliable – dare I say, a 'crap'? – gastroenterologist. Far from weighing down their inner organs as she had asserted, hops, at least according to Luther, nudged them into action. [107] This was a matter of great moment to him as Luther-on-the-Loo was a lifelong martyr to the agonies of constipation. He suffered mightily whenever he had to coax a reluctant hedgehog, all spines and ill-temper, or on better days a rubble baguette, to reverse through his back passage. And this struggle to clear his backlog was conducted in the Dark Ages before the discovery of All-Bran or the licensing of Dulcolax.

Days before he died in 1546, he wrote to his wife praising hop-based beer for its laxative properties. He announced with immense satisfaction "his three bowel movements" that morning. [108] Famous Last Turds, perhaps [109], awakening the dream of a near future in which he would meet his Maker face to face and perhaps, at last, enjoy a complete, conclusive bowel action.

Luther was entirely open about the many hours he spent in colonic auto-midwifery, contemplating the proper relationship between God, man, and Church, while waiting to catch a peristaltic wave. Indeed, he was perhaps too open, emitting too much information. When the lavatory in Wittenberg where the great Reformer had spent so much time in solitary confinement was discovered in 2004, the director of the Luther Memorial Foundation argued the importance of the find on the grounds that "it was where the birth of the Reformation took place"[110] – something that Luther confirmed. His famous "Here I stand I. can do no other" may well have had its origin in "Here I sit. I can do nothing", the eternal cry of *homo constipatus*. To borrow and modify what the poet Philip Larkin said of himself [111], constipation was for Luther what daffodils were to Wordsworth, though in the absence of Glade air-freshener (of which more presently) the Lutheran Loo would have been far from idyllic. Mrs. Luther would, I suspect, have happily offered a vast number of Hail Marys for a few fragrant sneezes of a can of Glade.

My attempt to ascend to metaphysics on what may seem to some readers to be a ladder of schoolboy giggles is haunted by the ghosts of Plato, Descartes, and Kant, all of whom have separated the conscious subject from the animal body. Plato's immortal soul, Descartes 'I' who thinks but is not part of the material world, and Kant's transcendental subject – all seem in their various ways to be independent of the body. Incarnation consequently becomes a kind of blunder or trap and the body an incidental, often foul-smelling, impediment. If this were the case, however, it would be unclear why Plato or Descartes or Kant should ever have been at a particular place (respectively teaching in Athens, growing up in Touraine, living in Konigsberg), or at a particular time (5th century BCE, 17th century AD, 18th century AD). Admittedly, Descartes did concede in his Sixth Meditation that "nature also teaches me, by these sensations of pain, hunger, thirst etc. that I am not only lodged in my body as a pilot in a vessel, but that I am very closely united to it, and so to speak intermingled with it, that I seem to compose with it one whole."[112] Even so, I am not in my body in the way that my body is in the tram and the tram is in Prague. But I could not be in a tram in Prague without my body being in a tram in Prague in the way that that tram is in Prague.

Depending on where we start, the mystery we are circling round is that of the incarnation of the person or the personification of the flesh. Neither partner has priority: they develop in parallel: thoughts are not trapped in a fat jacket of meat; nor does meat secrete thoughts that may in turn cause it to wrinkle itself in an attitude of puzzlement. And it is no use appealing to the proper-ties of the brain to explain everything. Embodiment is no less mysterious for being encerebration: grey matter seems no more thought-like than red meat. Nor is embodiment something that can be escaped – though Luther and those he quarreled with would have agreed on disagreeing with this belief. For them, the inner angel would one day escape from the dying body of the ape. For the tram-rider, however, what he calls 'my body' and what he calls 'I' have inseparable fates. That which thinks also bleeds, breathes, salivates, eats and drinks – all being essential for the production of rational and irrational thoughts, truths, and falsehoods – and of course defaecates. The Four Seasons pizza will have shared its calorific dividend between the I, who contemplates the history of the nation, the city, and the square where the food was consumed, and the 'it' that is the body inserting the food into itself.

In the light of these truths, there is no excuse for the on-tological snobbery towards the flesh of which we are made and on whose continuing viability we depend to be able to think. Not only our relatively respectable brain and heart, but also our humble kidneys, and least respectable of all, our genitals, and our gastro-intestinal tract. This was, perhaps, something that Luther wished to highlight.

The obsession with the evil of carnality unites philosophers and holy men who see the (usually female) objects of their desire as (to employ St Bernard of Clairvaux's characteristic clerical gallantry) 'bags of excrement'.[113] Bodies, so holy men and thinkers would tell us, are an all-consuming distraction from the business of thought. The endeavour to achieve communion with the deity or a transcendental reality hidden by our senses, is impeded by the appetites and needs of the flesh. Of this there is so much to be said that it is probably better to say nothing.

Nevertheless, a return to the gastro-intestinal tract, connecting headquarters with hindquarters, kick-starting things at one end with suppositions, and at the other with suppositories, may perhaps be in order.

The tract begins with the place where the humble tokens that make thoughts present are fashioned out of exhaled air. Soon it parts company with the wind-blown respiratory passage and disappears into anonymous innards where food and drink enter a darkness that belongs to no-one and declare their presence in rumbles and gurgles, in satiety and fullness, and pains and pleasures of an astonishing variety of kinds. Finally, it heads for the exit where the most substantial waste products of the human body, that make exhaled carbon dioxide and passed urine seem by comparison sophisticated and tasteful, are delivered to the extracorporeal world.

Thus, the riddle of two sphincters of the body. Matter at one end and 'matter' at the other mark the extremities of The Thinker-Stinker humbly awaiting a conclusive bowel action, a well-formed stool, with an eagerness that sometimes matches his longing for a well-formed formula at the end of a conclusive, even concluded, argument. *H. sapiens* united with *H. crapiens*.

In response to Jonathan Swift's famous lamentation about Celia, his mistress, 'Oh! Celia, Celia, Celia shits!'[114] we might note that "Jonathan, Jonathan, Jonathan shits" and that "Plato, Plato, Plato shits!"; and while Hegel probably did not die of cholera-induced diarrhoea – with the prophet of the absolute spirit going down the pan – he may well have perished of a gastric ulcer or some other abdominal condition. A reminder at any rate that to be embodied is to be enmired – something that Luther was happy to include in his public image. Indeed, he might have said of Celia, "You should be so lucky!".

If we forget this, it may be because dead philosophers – or writers of any sort – are presented to us as scentless, printed words or an odourless, inorganic bust or portrait. When we open Maurice Merleau-Ponty's great works, we cannot smell the tobacco smoke off the chain-smoking philosopher of the embodied subject whose habit stealthily furred up his arteries and brought the death that interrupted his thoughts forever at the tragically early age of 53. As for the author of the book you are holding, his instantiation in meat is as irrelevant to what you are reading as is the character of the light falling on the text and the physical effort you put into turning over the pages is irrelevant to the thoughts you may or may not be tuning into.

We have drifted back to the preoccupation of the Mistral Café: the strange state of being to which The Riddle of the Two Sphincters attaches a handle. As we move in the weightless element of metaphysical thought, it is salutary to remind ourselves of the indubitably weighty element of our bodies; to remember our beginnings as babies who (as Father Ronald Knox put it), are "A loud noise at one end and no sense of responsibility at the other."[115] And our endings may not be much different. *H. sapiens* and *H. crapiens* are bound together in a shared fate.

Thus, we endeavour to take hold of Purkinje's Embodied Spirit, Merleau-Ponty's Embodied Subject, or Tallis' Ambodied Subject – the ontological hybrid visiting a city created and populated by numberless other such creatures.

This long digression has been licensed by Martin Luther's Agony on the Throne but is he not a gatecrasher? What justifies Luther's presence? None other than Jan Hus whose impassioned followers, you may recall, hurled a septet of Prague worthies from the top of the town hall in Charles Square. As he suffered death by incineration, Hus' last words were recorded by a priest. Punning on the meaning of his own name, he reflected that "now they are cooking a goose [Hus] but in a hundred years' time they will hear a swan sing. They'd better listen to him".[116] And in a 103 years' time they did indeed listen to him and the future of Europe, of the world beyond the borders of Europe, and of this tram-rider were radically deflected. For the Swan to which Hus referred was Martin Luther. Courtesy of the Gutenberg revolution, he was able to spread his Word through printed documents while the Goose had only his exhaled breath, and a few documents painfully transcribed by feathers dancing slowly on paper, to broadcast his voice to those that had ears to hear.

The schism within the Catholic church opened by Jan Hus and one or two lesser-known figures was vastly and irreversibly widened by Luther. A hundred years on and we have the beginning of the Thirty Years' War, in which ruthless monarchs and their allies pursued extension of their authority, power, and wealth under the banner of transcendental concerns, of protecting one version of God and The One True Church against another.

# Hop-Off Caff and Kafka

So much for the hop-off. It was entirely internal, and I am still on the tram, with my face bathed in 21st century Bohemian light. In my left hand are my glasses, in my right a pen, and on my knees a notebook. In short, an ordinary moment weaving its own idea of trillions of other moments scattered over centuries, countries, and minds.

We (physically) dismount at Národní tŕídá [National Avenue] and the Quadrio Shopping Centre. We part company – one to do what the centre offers, and the other to take a seat in Costa Coffee to write and, sometimes, to think. This is a regular break in the journey, so memories are somewhat blurred by successive experiences. A particular occasion, however, stands out, when the bi-monthly 'Tallis in Wonderland' column for *Philosophy Now* needed to be completed.

The columnist was addressing the question, that may by now be wrinkling the brows of the reader: 'Is philosophy pointless?'[118] The case for the prosecution was strong. No-one really takes philosophical scepticism seriously when they are running for a bus or worrying about a crying baby or being caught stealing. Tram-riders may be embodied subjects, but they don't dwell on that fact or exchange inquiring, puzzled, or even astonished glances with the embodied subjects sitting or strap-hanging along with them. And even if philosophy *were* serious in a serious sense of 'serious', it doesn't seem to make progress: the problems that bothered Parmenides can justifiably bother contemporary philosophers (though in a different guise). The defence, however, was equally strong – or so the philosopher in Costa Coffee believed. If philosophy was pointless, it was pointless in the sense that being in love, or being awake, are pointless.

Steered to that conclusion, the article was submitted: it was attached to an email and delivered to the editor's computer by the kind of magic that we regard as entirely normal. What meaning the column contained could fly through the air faster than any imaginable glance or shout or horse-drawn carriage, train, or plane could transmit it to its chosen recipient.

Which is good, because the shopping is completed, and we are ready to resume our journey. But not before we have visited the stone-faced lady who runs the newspaper stall at the back of the Quadrio, next to a flower shop. Here we have a choice between today's *Financial Times* which is not our favourite newspaper and yesterday's *Guardian* which we would have preferred to have read yesterday. The babushka's irritation does not allow for hesitation: the time permitted by her impatience can accommodate only a monosynaptic reflex and no chin-stroking. Consequently, we always seem to make the wrong choice when selecting the latest helping of what is revealed by the "second hand on the clockface of history".[119]

Occasionally, we digress from our digression to visit the square behind the Quadrio Shopping Centre. It is not only handy for Tesco but is close to the office where Franz Kafka worked for an insurance company. Readers may recall that I set off on this journey determined to minimize the use of the K. word because that writer's association with Prague seems to be established at a Pavlovian level, notwithstanding that K. figures less prominently in the collective consciousness of Prague citizens than e.g., the contents of the shelves in Tesco. (This is conjectural as the relevant data are hard to come by.) Even so, the opportunity to see another of David Cerny's public sculptures is not easily resisted.

Franz Kafka, with his iconic ears and iconic tortured self-doubt, is portrayed as a vast head (11 metres high). Nicknamed Metalmorphosis (a pun that has survived crossing the English Channel), it is composed of 42 independently driven layers of stainless-steel tiles. The ripples that seem to pass through these elements compose and decompose Kafka's head, externalizing the many agonies experienced within.

That it is Kafka – or his representation on earth – or the part of the earth behind Tesco's – that has delayed our progression to the Castle seems highly appropriate. Indeed, so appropriate that it may raise the reader's suspicions that it is entirely contrived. I fear that by now I have already earned a devastating rebuke: "You are just using this city, aren't you, just as you exploited M. Luther, one of the giants of European history to justify a scato-philosophical knockabout, reducing him to an instantiation of the space between two sphincters". Well, yes this is true. Guilty as charged. But I am equally guilty of using myself in the same way. Yes, I am Raymond Tallis but he is here, in pages to be read by strangers, in order to be Everyman, Anyone, an Embodied Subject. (Perhaps I should have called myself E.S.) And if this text is driven by pretexts, isn't this true of other texts? What is different here is that the pretexts are not off-stage. They are up-front.

Before I dust myself down and we board the tram, I may as well get something off my chest about Franz Kafka. He is supreme among those writers I prefer to read about than to read. While I have struggled to the end of his short stories and *The Trial*, I have never finished *The Castle*, though I have begun it several times. (In failing to finish the novel I am in elevated company, because the author himself left it unfinished at his death. It ends mid-sentence.) I cannot, however, get enough of commentaries, criticisms, reflections on the man and the books.

I recall an enthralled reading many decades ago of an essay on the fragmentary notes Kafka wrote to his then girlfriend when, because tuberculosis had reached his larynx, he could no longer speak. And another essay - by Erich Heller on 'The World of Franz Kafka' - has been a much-visited favourite:

> [Kafka] thinks at an infinite number of removes from the Cartesian Cogito ergo sum [I think therefore I am]. Indeed, it sometimes seems that an unknown It does all the thinking that matters, the radius of its thought touching the circumference of his existence here and there, causing him infinite pain, bringing his life into question and promising salvation on one condition only: that he should expand his being to bring it within the orbit of that strange Intelligence. The formula has become: 'It thinks, and therefore I am not'.[120]

This last sentence has attracted a short biro mark in the margin of my paperback text, placed there by a youngster who had no idea of the oldish man he has, to his mild surprise, subsequently become.

Time to re-board our tram.

# Národni Trída to Národni Divadlo

That 'old man' – a self-description that manages to be both factually accurate and insincere – boards the tram, reflecting on the young man who went under his name and sported the same body. His thoughts transpierce 18,000-ish intervening days and hover on that out-of-focus location, where a distant RT was reading about Kafka, in my out-of-focus past, and I gratefully accept the offer of a seat before my Purkinje fibres and other circuitry are put to the test by the centrifugal force of the swing round from Národní trídá to Národni Divadlo.

The old man looks out of the window thinking not about Kafka but about David Czerny and two of his other public artworks: one of two men facing each other pissing into a pool in the courtyard outside of the Kafka Museum; and the other an installation in the Fortuna Gallery. The latter consists of two five metre high figures bending over with their naked bottoms accessible to be accessed by a ladder. The anal sphincters are windows through which the peeper can see a video-loop of President Václav Klaus and a one-time Director of the National Gallery in Prague feeding each other porridge. RT is distracted from this recollection by the sight of his own bespectacled reflection intervening between him and Národní trídá. It prompts the observation that it resembles a cross between Sigmund Freud and Harold Shipman the cuddly looking doctor who murdered between 200 and 300 of his patients.

Among the random items attended to when he looks through rather than at his reflection – such as a book-and-map shop, yet more cafés, a vast beer hall, the Drogerie made famous by my purchase of aperients *(vide supra)* – two locations stand out.

One is Café Louvre, established in 1902 and looking every inch a place where, as it boasts, Herr Professor Einstein sat and drank coffee (and doubtless wrapped his head round the universe), Franz Kafka sat and drank coffee (and perhaps tried to wrap his head round his anxieties), and Karel Capek sat and drank coffee (and probably tried to mediate between the cognitive monomolecular layer of Einstein's universe ironed out to equations and Kafka's three-dimensional, indeed bottomless, anxieties), as he, Capek, struggled with the lifelong curse of a spinal disease (ankylosing spondylitis) which killed him before he was 50.

I have learned the identity of these distinguished customers from large table mats made of paper that has the look and feel of parchment. One of them is beside me, as I sit here, 700 miles away. I read a welcome in calligraphic script coloured like red lipstick left on a paper handkerchief in three languages – Czech, German, and English. I am reassured by the writer that the Café is suitable for all my appointments. Its ambience is Parisian, with aproned bow-tied waiters looking as if they are on furlough from Sartre's Café de Flore. Their striped waistcoats, pleasingly rhyming with the striped wallpaper, offer reassurance as to the quality of the cakes. There is a billiard hall attached, though I do not recall seeing anyone playing. It is just round the corner from the Lucerna shopping arcade, where, the reader may recall, David Cerny has made another appearance: his sculpture of a battle-ready King Wenceslas on an upside down horse who, to judge from its demeanour, is dead. To take such piss from such a figure is brave indeed.

The other location glimpsed from the tram is Národní Kavarná – National Café – where Viteslav Nezval (accordion, stars, youth – *vide supra*), the father of Czech surrealism and friend of Paul Eluard and André Breton, was a regular. His patronage is commemorated in numerous black-and-white photographs on the wall. It is said, according to a source I have forgotten, that, on his frequent visits to Paris, he "rubbed shoulders" with these icons of surrealism – an innocent enough pastime but seemingly sufficient to transmit their vision. The best-known product of the period between Nezval's accordion-playing and his shoulder-rubbing was a collection of poems – *Abeceda* ('Alphabet'). Each poem began with a letter of the alphabet paired with a photograph of a beautiful-legged dancer contorting her body to evoke the relevant letter. This endeavour to collapse – or perhaps to celebrate – in writing the distance between word and body, a distance widened by all writing, but especially alphabetically-ordered writing, is arresting, but remains an idea.

The trouble is (perhaps) that Nezval's surrealism was driven by cock-a-snookery, an aggressive wish *épater le bourgeoisie:* 'acting the goat' as my mother would say - and with too much of a sideways look at the audience and not enough at the world. He rather despised the social democracy brought to the newborn Czech Republic by Thomas Masaryk, preferring something a bit more radical and dramatic – namely Marxist-Leninism. Well, he got it, as we know, in spades, after the Communist *coup* of 'glorious February' 1948.

After a courageous war in which he was imprisoned for underground anti-fascist resistance, he embraced the other totalitarian dream and headed the propaganda film department of the Czechoslovakian Ministry of Information. In the 1950s he was the official cultural representative of the Czech communist regime. Pictures show him as a stout *apparatchik* in an over-filled suit and his hair exemplifying not the flowing locks of the poet but the baldness of a man with a keratin-pinching skull, who has not a hair in place. His cameo head on the 5 Kc stamp is of a chubby-cheeked Czech smiling, one suspects, through gritted principles. And there is his portrait on the 200 Kc note, issued on his 100th anniversary, commemorating the laughing surrealist and glossing over the prolific poet who fell silent, unable to find an audience for his combination of accordion and the stars in a world where tractor realism and the worship of Stalin and of the local Stalinistas was necessary to keep bread on the table and one's head out of a noose.[121] The anguished precision of the poet would have been dismissed by the cultural guardians as being as pointless as a second hand on a sun-dial. Cock snookers snook cocks at their peril. The coin bearing his head, when pressed to one's ear, delivers not laughter but the sound of hissing.

I am tempted to reiterate something I wrote in the past about communist surrealists.[122] And since I, not the hapless reader, am in control of the agenda, I can succumb to the temptation. About 30 years ago, I 'went off on one' *re* the surrealists, especially those for whom Communism was their politics of choice. My target was Louis Aragon whose poem 'Red Front' has these deathless lines:

> I sing the violent domination of the Proletariat
>
> over the bourgeoisie.
>
> for the annihilation of this bourgeoisie
>
> for the total annihilation of the bourgeoisie...
>
> Death to those who endanger the October conquests
>
> Death to the saboteurs of the Five-year Plan
>
> Your turn Communist Youth...[123]

Much may have been lost in translation – but, alas, not enough. An obscure critic commented on these lines with industrial strength sarcasm:

> The world had to wait for the speeches of Leonid Brezhnev's last years before being offered such a feast for the mind and heart, such a combination of political insight, human understanding and historical sense, such immaculate verbal music.[124]

The attraction to many Surrealists of communism was based on little understanding of what it involved in practice. Too often, they embraced the doctrine out of a hatred, a loathing, of the *bourgeoisie* – the parents and teachers and bosses who told them off and didn't appreciate their poetry – rather than out of a desire to bring about an equality of opportunity and of prosperity that would ensure the well-being of all. The anarchic impulses of the surrealist poet did not sit well with the top-down control of totalitarian communism, backed up by every pressure ranging from finger-wagging, to sacking, to homicide. The initial violence of the revolution, with the slaughter or dispossession of the bourgeoisie, may have appealed to the poetic soul. But the dreary decades of rations and queues, smelling of fear and betrayal and demanding obsequiousness, in communist utopia most certainly did not.

I have succumbed to the temptation to xerox an old rant[125] – safe in the knowledge that auto-plagiarism is unlikely to be detected when one's sales are in single figures; but here or hereabouts there is a deeper point than that which may be made by noting the head-on collision between Surrealism and the revolutions some of its practitioners dreamed of. It is that there is something in life that goes beyond cock snooking and *épatant* whomsoever you want *épater.* Rebellion is a second order and, in most respects a lesser, impulse than an astonishment at the magic and mystery that is everywhere.

I think this as I graze the copy of yesterday's *Guardian* we have extracted from the stone-face *babushka*. It has a picture of the Queen (of England) carrying a handbag containing lipstick and who knows what else, instead of a sword, sceptre, or an orb. What would Libuse have said if presented with an inventory of the British monarch's handbag: camera, gloves, kerchief, reading glasses, and fountain pen?[126] Camera! Reading glasses! Fountain pen! Perhaps the gloves and kerchief might have made sense to her. After all, we may suppose that Royal noses dripped 1,000 years ago and that the princesses hands would have required protection from the cold. The rest, however, would have been revolutionary.

That magic is to be found – if ye have eyes to see – in the streets that Nezval walked before his muse was stifled by the need to survive and before, following his early death in his 50s, he was posthumously preserved in coins and postage stamps. And before his tingles of mystery and dreams of subversion were gathered up by scholars in the history of a capitalized Surrealist Movement over which they pore and about which they do not quarrel sufficiently or not in the right way; for they do not see that the surreal is everywhere and not merely in the fabled "chance encounter of a sewing machine and an umbrella on an operating table".[127] Think of the consciousness woven into the invention of the sewing machine, into the creation of the threads which it weaves, of the dyes that make dresses sing, in the very idea of clothes, intimate shelter against both thoughtless nature (for whom we are expendable) and the judgements or prurient curiosity of our fellows. I give myself permission to think momentarily of a mother who has had a little too much to drink, as a result of which her breastfeeding baby starts singing sea shanties or smutty rugby songs.

If, as the tram carries us down Národní Divadlo, I do not obey my own instruction – "Think…etc." – it is because have been distracted by a polythene bag (not so innocent as it used to be) on the pavement being chivvied by the wind: a hardy bubble, a bubble you can open, a bubble you can close and tie a knot in. It competes for my attention with an uncertain memory of the tinned sardines of my childhood whose keys opened the container by turning its roof into a rolled up blanket and, in doing so, gradually obscured the weathered face of the prototypical fisherman in those oilskins that climaxed in headgear named after the direction of a wind that prevails in certain parts of the world. Or of the poet Nezval's own head – reduced to a wafer-thin profile embossed on a coin – banging the heads of Thomas Masaryk and the bottom of a two-tailed lion as their involuntary companionship jingles in the little darkness of the trouser pocket of someone running for a bus.

The message is clear: no need to cock snooks, Viteslav. Better than the surrealist project of pinching one's self awake with poetic teases dressed up as dreams is the philosophical ambition of pinching one's self more awake with more wakeful attention to the contents of waking consciousness. It is not merely life-affirming but something more difficult: Tuesday-afternoon-affirming. We are spared the insincerity of pretending that the potatoes on the hob are chuckling to themselves in metaphysical revenge or are dreaming of Polish poets claiming that they (the potatoes, that is) dream of becoming vodka.

I fall to thinking of the idea of a citizen of Prague "rubbing shoulders" with Breton and friends in Paris and try to get myself to wonder how long the shoulder-rubbing was sustained for and what position the different parties would have to adopt to maximize the period of *frottage*. Thinking but not seriously (of course); rather playing – in order to highlight things even surrealists take for granted in a world whose magic they are trying to liberate. Actual, existing Surrealism stands on a solid base of 'the ordinary'. But true, sincere, authentic Surrealism would dig under that ground and not settle for brief arias of astonishment pitched into a long recitative of the taken-for-granted. The poet would not dismount or tumble from the wonderland constructed in his poems to express his irritation at the leaky pen he is writing with, at the shop from which he bought it, and at the poor quality of merchandise 'nowadays'. 'Nowadays'! The word stands on the presupposition of a glance that encompasses, or believes it can encompass, a fat time-slice of a wide world with more dimensions than any string theorist could dream up...

Waking out of the trance in which I am composing my sermon, I see the Nova Scena (New Stage) Magic Lantern theatre across the road from Nezval' s Národní Kavarná. The external façade of the building is composed of small squares of blown glass and the result is an overwhelming impression of a dirty bubble-wrapped parcel, overlooked at the back of a delivery van, or a box coated in 'frozen piss'.[128] It has worked hard to deserve its ranking as the one of ugliest buildings in Prague. Such anti-ornamental ornamentation is truly a crime and prompts a further reference to Adolf Loos – as cited in Walter Benjamin's 'Experience and Poverty' – "I write only for people with a modern sensibility. I do not write for people consumed with nostalgia for the Renaissance or the Rococo."[129]   How old-fashioned that contempt now sounds! One hundred years later, buildings that spoke to 'the modern sensibility' have lost none of their power to demoralize.

Hop off.

# Café Slavia

We have arrived at the entrance to Grand Café Slavia, having chosen it to represent the very idea of a Czech café. Quite some responsibility, given that Prague alone has 3,000 such establishments.[130] And it has many worthy rivals for our attention.

We have already visited Café Louvre. There is the Grand Café Orient in the House of the Black Madonna, a classic of cubist architecture right down to the light wood coat hangers that rise up as zigzags and the zigs meet the zags at stern angles. In acknowledgement of its cubist provenance, the tarts are square rather than round giving the pun-addicted writer the opportunity to test the tolerance of his companions with *Beano*-grade jokes about square meals. And then there is the beautiful, ornate café in the Municipal house, with its dozens of perfectly cutleried and crockeried tables draped with snow-white cloths, generously replicated in mirrors. Its high-ceilinged vastness gathers up conversations, the giving and taking of orders, and the movement of cake-laden trolleys, into whiskers of sound dying into a background cathedral hush. And, looking ahead in our journey, to the other bank of the Vltava, there is Café Olympia, which was once an illicit gambling casino. It welcomes with an impression of dark wood (paneling, furniture) and copper brewing kettles, somehow retaining the sense of the, just-crossed but now out of sight, Vltava intimated through large windows. A few yards away from Olympia, there is Café Savoy. Its magnificent entrance greets the clientele with a counter supporting a tidal wave of confectionary and a waiter whose courtesy extends even to the unbooked he has, reluctantly, to turn away. Those who are admitted to the Savoy have access to the best schnitzel in Prague, so it is said, though harvesting the necessary data to substantiate this claim would have been life-threatening. Our n=4 dataset, however, has presented no challenge to that claim, as when we consumed their schnitzels on my 75th birthday – frightening proof that reaching three quarters of a century, like death, is not just something that happens to other people.

I could continue – the battle for the short-list is fierce – but my point is, I hope, made: there is no single café in Prague, no equivalent perhaps of Café Central in Vienna where Peter Altenburg held court or Café Gerbeaud in Budapest, that can stand for all the rest.

There is, however, something that makes Café Slavia – part of the Lazansky Palace – qualified to represent The Café in Prague. To access this something, it is necessary to withdraw from the actual streets of the city to the idea of Prague, to stand back from the idea of Prague to the idea of Czechlands, and from the idea of Czechlands to that of Europe, to reach the edge of a theme that has two aspects as inseparable as the *recto* and *verso* of the sheet of the paper on which this will be printed: that of The Café in Europe and of Europe in the Café. My two guides are an unlikely pairing: the brilliant Croatian essayist Slavenka Drakulic; and the polymath's polymath Professor George Steiner.

In the title essay of *Café Europa*[131] Drakulic recalls how so many cafés in Eastern Europe before the fall of the Soviet Union, and the communist regimes it imposed, were called Café Europa, Café Wien, or some other name intended to invoke the world on the far side of the Iron Curtain. It was as if the names would magically transform the establishments into a part of the life and cakes over the rainbow. Europe was the longed-for future – a sentiment echoed in the slogan on which Havel's Civic Forum won the first post-communist Czechoslovak election in 1990: "Back in Europe!".[132]

And then there is George Steiner and his wonderful essay 'The Idea of Europe'[133]. Europe, he says, is *walked*. 'The cartography of Europe arises from the capacities, the perceived horizons, of human feet' – something that contrasts with the vast spaces of America, Australia, and Asia, where a thousand blisters' worth of walking would not take one to the end of a plain. It is steeped in *memory:* 'streets and squares are named after the statesmen, scientists, artists, writers of the past' – hence the gifts that have been offered to the tram-riders. There is 'a *twofold descent* from Athens and Jerusalem' – expressed in an extraordinary cultural richness and in the horrors of persecution climaxing in the Nazism that gave birth to the Holocaust, subjugated half of Europe, crushing the Republic of Czechoslovakia when it was just about to come of age, and opened the path for a further half century of communist oppression. There is *'the apprehension of a closing chapter'*, of the coming Fall – that even the present hospitable text cannot justify a digression to accommodate.

And then there is the *café:*

Europe is made up of coffee houses, of cafés. These extend from Pessoa's favourite coffee house in Lisbon to the Odessa cafés haunted by Babel's gangsters. They stretch from the Copenhagen cafés which Kierkegaard passed on his concentrated walks, to the counters of Palermo. No early or defining cafés in Moscow, which is already a suburb of Asia. Very few in England after a brief fashion in the eighteenth century. None in North America outside the gallican outpost of New Orleans. Draw the coffee-house map and you have one of the essential markers of the 'idea of Europe'... So long as there are coffee houses, the 'idea of Europe' will have content.

It is in such cafés that writers seek a place half-way between their own study and the flaneur's streets. Hence the shock Simone de Beauvoir experienced in New York:

> It is not customary here to do work where people drink...
> As soon as my glass is empty, the waiter comes over to inquire; if I don't empty it fast enough, he prowls around me.[134]

And the justification of Grand Café Slavia to represent the remaining 2,999 cafés of Prague? Well, there is its famous clientele. Bedrich Smetana of 'Ma Vlast', Karel Capek who invented the idea of robots, and the poet Josef Seifert, the only Czech to win the Nobel Prize for literature, sat in this space. And politics:

> In the Milan of Stendhal, in the Venice of Casanova, in the Paris of Baudelaire, the café housed what there was of political opposition, of clandestine liberalism.[135]

Václav Havel famously patronized the café along with many friends in the 50s, 60s and 70s, until he was goaled, along with his aperients and toilet paper, by the regime. It was in Café Slavia that he met his first wife in the 1960s and mildly caroused with his fellow aspirant *poétes maudits*, plotted against the Writers' Union, acquired his lifelong commitment to 'living in truth', gathered the first signatures for a letter defending The Plastic People of the Universe which ultimately gave birth to Charter '77...[136]

The connection between the Café Slavia, politics and Havel reaches beyond its tables, where subversive talk endangered those who engaged in it, through the wide windows in one direction to the magnificent but potentially dissident Národní Divadlo – the National Theatre on the bank of the Vltava – and in the other to the Castle. The National Theatre was built on a wave of patriotism and opened in 1881, rebuilt on a second wave of patriotism, after fire had seriously damaged the building, and reopened in 1883. It is neo-renaissance in style and crowned with a narrow oblong of gold, at the centre of its roof like a wide parting. It sports two mighty winged charioteers in an arrested leap towards certain death in the street below. As for the intervisibility of café and castle, it licenses us to imagine the gaze of Havel from his favourite table dreaming of overthrowing the oppressors within the Castle[137] ensleeving the gaze of President Havel looking back from the Castle at the café with nostalgia for the time when he sat at its tables unburdened by presidential responsibilities. A modest photograph of this modest man greets one at the entrance – a smiling, mustached face, shiny with the sweat of one who is slightly overweight and for whom the world is therefore typically a little overheated.

Actors, opera singers, and ballet stars doubtless crossed the road from the National Theatre to eat and drink in times past, but they seem no longer to patronize the place. They are present instead in the photographs on the walls punctuating the long, shiny-tabled, brightly lit, functionalist limbs of the L-shaped part of the establishment. There are entrancing photographs of two characters in striped shirts. In one photograph a fat man looks glum while a thin man is laughing; in the other the fat man is laughing, and the thin man is glum.

We pass them as we look for a table that will give us a view of the river and the Castle beyond. We are nearly always pleasantly surprised by how often they are available. The Laurel and Hardy figures are next to an alcove accommodating a pianist who skillfully wanders from tunes that we recognize to others that we think we do, creating an atmosphere borrowed from the 1950s and even further back to a time when the tables were occupied by people who exchanged their last glances before we were born. The gentleness of the pianist's finger work acknowledges that it is the duty of background music to remain in the background and not to act as insecticide on the buzz of conversation.

You know at once that this is not Alf's Caff or Alf's Decaff – one of those establishments where you have to bring your own ambience and they charge you corkage on it. Nor is this a place to write – except for a few notes – or even to read a book demanding committed attention. And the gentle veto applies to the book in your hands: if you are reading these pages in Café Slavia, look up and lay the volume aside, to be disregarded next to your glass of wine.

My personal ban on serious writing in Café Slavia may go against a much-treasured tradition. Writers in a café not only save on heating and lighting but have their material around them. This must apply especially to a philosopher whose subject is (let us say) 'Humanity in General'. Surely it helps to be surrounded by samples that you do not have to respond to as people. You purchase a morning's tenancy of space for the price of a coffee (and you get the coffee as well) and so you start to write, aware that beyond your page or screen is a world that, by its disconnection from your writing, is asserting its unreachable depth. As for the writer, if he is Jean-Paul Sartre, he will observe the waiter playing at being a waiter, pretending that his role is his essence, guilty of the Sartrean charge of 'Bad faith'.[138] Well, that is appropriate for a more ordinary café, for a little suburban dive in Vinorhady or Vrsovice or an English pub – the Wilfred Wood, the Dog and Partridge, the Victoria Arms – but is not an appropriate way of Being-in-the-Grand-Café-Slavia.

The maximum permitted distraction is an opinion column in yesterday's *Guardian*. If there are to be philosophical thoughts, they should be tied to the surroundings. This edict permits semi-philosophical reflections on the Castle; for example, that an upward glance touching its walls is effortless compared with any pedestrian ascent; that its presence can be extinguished by dropping a curtain of flesh with a surface area of less than 1 cm$^2$, reminding us that that presence is a mist of the mind; or that the clouds behind its bureaucratic ramparts are little different from those that Charles IV would have seen as he looked up from his newly finished bridge to the monument he had restored. Otherwise, it is a question of Being-Here-Now, and denying importance to any elsewhere; of arriving, settling down, and remaining arrived; of existing significantly just by sitting in this space and looking.

There is, of course, much to arrive at. Our fellow customers are obvious landing places. So many heads, so many voices, so much leaning forward and leaning back, index fingers putting statements in italics, meanings supported by open-palmed hands, paravertebral muscles underlining subordinate clauses, much waving and beckoning, much vertical nodding in agreement or horizontal shaking in dissent. Assertions and denials that 'such and such is or was or will be the case'; locutionary, illocutionary, and perlocutionary forces converging on some point in the space of interconnected consciousnesses.

It is evident that Café Slavia cannot take credit for much of what makes the café special – the thoughts, the conversations, the interactions. Take for example, that little boy over there reading about dinosaurs. The beasts had not anticipated the immortality provided by his 65,000,000-year backward glance. (He is one of our two much-loved Anglo-Czech grandsons – important reasons for our being in Prague.)

For a place so popular with tourists, it has a surprisingly large native clientele. It is good to eavesdrop on a world chattering to itself, to overhear conversations one cannot understand; to enjoy the richness and mystery, even the romance, of discourse without it being betrayed by the banality of content. This helps to explain what someone famously said, "People travel to faraway places to watch, in fascination, the kind of people they ignore at home".[139] It is the lack of interest rather than the fascination that would be indefensible; the reduction in one's own head of the over-familiar tropes of discourse – with all the riches underlying them – to 'Yadda, Yadda'.

I try not to notice one or two people reading their mobile phones. They are miles away from the miles away we are trying to inhabit, though we too may drift in thought to places unknown to the tables, chairs, and waiters, putting unmeasured distances from the spaces where we have come to sit. Fortunately, e-ttenuated consciousnesses, lost in electronically constructed elsewhere, seem less numerous than in any café in the UK.

As for non-natives, there seem to be many speakers whose tongue is as opaque to this insular character as is Czech. It is difficult to determine whether the slightly cavernous acoustic tangle among the orchestrated polyphony is Dutch or Flemish, Swedish, or Finnish. Images triggered by these voices enclose the bare names of these countries with a lingerie of connotations in which cliché and accident predominate.

First, cliché. Two persons a couple of tables away whom I suspect of being Dutch, their great altitude compensating for the two-dimensionality of their native land, are set among windmills and canals and dykes, mining their own versions of the Alps out of glasses of Schnapps.

And as for accident, nothing could be more unwarranted than an image that comes to me from Samos, the home of the second crashed toilet seat. It is of a quartet of cuboid, elderly Finnish ladies dancing the sirtaki in a favourite café not far from our apartment. They are moving with a grace that, if not amazing, is at least surprising. They rise and fall with the music as if their joints had not seen seventy years' constant service. Later, they tell us that they had spent the long, dark, cold evenings in Helsinki learning how to become Zorba the Finn. The idea of 'summermost' Greek sunlight illuminating the 'wintermost' Finnish darkness plants the seed of another idea of Europe that must be kissed awake by a glass of wine.

The wait for this alcohol-assisted awakening is such that we suspect we have been de-prioritized by the staff. Yes, with our rucksacks and just-in-case rainwear, we are in the lower centiles of elegance among the clientele. The seat on which I have draped my jacket that doubles as a *pret à porter* study wears that item with more aplomb than I do and the unpeeling reveals me as pull-overy. (After all, the dress code on trams is pretty relaxed. So long as the private and semi-private parts are covered, anything goes.) Eventually, however, we penetrate the strategic inattention of the waiter and an exchange, rimed with slight frost, results in an order being given and, after what seems a longer interval than might be reasonably expected, fulfilled.

The first sip of the first glass of wine spreads through the body, igniting real sunlight in the metaphorical solar plexus, one of the few parts of my body where Professor Purkinje has not left his name. As everyone knows, there is an enzyme in the body that turns sugar into alcohol. What is perhaps less well-known is that there is another enzyme that turns alcohol into adjectives, enabling the drinker to articulate the complex, layered taste of the wine as it enters his mouth and lights up the palate. I lack this second enzyme and instead think of a metaphor in Malcolm Lowry's *Under the Volcano* describing the moment when the Consul, an alcoholic, has his first mescal of the day: he is "like a burnt-out tree struck by lightning that flowers at the tips of its branches".[140]

Cue our inspection of the famous picture on the wall: Viktor Oliva's *Absinthe Drinker* which has caught the attention of Café Slavia's customers since 1920. It shows a terrified bearded man, his hands supporting his head, his newspaper discarded, staring at a beautiful, naked green apparition, her substance half-mist, half-flesh, mermaidenly sitting on his table looking at him. The vision's pleasing figure is emphasized by her perfectly shaped buttocks kissing the marble top. It is late: the other tables are empty, a lone waiter is waiting to shut up shop, and the coat stand is unencumbered.

Oliva, a Czech artist, who lived for some time in *fin de siècle* Paris, a genuine Bohemian among self-styled ones, had discovered absinthe in the City of Light. Luckily, he survived and returned to Prague to enjoy a long career as a prolific graphic artist, creating posters, illustrating books, and painting ceilings – producing unlimited quantities of what our unreliable informant Herr Adolf Loos would have dismissed as crimes.

Irrespective of whether absinthe makes the heart go fonder, Oliva's picture captures the dream of a deliciously decadent Paris, exotic in the eyes of citizens who would themselves have been exotic in the eyes of Parisians. Offshoots from that dream of decadence are to be found in the Green Devil's Absinthe Bar, the Absintherie Franz Kafka, and similar establishments scattered across the city. They offer a naughty-but-nice experience to those who want a change from beer in their Prague piss-up. The grammar of the advert for the Green Devil's Bar is authentically home-grown:

> We have a cellar from the 14th century! in which there is one of the steps even from the 13th century, when this area was inhabited by a blacksmith. We divided two floors as follows: the first floor is rather located in the shop and the bar is very downstairs with a very unique decoration. The atmosphere is amazing. We prepare our drinks before guests on a cart![141]

'On a cart!'.

The reciprocal dreams of Paris in Prague and of Prague in Paris remind us of a poem by John Keats – who died at a Mácha-ist age of 26: his 'Fancy' reminds us that 'pleasure never is at home'[142]. In spring we dream of winter and in winter of spring, because 'At a touch sweet Pleasure melteth/Like to bubbles when rain pelteth'. And we can recall Heine's pine tree in the arctic cold dreaming of the sunlit palm while the palm tree dreams of the snow-bound pine.[143] And we might be tempted to think of the playwright in the Café Slavia looking towards the Castle while the President in the Castle looks towards the Café. But this would be to stray deeper into a distraction from a distraction. It is time to recall where we are: here in Café Slavia, looking around us and out of the window.

I alight upon an asterisk of evening sunshine in the second glass of white wine and am reminded that 'here' is where light becomes eyelight and shared eyelight becomes weekdaylight. Perhaps it is because the wine is Moravian that I allow myself to unpack the asterisk to its imaginary source, an imagined landscape of its place of origin. The spark has been harvested from a vineyard far beyond the wooded Petrin whose outline forms part of the horizon of our present gaze, where the sun has set and Mácha's statue is starting to cool, after a hot day. The idea of Europe, harvested in this café, opens into that of a pilgrimage of light across the continent.

The pilgrimage begins in a Belgian café, say in damp, misty Bruges, where lamplight falls on a thick tablecloth, and on to the hangings that surround a small, cosy space. It ends at a table by the sea in Samos, where the not-quite-breeze in the stifling August heat causes the pegged down paper table cloth, bearing a map of the island, to tremble at its edges. The blue water between the café and the razor-sharp horizon tingles with pins and needles of light. Objects cast shadows so sharp that they look as if they have been cut with a knife. And between the beginning and the end of this pilgrimage of the mind, remote from any coast, is *Mitteleuropa*, this country, this city, this café, this table, this moment in this temperate Spring Day.

Here.

# Legii Most (Národní Divadlo to Újezd)

It is time to resume our outerwear and our rucksacks and continue our pilgrimage through the city of Prague. But not on the tram.

The interested reader (note the insightful singular) might like to know that the decision to proceed on foot is motivated by two reasons. First, we could do with a dose of fresh air to clear our heads and a bout of exercise to burn off a few calories. Admittedly, the pace we assume will hardly turn our bodies into a self-fanning inferno etherealizing our flesh into exhaled air. Even so, slow walking is a compromise between CBA and its Calvinist opposite. Besides, the bridge across The River has zero gradient. Secondly, the view is so wonderful that we want to sip it on foot rather than gulp it down through the tram window. And so, as we leave Café Slavia, rather than turning left to the tram stop adjacent to the bubble-wrap building, we turn right and head towards the Vltava.

Naturally, our decision to walk precipitates a change in the weather. It starts to rain, but not enough to justify erecting an umbrella. The individual drops are pin prick sized and they are not sufficiently numerous to qualify as drizzle. The sensation on our faces is like the feeling you have when you lift a freshly poured glass of mineral water to your mouth. This is a beautiful comparison, and I can say so because it is not mine. It comes from a mighty novel by Heimito von Doderer[144] which I read when it was translated into

English in (I think) the 1970s. Of its 1,400 pages I remember only a) that I thought them unforgettable, b) the behaviour of a character who became obsessed with *femmes lipides*, c) a handful of cafés and their different clientele, and – to get to the point – d) the reference to the gentle rain in the grand streets that seemed to stand for the Vienna where it was set. (For a Mancunian to define Vienna by rainfall may seem a case of the sea calling the land damp.) Besides, the shiny-pavement details in the novel remain sufficiently out of focus to prevent the rain from becoming just rain and the streets just streets and to protect the distance between the cities from collapse. This was the distance that was translated into a two-day coach journey in August 1791 taken by Mozart on his way to Prague – his spiritual capital ("My Pragers understand me") – to launch *La Clemenza di Tito* (which he said 'grew in his head') in the last year of his life.[145]

Thus, the origin of what I might reasonably call my Habsburg Leap from Prague to Vienna. I will pass over the fact that the relationship between the two cities was far from harmonious for the greater part of the period between 1526 and 1918, long centuries when the Czechs were unwilling junior partners in the Austro-Hungarian Empire and Prague was the lesser of the two cities. Connecting a piece of Prague with my confused idea of Vienna, mediated at this moment by an imperfect recall of von Doderer's novel, might have caused offence even at the height of the Great Resentment after the Battle of Bilá Hora and the Revival of Czech national consciousness climaxing in 19th century. Time therefore to return to Prague.

We take a backward glance at the glorious Národní Divadlo before we cross the Vltava. The glance penetrates the walls and many intervening days to remember a truly unforgettable performance of *The Cunning Little Vixen* on a brilliantly sunny May evening a few years past. The interval drinks were taken in a bar overlooking the river and offering a view across to Petrin and the Castle. Behind this musical occasion was a sense of the man, Janacek, unhappy in his marriage, late to success, and tortured in his final years by unrequited passion for a much younger married woman, and his unending sadness for the loss of his 20-year-old daughter. This seemed to be captured in the final reflections of the forester who has shot the vixen of the title. He falls asleep in the forest thinking of the passing of things and the music is charged with the melancholy of a stifling summer evening.

It is difficult not to think of a strange visit we took to Janacek's house in Hukvaldy on a hot, thundery August day. The house is next to a hill thickly coated with dense woods and the storks flying over it seem to express the heat. Nearby was the 'overgrown path' – or so we thought – that gave its name to the unbearably sad sequence of piano music he wrote in the wake of his daughter's death. The vixen herself has her share of immortality: she is cast in bronze, sitting on a rock, her sharp attention – the root of her cunning – signified in pricked up ears, her long, plump tail, draped over the stone. We also remember the shop set up in the school Janacek had attended as a child. It sold records of Dvorak, Smetana, Beethoven et al but not, at least when we visited, the local hero. The omission seemed to be both Czech and Janacek.

We cross the busy road running along the Vltava and join the *Legii Most* – the Bridge of Legions. TripAdvisor ranks the bridge as 182nd of 1,225 things to do in Prague. In any other city it would be in the Top 5 and this bridge would be The Bridge.

It was built between 1898 and 1901 "at the insuging *(sic)* of the entrepreneur Vojtech Lanna"[146], replacing a chain bridge. It was officially opened by Emperor Franz Joseph I after whom it was named. The tide of history rubbed out the emperor's name with the decisiveness of the sea erasing an image drawn on the sand and it became 'the Legion's Bridge' in 1919. The reference was to the Czechoslovak Legion who fought on the allied side in the First World War. Unsurprisingly, this name was displeasing to the occupying German forces. Between 1940 and 1945 it was renamed Smetana Bridge. It reverted to Legii Most in 1945, a title it retained until 1960, when it became '1st May Bridge' – morning or afternoon is not specified – in celebration of International Labour Day.

In 1990, after the Velvet Revolution, it reverted once more to 'Legii Most' the name it bears and retains as we cross the 345 metres connecting on one side Smetana and Masaryk Embankments and Malostranská (Little Town) and on the other Janacek Embankment. In short, it is a perfect realization of George Steiner's Europe whose streets are steeped in centuries past. Meanwhile the Vltava flowing under it continues relatively unmarked by history, rippling out into strange places, such as the mind of Smetana whose genius created the music my father whistled into the darkness of his last years. (I will not mention Bobby's Girl again.)

The bridge is placed in inverted commas by towers at each end. They were "used to select the having"[147] – that is to say, to extract tolls. Tolls are no longer demanded since a hold up at the booth would create a Prague-wide traffic jam. The neo-baroque Secession style of the bridge justifies the mighty bronze candelabras and the ornate stone railings whose main use seems to be to prop up tourists taking selfies – evidence that 'we were there' or 'that an exotic there was once our here' - and occasional, less egocentric, otheries. Photographing spares one the effort of looking; or postpones it to a time when you can do the looking in the comfort of your own home or even delegate it to another person who is too polite to express resentment at being the recipient of an unsolicited tour round the gallery on an i-phone or relieved to be shown bridges and spires rather than grandchildren in various modes of cuteness demanding authentic-seeming billing and cooing.

I offer these architectural details as affirmative action for a bridge that gets less attention than it deserves because it is such a magnificent viewpoint. The first law of gazing is that to look is to overlook. From Legii Most, we can glance back to the gift-wrapped, ornate cuboid of the National Theatre. It is especially spectacular at night when it is illuminated by a warm orange light, pierced at satisfying intervals by window-lights hinting at the luxurious interiors, and at the spaces opened in the imagination by drama, music, and dancing. In daylight, we can catch our first glance, at the far end of the bridge, of Malá strana or the Lesser Quarter with the boulevard-wide street on which are located the Savoy and Olympia cafés already mentioned as runners up to Grand Café Slavia.

We watch the swans (innocent of their Lutheran connotations) in the quieter parts of the river mirroring their necks to make curly brackets stolen from textbooks of algebra and their ripples wobbling the reflection of the contrail from an overhead plane, swan-shaped pedalo boats, numerous cruise craft, with music at a romantic distance rather than at earwax-melting proximity, and the torrents of the cataract that make it difficult to see how boats can travel unimpeded.

The bridge bisects Strelecky Ostrov – Shooting Island – which returns the compliment by bisecting the bridge, marking its midpoint. It is a lovely baguette of parkland with majestic trees – Keatsian 'green-robed senators' that, one warm September evening, quietly bombarded us with conkers – and a palatial 19th century restaurant. It was here that Charles IV arranged for his troops to practise long-bow and crossbow shooting. It remained a shooting range until the 19th century.

It would be perverse, given that we have mentioned Charles IV's name, to ignore his bridge, visible a few hundred yards upriver. It connects the Old Town with the Little Quarter, and its ends are marked by mighty towers – two at the Old Town end and one at the other. Almost as striking are the extraordinary statues and statuaries that form two socially distanced ranks of fifteen good souls and true facing each other across the bridge. They are 20th century replicas of 17th and 18th century originals, representing saints in their transcendental pomp. Most of the individuals honoured by petrification are kitted out with expensive accessories: crosses and, to reinforce the peaceful message of the Cross, swords, and shields, along with livestock, including the expected lambs and the less expected pet dogs, and wreaths. Some have attendants swooning in transcendental ecstasy or kneeling in pious acknowledgement of their bosses' greater piety. Stone hands, touching but unable to feel each other, are frozen in the posture of prayer, communicating with a realm beyond the sky, beyond all beyonds, that exists, so far as this infidel is concerned, only as the intentional object of linguistic signs that are the fossils of past consciousness. If I am mistaken in this view, it is a bigger mistake than all my others put together – and the competition for that accolade is fierce.

Just now, I remember one relatively disencumbered character whose head is adorned with what looks like the rotor on a toy helicopter. He reminds me of one of my schoolboy heroes – Flip McCoy, the 'Copter boy, who was propelled through the pages of *Topper*, by a similar device attached to a neat backpack, as he hopped from good deed to good deed, picture to picture, and week to week of my early childhood. Next to him, and looking upwards with adoration, is a well-upholstered, even welterweight, toddler, similarly equipped with a propeller attached to his head, clearly making an early start to his apprenticeship.

At the midpoint of the bridge stands the statue of yet another Jan: Jan Nepomuky (or John of Nepomucky) one of the most revered of Bohemian saints and the first to take up station on the bridge. At the heart of the much-contested story of his martyrdom is his death by drowning.[148]

On the orders of the Not At All Good King Wenceslas IV, who walked the earth 400 years later than his much-caroled namesake, Jan was flung off the bridge into the Vltava after having been tortured – a procedure that included "burning his sides". Nepomuky's offence, according to one story, had been his refusal to divulge what had been told to him in the confessional by the Queen, whose spiritual director he was. The King was eager for a transcript because he suspected his wife of having a lover.

Behind this seemingly everyday story of Royal folk is a vast hinterland of conflicting narratives, many of them added in successive centuries for different propaganda purposes, weaponizing Jan's life on behalf of the Counter-Reformation – the endeavour to reaffirm the sovereignty of the Catholic Church after the assaults of Hussites, Lutherans, and other Protestant troublemakers. Jan Nepomuky was also celebrated as a resistance hero, backing the Rome Pope's candidate for abbot of a rich Benedictine monastery against the Avignon anti-pope's choice backed by the king.

The story has been challenged. It has even been suggested that there were two Jans – the one who denied the king access to the contents of his wife's confession and the other credited with opposing the appointment of the king's choice of abbot. Pitching into the controversy as to who should have the last word on tasty appointments – the Crown or the Church, the Local King or the Foreign Pope – was highly dangerous.

The story that has a One-and-Only-Jan may seem to have prevailed. His image – scattered and adored over Czech Republic, Slovakia, Austria, Croatia, Slovenia, Germany, Italy, Poland, Lithuania, Alsace-Lorraine, and even Ukraine - often presents him as placing his finger to his lips, or with his mouth padlocked, enjoining silence, defending 'The Seal of the Confessional'. When his tomb in St Vitus Cathedral was opened centuries after his death a piece of reddened tissue fell out of his skull. It was his incorruptible tongue that had remained still in the face of torture. A clincher one would think. He was therefore canonized in the 18th century; and on the bridge he is in full saintly fig. His statue became a place of pilgrimage particularly for Czech nationalists.

In view of what we have already disclosed, this suggested some muddled thinking because Nepomuky was also an essential tool in the propaganda war of the Catholic Church – in particular the Jesuits – to support its claim to be the spiritual guardian of the soul of the very Bohemia that had the proto-Protestant Jan Hus as its spiritual patron. He was canonized because the Catholics wanted a martyr to counter-balance Jan Hus and he met the person spec. Those who by now have lost the plot are in good company.

The most striking feature of the statue is a tilted halo in the form of a ring with five stars encircling his head. The dun and dusty stone of his smartly dressed body make the stars look twice as bright. They are said to represent those seen over the Vltava on the night of his murder – 20th March 1383. According to another account, they refer to the stars apparently hovering over his head as he hit the water – which helped people find his body. One must set aside any reference to the stars which *The Topper* used to portray the pain and disturbed consciousness associated with collisions between heads and hard objects. As for the number of the stars, they have been interpreted in various ways. One ingenious scholar has suggested that it coincides with the number of letters in the Latin word **tacui** meaning 'I am silent'.

Jan's posthumous luck ran out in 1963, somewhere "between the trial of Lady Chatterley and the Beatle's First LP"[149] neither of which he could have imagined or, if imagined, approved. In that year, the Vatican reluctantly acknowledged that he was "a Jesuit fabrication" and that he was indeed the composite of two persons – the one who kept his mouth shut and the other who opposed the king's choice for abbot of a well-endowed monastery. He was stripped of his sainthood, though there was no record of his halo being recycled for another saint.

His statue had already narrowly escaped being tipped into the Vltava from Charles Bridge in 1918 by Czech nationalists asserting their emerging nationhood. The triumph of Hussite

Protestantism over the Catholic church to which Nepomuk belonged and for which he may have lost his life (whichever 'he' he was) was completed – and Jan-on-Jan action ended – only when Czech citizens were becoming increasingly secular and, of course, even worse things than confessional disputes faced the fledgling country. His statue remains, protected by ignorance, indifference, or respect for anything that bears the mark of antiquity.

It is best to see Charles Bridge from without and at a distance because it is Prague's most densely packed tourist destination. The saints exchanging glances across the bridge are separated from their opposite numbers by an unending flow of bodies not all of whom are photographing themselves. From Legii Most, the crowd on Charles Bridge looks so tightly packed that it is difficult to imagine how there is space for the artists on the bridge – the least talented of whom have more talent than the sum total of that possessed by the once-fashionable Young British Artists – offering to do instant portraits, and their slightly self-conscious clients seeing themselves committed to paper; or for beggars prostrated in a shockingly traditional posture of utter submission, of abjection, of literal groveling, with their caps laid on the ground speaking for them, as they hear the passage of feet that have come from all over the world; and little ensembles of elderly men, veterans of many decades of playing 1950s jazz in the open air.

Seeing the crowd from the distance of Legii Most, it is difficult to imagine that one has been part of similar random assemblies, fat-filing across the bridge. "People are afraid that all people are equal"[150] as Joe Moran said. A well-founded fear, given that, seen *sub specie aeternas*, we are all as insignificant as each other. Without the armour of unbroken self-preoccupation, reinforced by the consciousness of special people to whom we are special, beginning with the Lady on the Tram, we would see ourselves as what we are: contingent atoms in an out-of-focus crowd gathered up in a stranger's gaze, insignificant others beyond the horizon of selfies. The revelation of our equality reminds us that we are equal in the most fundamental sense: the brevity of the speck of light between the first opening of our eyes as we howl at the midwife and the unbearable brightness of the delivery suite and their final closure as we fade from ourselves.

So much for Charles Bridge.

Looking in the opposite direction from Legii Most, scanning the Dancing Building with a forbearing smile, and endless neo-Renaissance riches, our gaze reaches Vysehrad – 'the upper castle' – inside whose walls are the basilica of St Peter and St Paul. We have sometimes confused its twin spires (one for each saint we presume so there should no squabbling) with St. Ludmilla in Námestí míru. Also inside the walls is the cemetery where, a while back, we noted the re-burial of Mácha which marked the re-burial of the long-held, recently realized, dream of independent Czech nationhood. The fort and the church and the cemetery have seen more history than pretty well any other patch of land on the earth; and the fort was for a (very fat) while the superior rival to the Castle towards which we are headed.

With this thought, we re-direct our gaze towards the beautiful Petrina hill, to the right of it the Castle and the Cathedral, and to the right again the Summer Gardens and the great Letna park that overlooks the city as much as the Castle does. The park was an ideal location for a colossal monument to Stalin, realized in granite. The largest group statue in Europe, it took five and half years to build, being completed two years after Stalin's death and a year before Khrushchev's denunciation of his regime. A 50-foot high monster, Comrade Stalin was located at the head of a file of workers elevated on a vast pediment.

After Stalin's posthumous disgrace, his monument was an embarrassment to the Soviet Union and the Czech authorities. It was blown up in 1962, with the aid of 800 kgs of explosives. The sculptor – who had previously produced monuments to Jan Hus, Tomas Masaryk, and FD Roosevelt – horrified by the fruits of his labour had already killed himself a few days before the unveiling of this 'monument of love and friendship'. The fact that it was built by dissidents or other unreliable characters housed in a forced-labour camp may have influenced the fateful decision of the tragic sculptor who entered the competition for the commission not expecting to win it.[151]

The plinth involuntarily vacated by Stalin is now occupied by a vast metronome beating out what, for the want of a better phrase, we call the passage of time. It is explained by the motto "In time all things shall pass…" a not entirely reassuring sentiment. Time that buried Stalin also buried all those whom he destroyed and those recklessly brave individuals who opposed his successors, such as the Sage of Café Slavia. And the skateboarders who delight in the plinth may have forgotten or have never known the 'monument of love and friendship' that previously occupied it. Perhaps it is sufficient to note that, while the metronome marks the journey away from totalitarianism, it is not clear what paths that journey will ultimately take.

It is difficult not to return to brooding on the undeserved historical luck of those like us who have passed their lives without having had to fight tyranny at home and wars abroad, never had to weigh in the balance the safety and welfare of one's self and one's loved ones, against the perils of resisting evil. Our luck goes deeper. We have been brought up in what by historical standard was extreme softship:

If you take the history of civilization and clock it over twenty-four hours, the first twenty-three hours and forty-five minutes would be sheer misery. Only in the final fifteen minutes would civil society start to look like a good idea.[152]

Even so, it is difficult, after a sigh intended to stand in for profound moral reflection, to remain with, even less within, these thoughts. Reminding myself of the density of graffiti on the plinth supporting the metronome is attenuating my humility and gratitude at having escaped from the terror, poverty, and struggle that has characterized most of the lives of my fellow humans over history. Perhaps this is because I know that my historical luck will not hold; or, rather, it will be cancelled by the transience built into my being. A number will occupy the right-hand side of the hyphen on the inscription:

Raymond Tallis 1946-20**

A future reader, if there be such, will know when RT's ontological, metaphysical, political, and social luck ran out.

Our gaze drifts back to the Castle-and-Cathedral. Several things strike the most casual gaze. The first is that the Cathedral is by far the dominant partner. The second is that the Castle from this angle looks far too urban, even urbane, for something answering the designation 'castle'. My idea of a castle is a construction resembling Carnarvon or Warwick castles – with moats, ramparts and slit windows that ensure the traffic of arrows and other offensive weapons is one-way. Prague castle seems an entirely different kind of place. The long, medium-rise buildings that stand between us and anything looking like a fort, in beautiful yellow stone and gorgeously decorated, seem like Enlightenment office blocks where treaties are argued over rather than battles fought, the site of passages of prose rather than of arms, of quillwork rather than swordsmanship. It looks from this distance to be serene: we cannot see the crowds milling around it or the conversations and misunderstandings that fill its rooms and spill out into its corridors. We hear nothing of all those voices orchestrating muscles and directing the sedimentation of intention into a monument that has survived for nearly a thousand years.

This impression may be corrected in due course when, with the assistance of the tram, we storm the heights on which the Castle sits. For the present, we take one final opportunity to exploit the vantage point offered by the Legii Most. We look along the bank that connects this bridge with Charles Bridge and remember many walks along this perfect stretch that is both a park and a promenade. There is an art gallery from which we once took away a memory – supported by a post-card – of an extraordinary cubist sculpture of a head by Otto Gutfreund. It captures the tension between the inner transparency and the seeming opacity of the human bonce; between the regularity of the outer features and the inexpressible muddle of what it is like to be a looking, thinking, feeling, and perhaps aching, head. I regretted that it was rejected by the publishers for the cover of my book on the head.[153]

After a life that included two years in an internment camp in Provence during the First World War, for reasons that are not clear, Gutfreund returned to Prague. He established his reputation as a leading artist but drowned in the Vltava at the age of 38 again for reasons that no-one, not even Wikipedia, seems to be able to tell me. Meanwhile, he lives on in my life as having executed the most compelling portrait of the strange muddle that is the capital of embodied subjects, such as this individual who is transporting his head round the capital of Czech Republic, thinking of the strange muddle that is himself.

Just beyond the gallery, we encounter in our imagination another example of the work of David Cerny. Three massive, muscular bronze babies, crawling in different directions, are encountered bottom first. This increases the surprise value of their heads. (I was going to say 'shock value' but nothing so calculated to shock can do more than merely surprise.) They are hydrocephalically inflated and are featureless apart from a vertical oblong sphincter-like aperture that opens on to a blank. We always leave feeling that we should have made more of them, have become a bit clearer about how much piss[154] has been taken, and from whom. Needless to say, selfie-takers are attracted to these like bees to honey.

This public sculpture adds to the impression that the Czechs collectively have a rather special sense of humour as puzzling to other nations as English fart[155] jokes are to those across *La Manche*. The impression may not accurately mirror what the citizens are up to, engaged in, or preoccupied by. A little correction may therefore be in order. It is reasonable to guess that the citizens are busy (deep breath): describing something as a 'double whammy'... waiting for water to run warm, or a computer to boot up, while issuing a greeting...peering at something without understanding it or even struggling to do so...admiring the design of a cup, a bin, or a cathedral...testing the temperature of baby's milk with an elbow unsleeved for the purpose ...entertaining contempt for a stranger... stifling a yawn...adding something to a 'to do' list...posting a letter...wiping a surface clean...doubting a proposition...puzzling over a whirring sound...cleaning up after the baby...smoothing a sheet...complaining about the excess, the absence, or the shortage of something...being surprised at hearing a tune in their mouth or at what they are thinking of...taking advantage of the gastro-colic reflux to secure a bowel action...woofing down or toying with food...deleting emails...wondering whether to take a crying baby to doctor...kneeling in prayer...raiding the fridge...looking for a parking spot...covertly extracting a fragment of meat (1/100,000$^{th}$ of a pig) from between the teeth...sealing an envelope...erring on the side of caution...arguing over a contract...squeezing a tube of toothpaste in vain...rubbing a pregnancy bump...feeling the effect of the first drink of the evening...looking forward to a summer holiday...missing someone terribly...counting calories...checking their pulse...confirming the date of an appointment...anticipating such an appointment with fear or impatience...burning their tongue on a hot drink...counting out tablets...apologizing for having to dash...consciously using the vernacular...trying to remember the word 'vernacular'...speaking of dinosaurs...opening a can...reeling with a spasm of grief over a failed relationship...trying to identify a birdsong...pretending to erudition one does not have...fearing that 2 people are hand-in-glove...wondering what a trilobite is...

At the end of the imaginary promenade, our recollections come upon the lovely long, indeed oblong, Kampa square that is like a stretch of a wide boulevard and completes in cobbles the journey to Charles Bridge that towers – if that is the right word for a structure that is itself towered over by towers – over the final stretch of the journey.

We snap out of memories, pull ourselves together, and reluctantly descend from the bridge, Legii most, whose successive appellations have illustrated the randomness of the rules over the application of names to things, the arbitrariness of language. "Just imagine" I say, "if the answer to a quiz question 'What unites the last emperor of the Austrian-Hungarian Empire, a fighting force in the First World War, the composer who made a river world famous, and the first day of a Spring month?' were 'A Bridge in Prague'?" Imagine, indeed.

With such thoughts lying very lightly on our minds we continue, along Vitézna, to our next tram stop. We resist the pull of Olympia and Savoy on one side and of Bella Vista on the other. The Nostalgia Museum elicits a kindly, if slightly patronizing, smile. As for Krysta Chinese Ceska Family we share a 'Me neither' and one of us expresses surprise at the location of a large Air Flight Simulator which would enable us, if we could afford it, to have the experience of flying a Boeing 747 or an air balloon and to take off and land at more than 24,000 airports.

And so, we arrive at Újezd to await our return to tram 22.

# Újezd to Hellichova

And yes, before you ask, it is not as difficult to pronounce *Újezd* as the letters suggest – if, that is, you can remember how it is pronounced: 'Ooh yez' will do. But when it comes to unpronounce-ability, and unreliability, those who defend the English language are not in an unassailable position. 'Plough', 'though', 'thorough', 'rough', 'through' – I rest my case. Behind the arbitrariness of spelling is the greater arbitrariness of the relationship between words and whatever it is that they designate. That *arbre* means 'tree' must be arbitrary (the ground here is littered with unexploded puns) and equally so the fact that 'tree' means tree. And as for 'the', the definite article – something between a grunt and the bark of a Yap dog – the kind of work it gets to do is astonishing.

The story doesn't end with written words, of course. There are the letters that make them up. Just now, talk on the radio of the 'omicron' variant of Covid made me think about 'omega'. Omega looks like a 'w' that has had too much to drink or is bending in the wind – in the very breathe perhaps that is fashioning and transmitting it. Or melting in the heat of the end of things, as the journey from alpha is completed. (I say this in full knowledge that the best advice regarding the End of Everything after a nuclear war is that one should wrap up for it, as it will be bitterly cold rather than blazing hot.) At least 'omicron' ('o') – its junior brother – has a touch of rationality, seeming to depict a highly stylized pursing of any mouth uttering it, especially when it is multiplied and forms an orderly queue as it endeavours to express surprise – 'oooo!' – in response to camp gossip. (Though it can still go and spoil this when the trains of 'o's are buffered by an 'h' as in 'ooooh'.)

That I can work myself up to an astonishment at these thoughts about letters while at the same time using letters to record this astonishment should be an occasion for a higher-order astonishment. It isn't of course: there is still an unastonished ground on which the most worked-up astonishment stands. Kantian idealists running for a train that *must* be caught if they are to make the conference on Kant at which their attendance is obligatory take for granted the space and time through which they are hurrying, though their hero, their object of reverent study, denies the fundamental reality of the train and the space-time intervals that separate them from it.

Enough already. I am saying all this only as a roundabout way of apologizing for my insular bitching about a written language (Czech) that has the cheek not to be as easy, as transparent, as rational (I jest) as my native tongue. In short, I finish off what began when we reflected on 'Highbury' of the Highbury and Islington tube station. The point is that language does something extraordinary: it makes explicit the bump-into-ables of the world that surrounds us and transforms what-is into 'that-it-is'. It gives us the many and various powers that follow from placing Being in inverted commas. So, when I encounter a notice such as ZAZNI-LI VYSTRAHA OPJSTE DVERNI PROSTOR CAFÉ, I should refrain from churlish complaint. "Not everything or everyone is talking to you, mate", I remind myself.

Our short wait at the tram stop gives us sufficient time to note, and briefly bemoan, an extraordinarily dense outbreak of graffiti on a row of buildings whose state of dilapidation is the more surprising given their prime location. We did not dwell on this then, nor shall we now: enough has been said on this matter. Besides there is something more, much more, important: the Memorial to the victims of Communism.

The Memorial is composed of six bronze figures located on successive steps of a stone stairs at the base of Petrina Hill. The figures – naked, initially with anguished bearded faces, stooped in a posture of helplessness – are of the same man being gradually eaten away. On the second step a wide crack has appeared across his right shoulder and chest. On the third, his left arm and half his face have disappeared. On the fourth step, he has lost much of his torso and head. On the fifth, his head has entirely disappeared. On the sixth and final step he is reduced to a pair of legs. It reminds us how political prisoners were reduced to nakedness and beyond. Over 205,486 people were arrested, 170,938 were forced into exile, 4,500 died in prison, 327 were shot while trying to escape, and 248 were executed.[156]

The unveiling ceremony was marred by controversy.[157] The memorial had been erected by the Prague 1 local council controlled by the right-of-centre Civic Democrats, a party whose national leader was Václav Klaus. He was invited to the ceremony but Václav Havel, who loathed him, was not. There was an uproar, given that Havel had done more than any other person to bring down Communism. He was hastily invited but turned down the invitation and then Klaus did the same. Although this cast a shadow across the unveiling – another was feminist anger that all the figures were men, when many women had suffered under Communism – the memorial remains a uniquely poignant record of the iniquity of those in power and the helplessness of those who dared to oppose them and, as such, it may be a testament to the 'power of the powerless'.[158]

Our tram arrives and we are pleased that it is of the huge-windowed variety. On one side of the street there are the lovely gardens that form the hem of Petrina's wooded slopes. On the other, there are tasty, cobbled streets leading down to the Vltava and the Embankment along which we have a little while back taken our minds for a walk.

Just before we reach the next stop, we pass a pub, part of a chain, dressed in the livery of The Good Soldier Schweik. The yellow painted walls and the familiar stubbly face of the Good Soldier remind us of the interior and the traditional Czech food and beer to be had in the better-known U Kalicka.[159] There are quotations from Jaroslav Hasek's novel scribbled on the walls and replicas of the famous illustrations by Josef Lada, illustrating the life of the not-so-good soldier. It was Hasek's favourite pub, and it was here that he made an appointment to meet someone 'at 6 o'clock after the war', adding that it might be better if it was half-past six in case he was held up somewhere – or if victory were delayed. Visitors have included Lionel Jospin, Jacques Chirac, Boris Yeltsin and (of course) Václav Havel. Apart from Havel, it seems to have few Czech patrons – perhaps the price of the food and the accordion player visiting each table in turn (none shall escape) may account for this.

It is in the spirit of Hacek that the present writer makes his pilgrimage to the Schweikery without having taken the trouble to read the famous book. Given the choice between on the one hand reading something plus going to the pub and on the other just going to the pub, Schweik would have taken the latter branch of the fork.

But at this moment your tram traveller is taking the Schweikian spirit even further and failing to go to the pub. This non-visit, however, opens an opportunity to continue some unfinished business started by David Cerny's monstrous babies.

It is about what we might call 'the Czech temperament'. The first point to make is that Schweik' s attitude is not unique to Czech soldiery. "Bugger the war, let's have a brew lads" could have been excerpted from the table talk of any member of the poor bloody infantry in any nation over the last few centuries. The second is that the very idea that Schweik gives insight into his fellow countrymen is a measure of our tendency to transform a caricature into a reliable indicator of something called the collective consciousness. There is no good evidence, or none that I am aware of, that the frequency of non-Surrealist cock-snooking rises as we travel from e.g., Stockport Eng. (where I am currently writing) to e.g., Prague CZ (which I am currently writing about).

At the risk of banging on about the obvious, I will continue the list of the kinds of things that might fill the waking hours of the citizens of this city behind doors (front, bedroom, kitchen), windows curtained by sideways-blinking cloth eyelids or by reflections, round corners, inside trams, cafés, shops, theatres – what they might do, get up to, perform, dream of doing, refrain explicitly from doing. This might plausibly include wondering what the spouse is 'up to'...planning for Christmas with a transient mental image of candles and waning light...struggling with the top of a bottle... mouth washing...inspecting one's toes...declaring one's self on the brink of a breakthrough or of a breakdown... awaiting the result of a glucose test... rummaging in another's body and thinking it is lovemaking...looking for something just put down...throwing

a screwed up paper to a waste paper basket (wpb) and missing...
selecting a wpb from an overwhelming variety of choices available
in a department store...weighing pros and cons...fluffing lines on a
first date...taking a child to infant school...classifying something as
third-rate...wondering whether there is one or there are two s's in
Hussites...feeling overwhelmed by work...watching a volcano erupt
on TV...sneering at another country...being obsequious...feeling
badly let down or simply unlucky...snubbing or being snubbed...
actively controlling one's temper...hearing one's bare feet padding
and remembering last summer's holiday...confusing a button on a
shirt for a stain...checking a calendar while rumination over a snub
hardens into a well-formed grudge...galloping to get to the end of a
book or a pudding...belching...laughing at a belch...resenting the
weight of an object, or the attitude and tone of voice of a boss...
Nothing, in short, that would be out of place in the life of a citizen
of Stockport, Eng.

I would like to claim that it is my haste to visit a pub – even
a virtual one – that explains my omitting even to mention, never
mind describe, the beautiful music school and museum, and many
other attendabilia either side of the Schweik pub. But that would
be untrue. Rather, it is the embarrassment of riches; more precisely
(for one who would do justice to a journey through Prague and
capture its streets on a page) the hopelessness of riches.

Hence the relegation to a passing glance of an intriguing café
that is accessed via a post office/newsagents, whose tables are
mixed with banquettes (bald velvet surfaces), and honey cakes and
scented teas are served to a student-ish, metaphorically Bohemian,
population in an outdoor-indoor space fragrant with Vapes and per-

haps mind-altering substances and banishing many other enclosed spaces and architectural delights to a nowhere beyond this page.

# Hellichova to Malostranská námesti

The sleeve of our journey acquires a less opaque label: Újezd gives way to Karmelitská. It is not at first clear why the road should have taken on the name of the Carmelites. The journey from Mount Carmel in Israel, where The Roman Catholic Order of the Blessed Virgin Mary of Mount Carmel had its origin, to this section of the 22 tram route requires a bit of explanation. Actually, a lot of explanation.[160]

The Carmelites, especially the Nuns, have had a staggeringly high rate of visions. Whether this is due to dietary deficiency, suggestibility, or to a special *tendresse* the Virgin Mary had for this order, is unclear, though it has resulted in an impressive canonization rate, including some superstars – among them St. Teresa of Avila, St. John of the Cross, and St. Therese of Lisieux whose visions have prompted millions of pilgrimages and the sale of vast quantities of merchandise with wide profit margins.

What, then, are the Carmelites doing in Prague? Their present residence, which was built in 1611, began as the Lutheran church (I jest not) of the Holy Trinity. This designation was not to last. A mere 9 years later, after the Battle of Bilá Hora, and the victory of the imperial pro-catholic forces in the Czechlands, the triumphant Emperor Ferdinand II appropriated the church and bestowed it on the Carmelites – described as 'discalced' because they travelled barefoot or wore unfashionable, treadbare sandals. The monks did not hesitate to accept the gift and in 1624 they re-dedicated the once Lutheran Church to the Virgin Mary. To rub more salt into the Protestant wound, they gave Mary the additional title 'Our Lady Victorious' as a thank you to Ferdinand and an acknowledgment of the happy outcome of Bilá Hora. There is however no evidence that the VM took part in that conflict in which 4,000 Protestants were killed or imprisoned compared with 700 Catholics. As to whether she delightedly punched the air till it was bruised, when the result came through, there is no reliable information. A few years later a Carmelite *monastery* – aargh! – was added to what had been a protestant church.

To add vinegar to the salt rubbed into the wound, the church became the home of an idol. The item was imported from Spain by a Spanish duchess Polyxena Lobkowicz. She was to be married to a Prague nobleman and had, so the story goes, received the statue of the Infant Jesus from none other than St. Theresa of Avila, as a wedding gift. In 1628 she donated it to the Carmelite church where it became an object of veneration. It was said to have miraculous properties.

Just as the Infant was settling down in his new home, disaster struck. In 1631, not much more than a decade after the catholic triumph at Bilá Hora, protestant Saxons seized Prague. The monks fled and the statue was discarded as junk. When the monks returned to the church in 1637, the Infant was rediscovered by Father Cyril of the Mother of God. Alas, it had lost its arms. In his prayers, Father Cyril heard the infant Jesus saying that, if he were to restore his arms, peace and blessing would follow. This was an offer he could not refuse even had he the inclination to do so. The infant Jesus kept his part of the bargain. In addition to cases of miraculous healing, he was credited with saving Prague during the Swedish siege of 1639. As a reward, he was moved to a more public location in the church, so that he could be worshipped; and from time to time, he was carried in processions round Prague's holy places.

In 1651 he was adorned with a crown and, seemingly in response, the frequency of miracles continued to rise. Recognizing a winner when she saw one, Maria Theresa, Holy Roman Empress, personally donated an embroidered robe in 1754. The infant's luck then again ran out. Maria Theresa's successor Josef II launched a campaign against the monasteries and other institutions devoted solely to contemplation: their lack of productivity offended his Enlightenment sensibilities. The church and the altar on which baby Jesus was located fell into decay.

The story did not, however, end there. In 1879, the monastery was restored, and the Infant toured the convents of Prague on what was essentially a pre-digital crowdfunding mission, in which people carrying the icon, rather than electrons, were sent out to spread the word and, more particularly, to raise money for his own restoration. The rate of reported miracles throughout the Austro-Hungarian Empire again rose sharply.

The 300th anniversary of the installation of the Infant Jesus in 1935 was marked 'with great splendour'. For reasons that do not need spelling out, things monastic became a bit quiet between 1939 and 1989: veneration, such as it was, had to be low key. In 1993, four years after the Velvet Revolution, when the coast was again clear, the Carmelites returned to the church and veneration of the Infant returned to earlier levels. Pope Benedict visited in 2009 and gave the Infant a spare crown. The coronation of the Infant is still celebrated in the first week of May – except in 2020 when it was judged that his Corona was impotent against coronavirus.

All of this is said to have taken place just a short stagger from the pub bearing the branding of the Good Soldier Schweik and his creator. I have gone into some detail because the history explains two things. The first is the surprising capitulation of a proudly Protestant country in calling a main street in its capital after an idol-worshipping Catholic sect. From the standpoint of reformed churches, the icon was but a 'pented bredd'[161] – daubed wood – and to worship it was merely idolatry. The second is that it explains something that has always puzzled us as we glide past the church: there are invariably groups of people on the steps leading up to the main entrance. Now we know why: they are pilgrims. Indeed, they are 'Pilgrim Groups' or 'Mass Reservations' (no pun, I think, intended) who can book in advance. Importantly, as we are informed on the website, donations can be made in US Dollars, Euros, or Czech crowns by the press of a button, courtesy of the often-overlooked miracles of modern technology.

Just before we swing into *Malostranská námesti* we pass a gift shop and encounter in large print the lovely Czech word for gift: DARKY. I cannot resist becoming Dai-gression the Welsh raconteur, though I have more insight than he, recognizing that what follows has less to do with Prague than with the passenger looking at it and intermittently reporting some of what he sees; with the mind uncovering Prague for a distant unknown interlocuter.

The association of gifts with darkness invites me to dig into the deepest layers of the accessible past of this embodied subject,

Raymond Tallis, when Christmas meant gifts, and the anticipation of them was a torch shining in the darkness of Advent, of that month when nights were fatter than days, and darkness seemed the default state of the world. This journey through time was set out in space in the Advent Calendar, with each day a secret compartment.

I wake out of reminiscence to discover that we have passed the magnificent Palác Lazanskycho or the West-District Law Court. It was here that Václav Havel was sentenced to four years in prison, after a trial lasting all of 48 hours, for his role in Charter '77. Let Michael Zantovsky take up the story:

> Reading and hearing the accounts and recollections of Václav Havel and others who were there, in the dark, unfriendly building of the Prague-West District Court in Karmelitská Street, metres away from the baroque and Gothic glory of Prague's Lesser Town, it is impossible to escape the conclusion that Charter 77, the human rights movement that all the power, might and force of the regime would be unable to suppress, was born there that day.[162]

We are already embarked on the S-shaped trajectory that takes us into Malostranská námesti (Lesser Town Square). As we swing into the square, we glance at the fat-pillared cloisters stretching towards the Charles IV Bridge that, notwithstanding its elevation and its vast towers, somehow contrives to be out of sight. The cloisters shelter beer-dark cafés, some with cellar-like rooms that look as if they have been mined out of the material that makes up the walls that enclose them. We do not intend to dismount here, except in reminiscence. And there is much to reminisce about as this is one of the most travelled hubs of our many trips to Prague in the 20 years since we first arranged for our bodies, then in their mid-50s, to be transported to the city.

# (Mainly) Virtual Hop-Off:
# Malostranská Namesti

We have often sat in front of the cloistered beer halls, warmed by outdoor heaters. We have equally often alighted here to walk up Nerudova and Uvoz towards the Castle, before bodily antiquity made the principle of CBA more attractive. What we did not do was go inside Starbucks – which is the first establishment that greets us as we turn into the Square.

Starbucks, one of 20,891 such stores in 62 countries, is first and foremost a reminder of how even the most wonderful Somewhere has an interstitial tissue of Anywhere, of Nowhere in Particular. Luckily it is tidied away as the ground floor of a grandiose neo-Renaissance mini-palace, and it is largely hidden by cloisters. Nevertheless, the green logo of the Melusine – a cross between a mermaid and a siren, her hair like currents on water echoing so we are told, the seafaring tradition of Seattle ('What shall we do with a coffee-drinking sailor?') – is impossible to unsee.

Equally frequently, we have set off from here towards and across the Charles Bridge *en route* for the Old Town and the Old Town Square and we still do so when we have guests for whom the Old Town Square is a novel experience. On such occasions, we join the crowd outside the Gothic tower of the 12th century Old Town Hall, waiting for the astronomical clock ("the oldest clock in the world still operating") to strike the hour, something it has done approximately 5.25 million times. Vanity, Greed, Death, and Lust – a rather odd quartet – are set in motion and the 12 apostles process across the windows above the clock. The most striking item in the square – perhaps oppressively so – is the Jan Hus Monument. It is vast; indeed monumental. At its centre is Hus himself, standing upright. For company he has Hussite warriors, many of whom have fallen, fighting for the cause of various freedoms – from the Catholic Church, and from the Catholic Habsburg empire – of which freedom of thought was paramount.

It was a cause that must have seemed forever lost in the 300 years between the Battle of Bilá Hora and the emergence of the Czechoslovak Republic. The happy ending of a long wait was symbolized in the square by a young mother standing for national re-birth. The monument was unveiled in 1915 four years before the re-birth was completed and 500 years after Hus' martyrdom.

Hus' betrayal and incineration is summarized by Thomas Carlyle in his inimitable style:

> It was the way they had ended with Huss *(sic)*, with Jerome, the century before. A short argument, fire. Poor Huss: he came to that Constance Council, with all imaginable promises and safe conducts; an earnest, not rebellious kind of man; they laid him instantly in a stone dungeon 'three-feet wide, six-high, seven-feet long'; *burnt* the true voice of him out of this world; choked it in smoke and fire. That was *not* well done![163]

It is said that Hus sang psalms as he died: unimaginable courage amid unimaginable suffering and terror.

The flames that burned his body ignited the conflict of the Hussite wars until, by a particularly bitter twist, the Hussites turned on each other: Ultraquists against more moderate Taborites. Meanwhile, five crusades were licensed by the Pope against the Hussites. So things continued – with interesting technological developments in weapons of destruction – for over a decade until a peace treaty was signed. As time went on, the Hussites assimilated themselves to another nominalized adjective: they became Lutherans or even Protestants. By this time, the Czech lands were laid waste and the population in the century after the murder of Hus fell to half of what it had been in 1400. That was *not* well done!

The erection of the monument to Hus in 1915 was followed shortly by the demolition of the column to the Virgin Mary, that had been erected in Old Town Square to celebrate the end of the Thirty Years' War and to commemorate the role of the Czech Republic in bringing it about, though its consequences were unwelcome to them. For many Czechs, the Marian column had been a doctrinal and historical eyesore.

The whirligig of time has not, however, stopped whirling. In 2020 a replica of the Marian original monument was erected in its original place, notwithstanding many objections. Jan Hus and the Virgin Mary, representing proto-Protestantism and Catholic Mariolatry, are forced to be neighbours. How well they get on remains to be seen. The most effective guarantee of peace will be the total indifference of most citizens to the causes for which so much blood was shed. Atheism and agnosticism and, more recently, the worship of electronic influencers may act as a buffer between warring strands of Christianity thus reducing the chances of all-out-war or even chronic low-grade nastiness.

But today, we do not cross the Charles Bridge to the Old Town. We remain on our course for the Castle and have time to take in only one building and to recall one event.

The building is a church dedicated to St Nicholas. First, a fact or two.[164] Consecrated in 1775, St Nicholas' is the most famous Baroque Church in Prague. It took a century to build and engaged three generations of architects. The side-by-side slender belfry and the massive dome with its copper cupola give the church its distinctive outline, visible and recognizable from all over Prague.

The entrance to the church cannot be seen from the café in Malastransá námesti where we often stop for a drink after we have descended from the Castle. Notwithstanding our ambiguous relations with the waiters, arising out of the lack of clarity as to which waiter is serving which table, we patronize this café repeatedly. In part this is because of St. Nicholas' gigantic presence, and the pleasure of seeing two out of the four belfry clocks measure the passage of the afternoon toward evening or evening to night and the same evolution being measured out qualitatively by the sunlight that the belfry seems always to harvest. Sometimes the intersection, in the church clock, of time and eternity, of the actual present world and the possible next, infuses even this secular soul with an uneasy sense of chickens coming home to roast – though to undergo something as primitive as dying in this super-complex, super-sophisticated world seems rather regressive. The ancient, cloistered walls at the far end of the square, marking the beginning of Nerudova, add to the pleasure.

The café has a special place in our mind because it was here that we first learned of the expected birth of our first grandson, the little boy who appeared anonymously, reading a book about dinosaurs, in Café Slavia.

While we wait to be served, our attention to yesterday's *Guardian* is divided by the flaneurial pleasure of watching the crowd in different modes of stasis and kinesis – loitering, waiting, walking, strolling, running, tram-queuing being just a few – and the pigeons with chests puffed out with self-importance strutting between possibilities of food, their heads nodding in agreement with every step they take.

And the occasional incident.

One such incident that sticks in our mind began with a coach driver trying to perform a U-turn in a rather confined space on the far side of the square. After many attempts, he swung round with impatient resolve and bashed the rear of his coach into a wall of great antiquity, part of a run of cloisters. A large fragment fell from said wall to the ground. As seemed apparent from the demeanour of the driver as he got out to assess the significance of the collision, the wall had given as good as it got. Just what one might expect from a structure that had withstood all that the centuries had thrown at it – the Hussite wars, the Siege of Prague, the Habsburg empire, the Nazi invasion, Communism, and, in more recent times, the strong urinary jets of Prague stag weekenders, and the music of Karel Gott.

There was a collective raising of eyebrows. Eyes under the brows converged on the spot from which the sickening and exciting noise of metal on stone originated. Instant diagnoses were proffered. The coach, after all, was from Poland, the driver presumably Polish. No further explanation needed – at least to judge from the wisecracks and knowing glances between waiters and waiters, customers and customers, and waiters and customers.

The driver's fury and unfolding distress became a spectator sport for the crowd in the square, compounding the ordeal for a man who doubtless had had little prior experience of publicity. We imagined his passengers, even now returning from the Castle, descending Nerudova, negotiating the currents and countercurrents of bodies of other tourists, passing between splendid embassies, lovely bijou hotels, cafés, and innumerable souvenir shops whose contents spilt on to the pavements, to join their coach, innocent of the unsatisfactory climax of their visit to Magic Prague.

The collective knowing response to the event gave us permission for our own brand of knowingness – about the collective consciousness of Czech people of the collective consciousness of the citizens of the other nations of the Visegrád Four. The locals' response was articulated by our waiter, at last arriving with our drinks, "What do you expect of damn Poles?'". We did not say that we lacked prior expectations regarding Poles – damned or otherwise – and certainly any precise enough to be confirmed or corrected by the accident we had witnessed or that we lacked mental space available to be rented by such expectations. This was not due to an admirable resistance to inadequately evidenced general statements, on our part, much as we would have liked to have believed this of ourselves. On the contrary we at once formed the aforementioned general notion of our own: an idea of the Czech idea of their near neighbours. Or the consciousness that one nation (the one we were visiting) had of another nation (Poland) being gathered up in the consciousness of two representatives of a third nation (England) taking the first sip of their long-awaited drink.

Any tendency to pass adverse judgement even on this single Pole (who must now be described as 'hapless' or at the very least 'lean of hap'), never mind the nation whom his fame in the square had picked him out to represent, would have been pre-empted by our recollection of the driver's skill. He had, not long before the collision between the city and that which had transported him to it, executed a remarkable backward journey down the narrows of Nerudova where he had deposited his passengers. As one for whom backing into a carparking bay is a matter of successive approxima-tions towards an approximate realization of goal, or the impossibility of threading a rope through the eye of a needle, or inserting a leg into a finger stall, I could not but agree that it was hard luck, not nationality-determined incompetence, that had brought him to his un-pretty pass.

The *Grundlagen of Polentheorie* (the Foundations of Pole Theory) was in ruins and we were prompted to reflect a little on the idea of common knowledge shared through knowing looks:

> Common knowledge in the technical sense of something that everyone knows that everyone knows that everyone knows.[165]

Of course, knowing glances are more at ease with themselves when they are least informed. We suddenly have an insight into our status as a couple of strangers floating in an ocean of strangers borne up in a tidal wave of rumours.

We remember the opinionated taxi driver who drove us to Manchester Airport and the meta-opinionated platform from which we formed opinions on his opinions and we have a sense of grasping something that is falling through our fingers. Ish.

Ish indeed. For that consciousness was, of course, haunted by a meta-consciousness of its insufficient grounding. And the ish is many-layered. Most of our cognitive fields have to be out of focus so that we can be precise, avoiding that chair, this person, and the other conclusion, that lie to one side of our path. We are always reminding ourselves that the plural of anecdote is not data; but in real life, the singular of anecdote somehow multiplies itself into data when it lands on a prepared, that is to say prejudiced, mind: the kind of mind that elevates the cheekbones of an entire population in response to the idea of the descent of an Iron Curtain pushing a nation eastward in an inner map of Europe.

As we return from our virtual hop-off to the tram, we resume our habit of punching above our cognitive weight, navigating the world with the aid of assumptions of a vast and general scope that no life of finite duration could adequately confirm. We have the measure of something – not Poles, nor Czechs' view of poles, but…But what? Of ourselves, perhaps. Or bits of ourselves.

Perhaps.

# Malostranská námesti to Malostranská

The tram swings out of the square with a sharpish right turn. The passengers are now mainly tourists rather than polite and well-behaved Czechs, so we are not offered a seat. As is often the case on the ascent to the Castle, there is a disproportionate number of Italians whose excited conversations are not inhibited by the bodies of strangers interposed between emitters and recipients. My characterization of the Italian language as 'Latin soaked in wine' does not seem to extend to the insufficiently telegraphic exchanges shouted from one end of the tram to another. At the least it tests the sincerity of the metaphor.

After a short while, the street – Letenská – that picks its way between thick-walled government buildings, embassies, and churches, narrows to a single lane and we enter a short tunnel under buildings and imagine the rumbles that our passage transmits to individuals conducting their business in high-ceilinged and sash-windowed offices above us. The road widens and is reunited with its twin-lane, though it still seems like a cutting. Our backward gaze through the huge rear-window of the tram, is crowned by the dark spires of the Cathedral, as remote as ever, indeed seeming to rise as we recede, until it is obliterated as we turn into the vast openness of Malostranská.

A few yards from the stop is the entrance to the Wallenstein Gardens.[166] We decline the opportunity to ascend to the Castle through this extraordinary geometrical early 17th century Baroque horticultural masterpiece, notwithstanding the attraction of a garden pavilion, a grotto, an aviary, and an artificial lake where there was one of the earliest successful tests of a steamship, something that would be of particular use if Bohemia managed to grow coasts. As a result, we also miss out on the opportunity to visit another masterpiece: the Wallenstein palace situated in the gardens – a complex of 26 buildings and 2 brickworks that is now the seat of the Czech senate.

The gardens and their contents were constructed at the command of the eponymous Wallenstein, probably the most brilliant general in the Thirty Years' War and, as a result of two marriages and the spoils of war, one of the richest men in Europe. His up and down relationship with a justly suspicious Emperor Frederick ended in his assassination at the age of 50. Into that half-century of brutal, visionary, recklessly courageous, boundlessly ambitious, existence he had packed more than enough event, activity, and achievement to fill a dozen lives – and all this despite being crippled by agonizing gout for his last 14 years and, towards the end, suffering the added torments of late syphilis which meant that he could scarcely mount a horse.

Not for him the CBA principle that binds us to the tram.

# Malostranská to Královsky letohrádek

As a result of some fancy footwork, we manage – between the efflux and influx of passengers – to annex two seats, window seats what is more. We are doubly motivated. The first is that we are at last about to begin our ascent. The broad avenue along which we continue suddenly takes a sharp turn to the left, then with an equally sharp right turn enters a hair-pin bend before finally straightening out. The pressure on bodies under the influence of the inertial framework of the distant stars would have overcome our capacity to remain upright. Secondly, the hairpin gives us a panoramic view of the Little Town (with the great-domed St. Nicholas), of the Old Town (with the towers of the Charles Bridge and the Old Town Hall), of Vinorhady and the twin spires of St Ludmilla's church in Peace Square, and alas the Zizkov Tower, about which I shall say nothing more. (It keeps on popping up and saying '!', 'Here I am!', 'Look at me!' "Just take no notice, we say to ourselves".) It is as if great stretches of our journey have been gathered up so that what had to be experienced in succession is now presented simultaneously. The headwear – something between a crown and a bun – of a rather self-conscious stone lion occupying the apex of the bend makes us laugh.

The panorama is lost as we turn again, continuing our ascent along a wide, tree-lined avenue which permits sideways glances at an impressive succession of palatial buildings. We are richly compensated for the loss of view. We can now see the Cathedral a little closer and from what hitherto been its back view. The Castle is starting to look a little more like what it says it is, thanks to a deep, wide moat, on the far side of the avenue. But first we are offered Královsky letohrádek which means Royal Summer Palace. It is here that the Exhibition commemorating the 30th anniversary of the Velvet Revolution was held. The short, rueful statement that greets the visitors at the end of the exhibition, and which we anticipated on our return from Grébovka, deserves a second hearing:

> Because the ethos and ideals of the November legacy have not yet been fulfilled and, to this day, remain a vivid challenge for us.

The Summer Palace, otherwise known as the Belvedere (or Great View), is yet another renaissance masterpiece. It was built in the Royal Gardens of Prague Castle by the Holy Roman Emperor Ferdinand I (doubtless with the assistance of others). It was a gift for his wife Anna. Construction ran over time (and doubtless over budget) and the palace was not completed until 1565, 27 years after starting. Queen Anna had by then been missing for nearly 20 years, having died giving birth to her 15th child (13 of whom lived to be adults), her fertility providing what would be a challenge to anyone's numeracy. King Ferdinand had already left Prague some six years before her death, though one assumes that he returned from time to time for conjugal visits to maintain the seemingly unbroken flow of descendants from his wife's fertile womb. The gift of the palace therefore never reached its intended recipient, though the couple are commemorated in one of the many frescoes in the palace: Ferdinand, wearing the Order of the Golden Fleece (an honour he shares with Queen Elizabeth II of Great Britain and the bicycling Queen Beatrix of Holland), is offering Anna a fig-tree blossom. The Palace was subsequently used by Emperor Rudolf II for an observatory and his staff included Tycho Brahe and Johannes Kepler of whom we shall hear more presently.

# Hop-Off Královsky letohrádek

The temptation to dismount here is heightened by memories of hot, very hot, summer evenings in the Summer Palace Gardens that are a miracle of stillness. There is insufficient breeze to make a flower nod; not the slightest fidget from the tallest tree; distant voices cancel their distances. We are prompted to cite PG Wodehouse's reference to "those still evenings you get in the Summer, when you can hear a snail clear its throat a mile away".[167] A doomed competitive instinct prompts me to attempt unwisely to cap this with (say) a worm permitting flatus to leave its body with utmost discretion. Or the silent settling of eyelids shutting out Prague, inscribing a short hyphen in the evening light, terminated by a clickless opening. At any rate, as Coleridge expressed it,

the mute, still air

Is Music slumbering on her instrument.[168]

The stillness of the Summer Palace Gardens unpacked itself into a sense of Bohemian distances around us and, beyond that, the *Europa* that those distances are in the *Mittel* of.

In Prague such evenings seem commoner than at home perhaps because they echo more sonorously in the memory. We remember so many evenings (and afternoons) when our own mobility, creating a soft counter-current, awakens 'air' from being the most delicate of mass nouns to the least muscular of verbs:

the air airs. Such stillness seems miraculous given that, as Kepler discovered, we are located on a small, air-fleeced planet drawing ellipses at 67,000 miles per hour through largely empty space.

The city of Prague is quieter than one might reasonably expect of a capital city. Excellent public transport means that traffic jams and angry, hooting drivers are rare. The quiet was brought home to us once when, walking up to the Castle in light rain, we were passed by a tourist from the Far East descending in full waterproofs. The whispering of one over-trousered leg rubbing against another was the loudest sound of that moment.

Something else adds to the force-field of the temptation to de-tram. I quote from a Guide book:

> Instantly across the road are the Royal Gardens and the Royal Summer Palace, which *fragrantly leads to a public toilet* and to Prague Castle.[169] (Italics added).

The Castle can, of course, wait; indeed, must wait, for other things are, shall we say, more time-sensitive. There is one (the she) who has been assailed by a signal from within, mirroring those received with increasing frequency by the other (the he) who has acquired in the most recent decade an Unbearable Tightness of Peeing (a possible title for Milan Kundera's unwritten novel about late life). It is the she on this occasion for whom the vesical imperative is most insistent. They therefore exit through the accordioning doors of the tram and cross the road.

He settles on a bench while, taken to one side by her body insisting on the business it must transact, Mrs. T. makes her visit – one out of a lifetime's total of about 250,000 – to 'the smallest room'. Such waiting is always an opportunity to think; and, if thinking generates words that seem to have a potential home outside the moment, to make notes in a notebook. We are after all getting closer to the Castle and it seems time, perhaps, for a backward glance.

That glance looks past the tram-ride, past our flat in Norska, our arrival in Prague, to the house in Bramhall, Stockport, from which we departed. Thoughts turn homewards and the Philosopher on the Tram finds himself recalling a place, as seasonless and placeless as thought itself: the version of the smallest room in the house he left a week or so ago. "The end of all our exploring will be to arrive where we began and to know the place for the first time".[170] Or to reclaim for proximity the enchantment lent by distance.

This imaginary homeward journey is fueled, for some inexplicable reason, by a thought about vowels, or the lack of them, in the Czech language. The thought alights on a copy in the toilet of Valley Road Bramhall of the satirical magazine *The Onion* ('The Finest News Reporting') and a headlined article on an emergency drop of vowels into Serbia authorized by President Clinton. (Other articles include the claim that Microsoft are planning to patent 1's and 0's.)

Thus, is sown the seed for The Recollection of The Third Toilet, illuminated by the guttering matchlight of memory. Facilities 1 and 2 have already been introduced to the reader: there was the item in Norská where Blu-tack failed; and the other in Samos where Purkinje's secretion lost its grip on the thighs of the sitter. The seats sent their pistol shots through silences several hundred miles and many months apart, stitched together in the consciousness of the man sitting on the bench in the Summer Palace gardens.

What follows is to some extent an after-spark of that (fairly) friendly quarrel with Viteslav Nezval and his Surrealist friends that flared up in Národní trídá: a recognition of a second type of embarrassment in the toilet – an embarrassment of riches. As I await Mrs. T., I start an inventory, to be completed on my return, that will eventually run into more items than it is appropriate to rehearse in this place, unpacking what, from 700 miles distance (and even close up when the gaze is right), seems like a treasure chest of rich affordances.

Mrs. T. exits the toilet enriched by a further datum to support a general observation. It relates to The Great *Bouleversement* (for she is learning French as a second language, Surrey English being her first) with respect to the olfactory properties of British and Continental toilets. There has been general improvement both sides of the channel since we first ventured beyond the shores of our native land; but there is no doubt that Continental toilets are now ahead of their British counterparts as regards the desirability of what is mandatorily inhaled by the customer when making his or her own contribution. The promise of 'fragrantly leading' to the facility is honoured on arrival.

Mrs. T. reminds your author of an anecdote reflecting the suspicion of 'The Continong' *(sic)* prevalent among Britons in the early post-War period of their childhood. Her aunt, having taken Mrs. T's younger brother for a daytrip to Calais washed him in Dettol on his return before handing him over to his parents. There could have been no more compelling evidence of The Great *Bouleversement* than the embarrassment your author experienced when he took Jan Halák to one of the most famous pubs in the city of his birth and both parties were appalled by the Billingsgate perfume of the gents toilet.

Time to admit that the entry in my notebook written while waiting for Mrs. T. may have been an invention; but the inventory there conceived, and the surreal reality of daily life that it intended to highlight, most certainly is not. And if I have skirted round the edges of the traditional 'Magic Prague' of Angelo Maria Ripellino and others it is not only because they have done something better than I could have done, even had I got there first, but because the magic of Prague resides at least in part in its capacity to cast light on the magic of elsewhere. Its magic, that is to say, is generalizable – even, dare I say it, to Bramhall, to Stockport, to Manchester. Or, to return to a starting point: the items cohabiting in the Third Toilet add up to something that beats into a cocked hat the meeting of an umbrella and a sewing machine on a dissection table.

It is time, however, to reboard the tram and continue our quest – that of two embodied subjects seeking to find a city and finding through seeking; finding through not-yet-finding.

# Královsky letohrádek to Prázsky hrad

The new tram is as well provided with excited Italians as its predecessor, but they are all standing up – and indeed more excited – because the next stop is the first real option for accessing the Castle via its North Entrance.

*Prázsky Hrad!* Prague Castle. In case we do not grasp this portentous fact, the stop is also announced in American English. 'Exit here for Prague Castle'. We have arrived at our destination.

Except that we haven't.

Our fellow passengers gather themselves up into a voluble blob and file out taking their heads and fading voices across the road to one entrance to the Castle.

This, the Powder Bridge Entrance, is perfectly respectable, indeed beautiful. A cobbled bridge crosses over the steep moat-like dip that separates the Castle – or rather the Castle complex (a word we shall revisit) – from the road. It delivers a lesser sense of approach than the one we intend to take. It is enough to note that the charming Tour Guide captured on a video informs us that the extremely smart blue uniforms of the boxed guards either side of the passage into the Second Courtyard were designed by the same individual who created the costumes for the multi-Oscared film of *Amadeus* and that they had been name-checked in *The Simpsons*.[171] The costumier in question – Theodore 'Doda' Pistek – was an old friend of Václav Havel.[172] They had been fellow members of a wild association of artists, filmmakers, and athletes. 'The Fatherland's Palette' specialized in pranks and hellraising in the most desperate and dispiriting years of communism. In 1971, their annual Rallye Monte Fatherland "counted among its drivers a Mexican-looking gentleman in a big black Mercedes car". The gentleman was none other than the future leader of the Velvet Revolution and subsequently the occupant, as Prime Minister and President, of the Castle.[173] 'History has many cunning passages/Contrived corridors'.[174]

# Prázsky Hrad to Brusnice

We continue our journey, creaming along the broad, open carriageway, still ascending as the tram sees off the last of the Castle Complex, on our left. According to the *Guinness Book of Records* it is the largest such complex in the world, occupying an area equal to 45 football pitches – a unit that would have meant little to most of those associated with the Castle over most of its history which itself has lasted between 5 and 6 million standard football matches, excluding the half-time break and any injury time. The receding castle on our left has caused us to overlook something rather special, hidden in the land that slopes away to the right. So also, to judge by the paucity of intake and output from the tram at *Brusnice*, has the rest of the tourist population. It is the ancient village of Novy Svet.[175]

Novy Svet means 'new world' or 'new community'. As is the case with Oxford's New College (founded 1379), the name reminds us that 'newness' is relative; for it was built in the later 14th century to house the servants employed in Charles IV's shiny new castle. Their terms and conditions were not exactly generous and the dwellings in which they passed or eked their hungry, huddled lives were tiny. Either out of wishful thinking or irony, many of the houses were given names such as 'House of the Golden Star'. Words are cheap. (It would have cost us nothing to rename our modest dwelling, 'The Manor House, Bramhall.)

Six centuries later, the little houses are no bigger. Nevertheless, gilded by antiquity, and equipped with hot and cold running water, gas and electricity, and made over in other ways, they look cute, picturesque, even edible; and the cobbled streets that run between them, and the baroque defensive wall that surrounds them, give no hint of the aching legs that walked to work in the Castle or the stench of the excrement that added an extra layer to the cobbles. Two big fires – one in the 15$^{th}$ century during those obtrusive Hussite wars and the other in the middle of the 16$^{th}$ century – destroyed all but one of the wooden houses and kick-started the process of upgrading.

Among Novy Svet's distinguished inhabitants have been two filmmakers (Karel Kachyna and Jan Svankmajer for the super buffs) whose talents were displeasing to the communist authorities, and Tycho Brahe – though strictly he was a visitor, staying at the Golden Griffin Hotel before his ascent to the podium he now shares with Johannes Kepler, where he is awaiting us at the end of our tram journey. Accommodated outdoors there is none other than our old friend Jan Nepomuk, this time with headgear less wildly Ascot than the starry halo worn on Charles' Bridge.

Through the town runs Brusnice stream whose most salient achievement (from the distorted viewpoint of this narrative) has been to confer its name on the tram-stop. My only encounter with this stream has been courtesy of Jesse and Jonah Marks. The brothers travel the world, harvesting sounds from Panama, Mexico City, Vietnam, Cuba, Croatia – and Novy Svet.[176] They have recorded the sound of the Brusnice stream as it passes through a tunnel system that leads into the Vltava. The frantic coarse-textured sudsiness is also available visually as a flickering map of frequency and amplitude. And so, courtesy of the Marks brothers, a minor branch of the Vltava my father shared with Smetana and many others, is gathered up into an on-line space shared with: ocean waves in Troncones, Mexico; Gunflint Lake Ice in Minnesota; the dawn awakening of the jungle in Guatemala; and Merengue Musicians in Dominican Republic.

I mention the brothers' project because it has something in common with the ambition of the present work. They are trying to achieve something by sewing together widely scattered fragments served up to their minds by separate accidents, by gathering up the voices of disparate parts, to turn scatteredness on its head by making it a revelation of expansiveness of the world in which they pass their lives. In my narrative the brothers have themselves become such fragments but rather special fragments that (perhaps) entertain the hope that by capturing scattered butterflies they might also capture the spaces between them and hence enclose the world between their cupped hands. This is not so grand, or self-aggrandizing, as the ultimate purpose of my own (verbal) engagement with things: to reflect on the way 'and' both connects and separates and, by highlighting connecting links, also highlights and reaffirms connectedness.

"We must go there – and soon" we think as the tram pulls away from Brusnice tram stop. Even we are unable to measure the sincerity of our intention. The visit to Novy Svet recorded in these pages has been a virtual one, courtesy of the World Wide Web, perhaps the greatest *Wunderkammer* of them all, where fingers on a keyboard fling open an infinity of doors.

# Brusnice to Pohorelec

> The ravings of alchemists, birthday horoscopy, the elixir of life and the philosophers' stone, Tycho Brahe and Kepler, the Golden Lane, the animal and vegetable physiognomies of Arcimboldo, Rabbi Loew and his homunculus Golem, the fearful, misshapen Ghetto, the old cemetery and the Emperor's *Kunstkammer* – these are the images, the components of that bewitched kalei doscope we call Rudolfine Prague.[177]

We are on the last stretch of our seated journey, the final hyphen connecting tram stops. The still, boulevard-wide road – called Keplerova for reasons that will become obvious as we reach the end of this paragraph – continues and, because it sweeps round another curve, we postpone our assumption of the upright position until the last minute. We will shortly embark on a celestial journey courtesy of two of the most extraordinary heads human flesh has generated: they belong to two old friends – or perhaps frenemies - Tycho Brahe and Johannes Kepler.

As always, we pause after we have de-trammed to offer the gentlemen the gift of our attention. I can look at the statues at this present moment because they are portrayed in my computer's picture gallery, located between 'Brain' and 'Brentano', two along from 'Brexit and the NHS' (very bad news), and below a Pinocchio-nosed Boris Johnson (terrible news). My dependence on this machine that I am feeding with my finger-tips accounts for the fear of a particularly modern kind of defenestration, a digital successor to the analogue horrors: being expelled from Windows and effectively silenced, all passwords spent.

The processes by which Brahe and Kepler have arrived in the computer gallery in which they are stored is unimaginable. They would have been even more so to the two gentlemen making us extend our necks to gaze at their ungazing heads. The Cloud where their images are stored, and how we pull them down, are true miracles. They are the recent products of a 500-year intellectual adventure, of an engagement between mind and universe, that they had such a crucial role in starting. It will be evident that our pause by their effigies is infused with gratitude. We inwardly genuflect.

The side-by-side statues look ancient, with verdigris well established in the folded bronze. In fact, they were erected in 1984. Brahe is looking slightly downwards. In his right hand is an astrolabe, one of the various instruments – sextants, hourglasses, armillary spheres being some of the others – that he used in subjecting the heavens to an unprecedentedly sustained and accurate gaze, unpeeling the universe to human consciousness as it had never been unpeeled before, notwithstanding that he was unaided by telescopes. Kepler's gaze is upwards towards the heavens. This is perhaps a little surprising, given that it was Brahe who was the more assiduous sky-watcher and the source of much of the data Kepler used to arrive at his brilliant and near-heretical account of the orbits of the planets as not circular but elliptical. Brahe's report on his detailed examination of a supernova (proving that the heavens are not unchanging) – its title, too fetching to be exiled to endnotes, is *Concerning the Star, New and Never before Seen in*

*Anyone's Life or Memory* – published in 1573 was reprinted twice by Kepler. Kepler was an extraordinary mathematician – and visionary thinker – and this was what he brought to the collaboration with Brahe. Hence the scroll – on which are written his cosmic laws – in his hand.

Their collaboration had its ups and downs: Brahe was not entirely happy with Kepler hoovering up data he had acquired over thousands of often bitterly cold nights. No wonder they are as socially distanced on their shared plinth as is possible without one of them falling off. Indeed, they look as if they are about to walk, or even flounce, out on each other after a sharp exchange of wounding words. Nevertheless, the expatriate Dane and the refugee Austrian fleeing from religious persecution found a shared home in Prague and in the court of the infinitely curious and distinctly bonkers Rudolf II.

Their productive partnership laid the foundations of 'celestial mechanics', a term that captures a dramatic transformation of our collective vision of where, and perhaps who, we are, by bringing the heavens down to earth. It lies at the beginning of a journey towards a disenchanted world in which magic is to be found in technologies created on the basis of the laws of science. That kind of magic enables us to paint a perfect portrait of the statues of Brahe and Kepler with the click of a button and to send that portrait – bouncing it off a satellite circling the earth – to a similar device held in other hands hundreds of miles away, so they can look at it, smile, and share it. A hand-held *Wunderkammer* beyond the wildest dreams of the two men forever united in the history of humanity's penetration of the universe in which it finds itself.

The memorial, where patient observation and bold hypothesizing stand side by side, is thus wreathed in ironies. The geniuses hired by Rudolf II to assist him in his mystical and alchemical quests started the process by which astronomy distanced itself from astrology and the pursuit of knowledge and understanding was increasingly dependent on sober observation, measurements, and mathematics. And there was another irony, not as global in its implications but perhaps more poignant. Towards the end of his life, Brahe eventually agreed to Kepler's having access to all his data but on the understanding that Kepler would use them to verify Brahe's cherished belief that the earth was unmoving and that the other planets orbited the sun. Kepler found otherwise.

Brahe's posthumous existence has been haunted by two stories – one true and one endlessly debated – but both characteristically, even David Czerny-istically, Czech, though the astronomer was in the country for only a few years.[178] He had a prosthetic nose reputed to be made of gold or silver. It was a replacement for the one he had been born with that had been sliced off in a duel. The *casus belli* has been disputed but the most respectable version is that it was prompted by a disagreement with a fellow student over a mathematical problem. When proof fails, try swords. The largely respectful funeral oration referred to the golden hooter, and this caused an international incident: the King of Denmark – Brahe's earlier patron – wrote a letter of complaint to the Elector of Saxony.

More vigorously disputed has been the immediate cause of Brahe's death. The most well-known and snigger-worthy explanation concerned his urinary function. At a banquet with the king, he was seized by the need to take his horse to water but felt that it would have been impolite to leave the table before his royal host, notwithstanding his desperation. He progressed from being metaphorically to literally bursting, which took him from metaphorically to literally dying for a pee. Other explanations – such as mercury poisoning by a rival – have been proposed as his cause of death. The most recent inquiry, instigated by the Danish government, reported in 2012. It included a high-tech autopsy, in which the astronomer's remains were subject to some of the fruits of a vast scientific endeavour he had unwittingly set in motion: his star-ward gaze had helped us understand the earth. There was no evidence of mercury poisoning and nothing to contradict a story which, since we are still in Czechia, we may designate as another instance of 'the unbearable tightness of peeing'. And to add insult to injury, the pathologists claimed that there was evidence that Brahe's prosthetic nose was made not of gold or silver but of brass, thus putting it posthumously out of joint.

Before we leave the two men and the extraordinary merging of their two minds it is well to give the last word to Kepler:

> I measured the skies, now the shadows I measure,
>
> Skybound was the mind, earthbound the body rests.[179]

And so, we set off on foot for the last stage of our journey to the Castle. Our earthbound bodies wait to cross the road.

# THE DESCENT TO THE CASTLE

# More Disclaimers

I approach the task of doing justice to the final stage of our journey with an intensification of the sense of defeat that has haunted my narrative. Since we have descended from the tram, our excuse that we were swept past what we see no longer holds up.

A few decades ago, I published an article that argued against a belief, popular in certain circles, that realistic fiction was no longer a viable art-form. Amongst the reasons given for this by various critics who claimed that the cinema had killed the novel, the least daft was that fiction could not compete with the cinema as a representation of reality.[180] In some respects, this was a re-run of the argument in the 19th century over whether photography had rendered representational painting superfluous. My counterargument was that, unlike snaps and daubs, realistic fiction and realistic cinema are not in direct competition. They are trying to do different things. Indeed, there is much that fiction can do that cinema could not attempt. While the pen could scarcely compete with the camera as an instrument to articulate the visual appearance of things, it had the upper hand when it came to capturing what that visual appearance *meant* – or did not mean – to the person or people to whom it was appearing; how, for example, it fitted into their lives and relationships and their wider sense of things.

The article satisfied me when I wrote it; not the least because it was accepted for publication at a time when my non-medical publications could be counted on the fingers of one hand while the legs of a nest of millipedes would have been insufficient to count rejections. Nevertheless, I secretly sympathized with the notion that a picture was worth a thousand words – a sentiment I share with Fred R. Barnard in the advertising journal *Printers Ink* and Leonardo da Vinci who wrote that "a poet would be overcome by sleep and hunger before [being able to] describe with words what a painter is able to [depict] in an instant."[181]

If I am acutely conscious of this as I have tried to share the tram journey from Norská to The Castle it is in part because I have refreshed my memory of this path through Prague by looking at pictures and – brace yourself for a confession – several *videos* of the 22 tram route. I have started, stopped, and looked at these portraits of my journey innumerable times. Relying on videos is no more cheating than visiting the city with a notebook or a camera in hand; but the failure to do justice to what I see on the video highlights what is lost in the move from seeing to writing, from the eye to the pen. It is easier, of course, to specify the style of a building than to describe one brick. And I have no conception what "19th century neo-Renaissance" will ignite in the consciousness of the reader – what image, what idea.

Not that anyone would want a brick-by-brick account of the city or an unpacking of its infinitely folded surfaces – walls, rooves, windows, passages, avenues, carvings and facades, parks and gardens, daylights and shadows, skies and cobbles, vistas and close-ups, nooks and crannies – in an unending skein of sentences. Words fall short of the thisness of things (and by the way things return the compliment). Particulars slip between the meshes of terms that are necessarily general if they are to be used in an indefinite number of circumstances by a boundless chorus of speakers.

What you have read so far has not pretended to be a guide to Prague – to its present in space or its past in time – or even A Personal Guide to a Path Through (a Bit of the Stretch of Space-time That Is) Prague. So why the fuss? Simply this: we are closing in on our destination and there may be higher expectations of delivery than have been met so far. The tenuous connections and quirky angles and the faithful imitation of the aforementioned Dai-gression the Welsh *raconteur* may no longer satisfy the imaginary recipient who will not be mollified by being addressed as 'gentle reader', since gentility may not, and should not, be taken for granted.

In short, I am aware that you out there have grounds for complaint, and I can no longer disarm you with promises. Even had I been able to give you your money back (which would include your petrol or bus fare had you travelled to a bookshop to purchase this book, thereby doubling its sales, rather than sent electrons as your emissaries) I would not be able to return your time lost – time that might have been spent reading Shakespeare or Tolstoy, improving your competence at your profession, continuing your charitable activity, helping someone with their homework, sorting out that leaky gutter, or playing Snap or Monopoly with the children (if you have any to play with), or simply having a drink on the terrace with your spouse pretending that it is a distant cousin of The Balcony of Europe. Or working overtime to save up for a trip to Prague.

I cannot imagine talking in the manner of the author of several of my favourite books, Joseph Roth, who wrote thus of his arrival in Lyons on a Sunday afternoon:

> This city lies on the border between northern and southern Europe. It is a city of the center. Equally amenable to northern seriousness and single- mindedness and to the easygoing South, it smiles and works.[182]

'Smiles and works!' The reader will know already what I speculate might occupy the citizens of Prague, or rather a subset of them with whom I have shared a tram. At a great risk of overstating a case, I will add some supplementary expectations: that at a given time, a certain number of citizens will be...concluding from the need to use a hearing aid that old age is creeping up...bewildered by the range of offers in the department store they trust... struggling to remember who the Hussites were...sniffing, literally and metaphorically at something someone has said or a piece of equipment that has jammed or at the lack of resources in a hospital or at what they gather up as 'the political situation'...scoffing at the supposed philistinism of engineers...being obsequious... being angry at a washing up machine or the hand one has been dealt in life... actively controlling one's own temper...trimming a reluctant baby's fingernails...grasping a steering wheel with fury...

being overwhelmed with joy…noting the dissonance in another's face…plumping pillows…cracking jokes that misfire…mis-whistling Beethoven's 3<sup>rd</sup> symphony…peering through a windscreen… stepping in dog-dirt (less likely of late – *vide infra*)…being irritated by another's whistling…struggling with a zip …throwing a teddy bear across a room…being callow…having the mother of all chinwags… being aware of being callow but not having the word for it…sighing with pleasure at the appearance of a carpet….resenting being chided for speaking with a mouth full of food…tweeting…taking a laptop to a repair shop…feeling wistful…heading off to a distant war…sorting rubbish into municipally mandated categories…blowing out cheeks with surprise (have I seen this?)…comparing prices grumpily…catching sight of the frizzy outline of one's beard on a wall…being surprised by happiness…In short, Herr Joseph Roth, more than can be classified under 'smiles and work'.

We do not have to try – and fail – to be true to the panoramic views that every city offers us, even less to capture the consciousness of swarms of its citizens, to encounter something that lies beyond the reach of our powers of imagination and articulation. What the eye sees on any occasion cannot be mirrored in ink. The magnificent failure of the French poet Francis Ponge to speak with 'voice of things' – entities such as potatoes, cigarettes, and the 'magic stone' that is soap – was lifelong. Though to appeal to a failure so radical – and shared with all – is to protest too much and readers may suspect that I am doing so to distract from my own distinctive failures. Yes, the city cannot be hoovered up in a finite number of sentences, but some sentences carry more truth than others. So, armed with disclaimers, I take you to the Castle, having I hope pre-empted your reasonable expectation of a special kind of arrival at a place, at a climax or resolution, a convergent focus for so many   glances or even a home for something like a collective consciousness...

At any rate, don't hold your breath. You may go blue with hypoxia.

# Hradcany (The Castle District)

The final stage of our journey, like nearly all that has gone before, is beautiful and history-laden. What's more, it is (slightly) downhill and we are quietly rejoicing that the tram has left us with the parting gift of potential energy which we can now cash as kinesis. And so off we go, largely self-propelled with a little gentle assistance from the gravitational field.

As we cross the road from Tyche and Johannes, we are aware of the Strahov monastery above us on our right. It has the triple attraction of a cobbled courtyard, an extraordinary library, and proximity to a restaurant that sells traditional Czech food and beer that, according to Mrs. T. is the one of darkest, tastiest, and strongest in Prague. One of our favourite venues, it is, however, a trip for another day, and perhaps another volume – *Prague 22a. A Book of Even More Tenuous Connections.*

A short walk sleeved in cloisters takes us to the first of two magnificent squares: Loreta Square. En route we are usually assailed by the irresistible aroma of spiced, hot, mulled wine reminding us that Czechia is part of Europe. Whether or not it is authentic Glühwein that is speaking to us is not clear as umlauts do not have specific flavours. Irresistible or not, we resist it.

On our left is the vast oblong Czernin Palace, the largest of the Baroque Palaces in Prague. It has an almost Brutalist simplicity. As cheeky Emperor Leopold said of it: 'It is a big barn without a door' and thus effortlessly adding to the sum of taken offence in the world. But that was when it was half-completed. It is now deservedly judged to be one of the many jewels in Prague's over-encrusted crown.

It was constructed at the behest of Count Humphrecht Jan Czernin, a Czech aristocrat who 'disliked the disdainful attitude of the central Viennese government to the Czech countries'.[183] As we have seen, the understandable resentment of the Czech people of Austro-German attitudes that dismissed them as yokels or bumpkins, speaking a language barbarously remote from the ones they were familiar with, had vast consequences. Shortly after the Czechoslovak Republic was created, the Czernin Palace was allotted to the Ministry of Foreign Affairs and has remained the Foreign Office since then.

We have already met one of its most distinguished inhabitants, the Foreign Secretary Jan Masaryk who in the late 1940s was marginalized by the Communist Party. His progressive liberalism was judged increasingly offensive and, unlike Emperor Frederick, the offence he caused was not without price. And we have already met one of its windows – the one from which he fell, or was propelled, to his death. He would have been gratified to learn that it was in this building that the Warsaw Pact – of which it has often been noted that it was the only military alliance in history that attacked its own members – was formally dissolved in 1990.

Opposite the Palace is Loreta, a gorgeous Baroque church. It is famous for its bell tower which every day since August 15th, 1695 – hourly from 10 a.m. to 5 p.m. – has played "A Thousand Times We Greet Thee", the Thee in question being The Mother of Christ. A calculation performed with the aid of the computer on which these lines are being typed finds that the greeting has been issued nearly a million times – a thousand thousand occasions on which Hussites, Taborites, Lutherans, and others have seethed at this shouted Mariolatry. It is perhaps a good thing that nowadays the holy places of Prague are for the most part mute – or that, at any rate, we have rarely been animated by the hesitant avalanche of sound that even the most modest of English churches emits to call the faithful and celebrate the fact of God's existence.

For this infidel, it prompts further thoughts about the intersection between time and eternity expressed in the clock-watched communications with God. There is something slightly comical about the idea that God is to be spoken to at certain times of the day, certain days of the week, certain weeks of the year. At this moment, I am joined by Kepler who has stepped down from the podium he shares with his co-worker Brahe, leaving him drowning in the data he harvested from his tireless gazing at 10 thousand night skies.

I resume tracing the intellectual trajectory from Kepler to Galileo – who saw that there should be one physics applying to celestial objects and ordinary terrestrial objects, thus bringing the stars down to earth and opening the way to a great democracy of matter according to which planets and pebbles are made of the same stuff and subject to the same laws – and thence to Newton and the emergence of the idea of the universe as a gigantic clock. God is marginalized as the clockmaker and clock-winder who created the stuff, laid down the laws, set the initial conditions, and then withdrew.

At this point, I run into my own 'happiest thought', not as satisfying or numinous as the one that occurred to Einstein and which I rehearsed on the escalator taking me down to I.P. Pavlov Metro Station *en route* to seeing Jan the Philosopher. The thought is this: If we really were clockwork items in a clockwork universe, would it be possible to explain the origin of items that count as clocks, that locate events in time and measure their duration, and of entities – people like Kepler and Me and Mrs. T – who turn time into a verb and *time* things? It was something that Einstein – who brought classical mechanics to its glorious conclusion in the General Theory of Relativity – worried over. He acknowledged that there was no place for clocks and measuring rods, and indeed measurement, in this clockwork world. The General Theory of Relativity could not accommodate the existence of The General Theory of Relativity – of the theorists and their kit and caboodle, their thoughts, and observations, that led up to its formulation. This was his unhappiest thought.[184]

While Einstein would have agreed that 'to be ignorant of motion is to be ignorant of nature', he was not clear how it was we were able to get to know the universe; how the cogs in the machine could come to describe the machine and themselves as cogs in it. As God has been marginalized in the world picture of so many, humankind seems to have come to replace him. Enter 'the ghost in the atom' – the ghost of the observer. Enter the dense, tangled, opaque muddle of quantum theory and a world which (so we are told) has a determinate characteristic only when it is measured. Enter Man as God who re-creates the universe by making it explicit and even furnishes it with a Creator who is worshipped in many ways including with the bells of Loreta.

Thus is a four-hundred-year history of human self-consciousness and world-consciousness gathered up in a few asides as we pass by the Loreta. Kepler returns to his podium next to his friend and to his place in the 16th century. And we resume our pilgrimage, close to the spot where Drahomirá met her end.

You may recall that she was St Ludmilla's daughter-in-law-from-Hell. We discussed her between quadrants of pizza at Grosseto.[185] One day, after she had spent many miserable years being ostracized for the murder of her mother-in-law and her son The Good King Wenceslas, she decided to leave Prague. Her coach had reached Loreta Square when her carriage stopped so that her servant could pop into Loreta church for a quick prayer – rather surprising, not to say tactless, considering the trouble Drahomíra had taken to reinstate Paganism in Bohemia. The Devil, with whom she had a pact, reappeared. She had clearly not taken sufficient legal advice nor read the small print when she signed the agreement: it included a one-way ferry trip across the Styx. A chasm opened in the square and Drahomíra went down, along with her carriage (and presumably the innocent horses) and was engulfed in flames. The place of Drahomirá's engulfment used to be marked by a column but it was torn down in 1788 by an order from the City Council – that may have been chary about being held responsible for potholes. All that remains to mark her exit route is a small circle, which we have not found because we keep forgetting to search for it.

Behind its ornate walls is the Loreta treasure which includes the 'Prague Sun', a receptacle in which the consecrated Host is displayed for veneration. It is encrusted with 6,222 diamonds. Pilgrims to the church can address fleshly ailments as well as spiritual ones. Capuchino Balm – a medicine that dates back to Rudolf II and is still concocted in the pharmacy of the Capuchin convent according to a traditional recipe – can be purchased from the Museum.

Alternatively, it can be ordered by email: "Mary, Mother of God, Deliveroo us from our suffering". The juxtaposition of Rudolfine cures and electronic communication is a remarkable illustration of how astrology and astronomy, alchemy, and science, may still peacefully coexist in certain cultures – or less peacefully as in the case of religiously inspired beheadings that are broadcast to the world at large through Facebook. Or anti-vaxxers using science-based communication systems to spread their fatal anti-science lies.

The juxtaposition prompts me to cite Sartre's reference to a nun he saw on a motor scooter as a spontaneously occurring surreal object. And to note a comparable incongruity in the image of President Václav Havel, fed up with the endless corridors in the Castle, taking to a scooter. The story is told by the indispensable Zantovsky:

> Bara Stepanova, the actress and 'prankstress', who had become notorious as the leading light of the Society for a Merrier Present, provided Havel with a scooter after she had heard him complain on the radio about the endless corridors in the Castle.[186]

A short walk along Loretanská takes us past what was once Hradcanská town hall to Hradcany Square, the vast ante-room to the Castle. A catastrophic fire in 1541, which destroyed the moderate houses and life-chances of the residents of Hradcany district, cleared a space for the wealthy to build palaces conveniently close to the Castle, making it possible to nip next door to speak the right word in the relevant ear.

Here the failure of language is complete, and prose disintegrates into lists. But what lists!

On our right as we enter the square, next to St Benedict's church and the Barefoot Carmelite Monastery, is the early Renaissance Schwarzenberg Palace (built 1445-1567), which in turn neighbours the much junior Salmovsky palace (1800-1810). Across the square are the Archbishop's Palace and the Martinicky Palace – both children of the Catholic revival after that business on the White Mountain. At the end of the square opposite the Castle is the Toskánsky Palace – built in the late 17th century for the Duke of Tuscany.

Your guide is conscious of falling short of the grandeur and architectural beauty of the square. It is something of a relief (wrong word) to descend to details that our imagination can accommodate. We switch our gaze to the middle of the square. Set in a smooth lake of the perfect oblong stone pixels of the road, there is a tree-filled island which provides a refuge from the modest traffic for a regular visitor to these pages: none other than The Virgin Mary.

She is elevated on a Plague Pillar commemorating the epidemics of 1713 and 1714. Its building came with a request that the Virgin might ensure that the then-monarch Charles VI should have a son. No luck: he had a daughter. But what a daughter: Maria Theresa, who would outshine a thousand bone-headed Hapsburg males. The Virgin's halo is fragmented into a ring of 12 stars. Below her on the pillar are various transcendental dignitaries including St. Wenceslas and St. Vitus in the top drawer and further down the ubiquitous Jan Nepomuk, who remains *in situ* notwithstanding the Vatican's decision that, as we have mentioned, he was either non-existent, an imposter, or a fusion of two different characters blended by the confusions of history fomented by the political need for a Catholic hero.

Further down, there is one of our favourite pausing places: a huge candelabra night-lighting the square. A relative *parvenu* – it was built and installed in 1876 – it looks very much of its time. The base is a burly oblong stone on which stand four beautiful bronze maidens. They are elegantly gowned, and, for a change, their breasts are not uncovered as if to commemorate the Great Bra Famine of 1837. They are presumably virgins, though it is difficult to tell from where we are standing. Further inquiry or examination, aimed at placing this assumption on secure footing, would be intrusive and a mark of a dated patriarchal preoccupation that, as we have seen in the case of the Mother of Christ, still has the power to cause boundless harm.

Perhaps rather late in our journey, and after many encounters with the lady in question, it strikes us how strange it is that The Virgin Mary should have this status broadcast in her very name. Every introduction – 'Let me introduce you to Mary, she's a Virgin you know' – would draw attention to the absence of a certain experience in her life – what she has not undergone or missed out on. It is as if this lack were a state and the state were a status or an office or a qualification – like 'Dr' or 'Professor'. She had a flying start in the purity stakes, having been herself conceived by a kiss between her parents, Anne, and Joachim, and being fed by angels – presumably on primordial Angel Delight. More seriously, her status seems to imply that those women whose babies have the standard causal ancestry are a bit mucky: the immaculate conception makes the usual mode of conception maculate. The shine of her example casts a misogynist light on her own sex. We remind ourselves of the horrors inflicted on mothers who conceived out of wedlock, and on children who were foolish and wicked enough to start the autopoietic journey from a zygote to Someone, outside of a legal framework.

This is clearly not a Prague-specific issue, especially since Protestantism, Communism, and secular humanism, have made her presence all over this city less than entirely welcome. I don't know whether much blood has been spilt over the question as to whether the Lady was or was not an Eternal Virgin or whether Jesus' four brothers and two sisters came from the same womb as He did himself.

The status of the statues on the candelabra as virgins or no-longer-virgins is not relevant to the discharge of their functions in the present context. The ladies' heads have the unenviable occupation of supporting a tray from which there grows a teased-out bouquet of six lamps perching on the end of branches. Being a mechanical prop is a strange use of something as rich and complex and multi-talented as a head. Be that as it may, the item we are looking at – the gas lamp – is typical of those of the second half of the 19th century which provide subfusc illumination paradoxically highlighting the dark they are employed to banish and giving nourishment to thrillers and horror stories. The monument continues upwards in the form of a slim Corinthian column. This provides support for a further, generically female, figure wearing something that looks like a half-hearted crown. The lamps are tethered to this column by chain-mail leashes dipping elegantly.

It is difficult to overlook the sgraffito decoration of the Schwarzenberg Palace that has a *trompe d'oeil* effect creating the illusion of little pyramids implanted in the stonework. It surfaces in our minds at odd times. Most recently, I was returning in the rain from the bank in a particularly forlorn stretch of Stockport Market (and there is some tough competition for that accolade). I passed an advertisement that used a *trompe d'oeil.* By the routine magic that is autonoetic memory, I remembered myself just by Prague Castle discussing it with my brother-in-law as I had done five years before on the occasion of my older son's wedding. It is in such haphazard fashion that your informant hangs together in the interstices between the scaffolding of duties, promises, plans, projects, and appointments that structure his days and give them the coherence necessary for life to be 'everyday' rather than "one great blooming, buzzing confusion" of experiences[187].

# Arrival?

We have reached the great courtyard in front of the Castle. To our right is the statue of Thomas Masaryk, father of the nation and also of the tragic Jan, standing exactly where he should be. He died in 1937 and was consequently spared the anguish of knowing that the Czechoslovakia he had made possible would be crushed first by the Nazis and then by the Communists. His mustachioed face, resolute and severe, looks into the future and one can only be glad that he cannot see it, though he was one of the first European statesmen to acknowledge the threat represented by Hitler. His hair parted down the middle, frock coat, tie, and fly-away collar, makes this man of all time a man of his time. The bronze podium on which he stands is etched with TGM in large letters, with G standing for Garrigue, his wife's surname, in a proto-feminist gesture of taking on her name as she did his. He is younger than the balding, bespectacled, bearded individual whose face is featured on some of the stamps of the country he fathered.

The continuing unfolding of history and the fragility of the present against the past is symbolized by the flowers laid next to his statue, petals next to bronze, usually by individuals and groups protesting what has happened to his country. Today, the protest is about the present President Milos Zeman cozying up to President Putin – a *tendresse* he found it expedient to outgrow when Putin invaded Ukraine for a second time.

We are facing the Western entrance to the Castle and behind it is the Castle courtyard. This is the start of the final phase of the process of arriving, or trying to arrive, at the Castle. We pass between the gate piers, each furnished with toy soldiers that surprise younger children by moving as they change places with other toy soldiers. We add our bodies to the estimated 1.8 million similar items that converge annually on this spot from all over the world.

To assist the transformation of my bodily arrival into a genuine arrival, I reiterate two things noted earlier: that it is the largest ancient castle in the world; and that it is not a castle – or just a castle – but a collation of buildings of huge variety, constructed and destroyed, beginning in 870 A.D. with what remains of the Premyslid Fort and the Church of the Virgin Mary.

This does not quite deliver self-delivery as we wander between a bewildering variety of towers (4), fragments of fortifications, churches (5), palaces (4), courtyards, mighty halls (5), gardens (8), and other major structures (7) – variously built, occupied, and vacated by kings, Holy Roman Emperors, invading tyrants, and Presidents of the interrupted Republic. The 'castle' complex is dominated by the cathedral, an acknowledgement that the powers spiritual and temporal are knotted together: that Popes and Kings, Archbishops and Dukes have competed to occupy the same power spaces, expressed in the uncertainties as to who should be kneeling to whom. The grain of our attention scales up to walls, spires, naves, and buttresses, and scales down to gargoyles, a startled face in a saint-stained pane, patterns on an altar cloth, and a dimple in a golden arm. We take a non-metaphorical pew, lift our gaze, listen into the softly echoing spaces, our bodies at rest at last, and our minds attempting to match them. Attempting, that is, to arrive.

The Cathedral cannot be contained by a head and yet it was unpacked by heads, by the sharing of an idea of a hidden Power, in a manner utterly unlike anything achieved by the forces of nature. I feel a pang that I cannot transform the various aches within me into a master-ache, my fears into a master-fear, my joys into a master-delight, here embodied in stonework, that reaches out to Something transcending Everything. I pre-empt envy by performing a perfunctory calculus, hopelessly underpowered by facts, concerning the balance of good and evil brought into human life by the idea of God.

In trying and failing to arrive at the Castle we are in distinguished company. There is no way of arriving at the place that Havel encountered when he assumed the presidency of his country:

> [A] building four storeys high, a kilometre in length, and a hundred and fifty metres wide, with a multitude of satellite buildings, gardens, courtyards, cellars and dozens of miles of corridors, and hallways.[188]

If our failure is the fulfilment of a cliché, it is one that, like many clichés, takes its rise from a lived truth.

We wander – a second cousin of loitering and third cousin of gadding about – inside and between buildings until we have had our fill. Our plans to visit the bronze sculpture 'The Parable of the Skull' are once again unfulfilled, though the item deserves a place in these pages. Created by a surrealist sculptor Jaroslav Róna in 1993, it is of a beggar in that posture of total abjection we had seen on the Charles Bridge. On his back is a huge skull and between his legs dangles a vast testicular apparatus. He has been moved to the convent of St. Agnes – without one imagines her permission – which is now an art gallery. We settle for a post-card of the work which invites us to think about the skull, the head unpeeled of that thin coating where smiles with an infinity of gradations, and scowls and grimaces are fashioned, of the bone outlasting the person whose headquarters, indeed life-quarters, it was. We shall accept the invitation but not at this moment.

We leave the Castle complex, suspecting that our visit – like previous ones – may be the most acute expression of our failure to arrive at or in Prague. We blame the intrinsic dynamism of our own consciousness that is, and must be, always seeking but never finding a significance that is content with itself. The concrete castle dissolves into an unfolding smoke of experiences that will be dissipated by their successors. We are not deluded into photographing what we cannot experience, in the hope of experiencing it later.

We decided not to return from the Castle via the Summer Palace nor to call in on the Kafka family in Golden Lane. Instead, we exit by the route we entered, passing the toy soldiers. Turning left, out of the main gates, we descend slightly and reach the ultimate terrace of a city that has many terraces. We lean against a low wall, having found a gap in the thick phalanxes of selfie-takers.

The relationship between viewpoint and view that has dominated our journey is now reversed: we see Prague from the Castle rather than the Castle from Prague. We look past the permed terracotta tiles of the rooves of the narrow streets, the green copper cupolas, thickly shrubbed Petrin with its toytown Eiffel tower, the multiply-bridged river, Vysehrad castle where Mácha is still buried, a V-shaped high-rise block that is competing with the Zizkov tower for the accolade to which we have already referred, and we arrive at – guess what? – the twin spires of St. Ludmilla in Náměstí míru. Thus, are we connected with the place where the long curve of our journey got properly started, by the magic of the gaze, a taut thread of light linking the beginning and end of the bow.

Our next move will be to follow the example of our glance and head home to Norská, though our return journey will not be as wriggly as our outgoing one.

# Return

We shall not therefore retrace our steps to Pohorelec and the two astronomers. Instead, we shall enjoy the euphoria of spending on foot the altitude we have acquired on the tram. There are many ways down from the Castle: across to Petrin and a zig-zag path through the woods – opening from time to time to reveal breathtaking (a word that I have succeeded in avoiding until this moment) views of the city; through the Summer Gardens and Letna to Cechnov Bridge; by way of the Schonbrum Gardens to Malostranská; or descending via Nerudova to Malostranská námesti. The names may mean nothing to you, gentle reader, and may turn you into a gentle or even frantic skimmer. So, I will confine my story to our favourite route, the one that passes down Nerudova.

In fact, the first part of our descent is down Uvoz street that skirts the base of the Castle complex and enables us to look side-ways across vineyards to Petrin and forward into views that are idealized prospects of the city. It was here that we once heard the aforementioned whispering trousers of the man from the Far East whose audibility highlighted how quiet Prague was for a city – never mind a capital city and one that attracts 8.5 million tourists a year. We again taste the quietness – also highlighted by the localized rattle of my calorie-free sweets in their little container – and praise the public transport system that takes the jams out of the streets. The sound of our own chewing is broadcast to us undiminished.

The passages of cars are sufficiently separated for us to savour how the sound of tyres on cobble is like a broken splash. An occasional motor scooter unzips the silence.

We pass a café that claims an association with one of Prague's most famous poetic sons, Rainer Maria Rilke, and I immediately commence an 82% accurate recitation of the English translation of the opening lines of his Duino Elegies. 'Who if I cried would hear me among the angelic orders…?'[189]

Uvoz evolves into Nerudova, one of Prague's most beautiful and complex streets, and another daunting challenge to the endeavour to transfer the city to the page so that readers might subsequently unpack from the written text something corresponding to what presents itself to an unhurried stroller. In short to get an Archaeopteryx or a Roc to perch on a twig.

Nerudova is named after the national poet – Jan Nepomuk Neruda –– whose first two names illustrate the power of that apocryphal saint to muscle in everywhere, even between a Jan and his family name. Neruda's surname is more familiar to us than it might otherwise be because it was assumed as a *nom de plume* by the teenage Chilean poet Pablo Neruda to hide his poetic career from his father who wished him to go into law. We love that poet because of his poem 'Walking around':

As it happens, I am tired of my feet and nails,

My hair and my shadow.

As it happens, I am tired of being a man.[190]

And he seemed to be on the right side of Chilean history when the blood-boltered Augusto Pinochet launched his murderous coup against the legally elected Salvador Allende – supported by a US foreign policy particularly associated with the loathsome Henry Kissinger. We came to like Neruda less when we discovered his love of Stalin, expressed in a *Nuevo Canto de Amor a Stalingrad*, and learned that he had been the recipient of the Stalin Peace Prize in 1953. The peace that Stalin distributed so generously was available only to corpses.

We therefore return the subject to the 19th century Czech poet from whom the 20th century Chilean poet borrowed his name. Jan Neruda is often described as 'a romantic nihilist'. This was certainly true of the young poet, but his views changed in middle age. Perhaps it was because the hourly pay for nihilism is rather modest; or possibly he discovered that when he looked into the void it winked at him and said, 'Cheer up!'. For the rest of his life, he seemed able to reconcile his personal despair with the hope of a future independent Czech nation, a cause to which he devoted himself. He was also responsible for rescuing Mácha from the execration that had buried the latter's reputation for the decades after his death. Neruda and a circle of like-minded friends felt that they were carrying a posthumous torch for the author of *May* whom we met in a street off Krymská and again in Petrin. Neruda clearly deserved the crowds who attended his funeral, the outburst of nationalist sentiment it occasioned, his place near to Mácha in Vysehrad cemetery, and his statue in Petrin, a few hundred yards from the earlier poet.

I have often thought – or said that I have thought, perhaps to keep a conversation going – that I would like to have a pub named after me and thereby be licensed to imagine people saying things like "We went to the Raymond Tallis Arms and got absolutely rat-arsed".[191] Alternatively, I might have a unit – for example a unit of pleasure or of luminescence – bearing my moniker. Or my name might denote a kind of mathematical entity like a Hilbert space or a logical one like a Ramsay sentence. Another possibility would be a disease, as unfortunately Purkinje and others have already bagged the best seats in the body. The trouble is the illness in question might not be terribly savory: 'Tallis Itch' might be located in the unwashed shrubbery around a sphincter or regularly bathed in malodorous discharges seeping out of the bodies of a billion strangers. It would be less risky to donate my name to a city street. If I had any say in the matter and if Neruda hadn't got there first, Nerudova would be my choice. Perhaps we could share it between us: he would label the uphill direction and I the downhill. After all, contrary to what was claimed by the pre-Socratic philosopher Heraclitus, the way up and the way down are not the same – though admittedly, as noted earlier, they are not usually separated from one another outside of escalators.

Nerudova always strikes us as one of the most Prague-packed of Prague streets.[192] In part, this is because it goes back to our first visit and on subsequent visits we feel we haven't fully tasted the city until we have walked down Nerudova. Those who know Prague well, in particular natives of the city, are a little shocked by this, as it is so 'touristy'. There is, of course, quite a thick fluff of shops with merchandise that spills out on to the pavements, outlets for Russian dolls, balloons, absinthe, souvenirs that may be an alternative to actual memories, and ice cream, and a tide of tourists to whose wallets they are addressed. But it is not difficult to look past this intermittent Blackpool coating of ground floors to the continuum of Renaissance and Baroque houses either side. Several qualify as palaces and many have been transformed into hotels so steeped in Czechness that, unlike some establishments we have been to in our native country, they do not cause imagination to stop at the surface of a table or the meaningless squirting and burping of a coffee-making machine.

The houses are washed in different colours – yellow sits next to brown, brown to orange, and orange to light green. Strictly, we are talking shades rather than colours: they are not the slightest bit gaudy. Some of the larger buildings sport flags: they are impressive embassies. While Prague was ahead of the curve when it came to giving houses numbers – the Czechs did not wait for Napoleon to codify postal addresses as he did so many other aspects of life – many ornate signs remind us that this was once the Royal Route- the coronation route of the kings of Bohemia as they ascended to St Vitus' Cathedral to be crowned.

We pause to look at The Golden Anchor, the Red Eagle, the Red Lamb, the Golden Chalice, the Golden Key, the Golden Wheel, and other houses. Three attract our particular attention. The Three Little Fiddles was not the office of accountants but the domicile and workshop of a family of violin makers and they are signified by a trio of violins beautifully framed in rococo curlicues of stone. At Nerudova 18 there is a relief of that discredited but pushy saint, St Jan Nepomuky. He shares this address with St. Florian who is afforded a statue and is the patron saint of firefighters (and brewers, chimney sweepers, and soap makers). And last, but not least, there is the House of the Two Suns at Number 47.

This is where Jan Neruda lived for many years, whence he looked and listened and walked up and down and wrote his stories about the Little Quarter in which he lived. Each of the two suns has a rather glum human face painted on it and is encircled by a ruff of formal flames. These giant emojis are set in an ornamental frame which has a long-haired brown head above and between the suns and two further heads with generous quaffs of hair looking angrily away from each other, up and down the street. The *casus belli* is not clear.

The poet himself is commemorated by a large metal plaque occupied by an androgynous figure, loosely draped in timeless cloth that seems to suit a deity, or a classical hero, in one hand holding forever unwilting roses by their bared thighs and elevating a shield in the other. In short, not at all like the bearded, bespectacled, rather overweight, melancholy, frock-coated man, with a thick mullet, temporarily immortalized in bronze in Petrin Hill, but perhaps truer to the free spirit he would like to have been.

The remainder of our descent is punctuated by numerous pauses as we renew acquaintance with toys we might buy for grandchildren who do not yet exist, or have just come into existence, or are now growing past them, a stop for a coffee or a glass of wine, or to relish ornamentation that Adolf Loos would have had no hesitation in classifying as criminal. We are often moved to give the time of day to a pair of statues supporting a balcony with their bent heads – two chained, muscular Moors with justifiably angry, defiant expressions, an *Invictus* look mysteriously emanating from blank eyes and poignant, cherubically curly hair and exposed but odourless armpits. There is a job for everyone in this world but the terms and conditions – on duty 24/7 and 365 days/year – are not attractive. Above them are busts of a young man with a smiling sun on his chest (symbolizing day) and a young girl wrapped in a shawl (symbolizing night) – somewhat easier billets than that of the unlucky, enslaved Moors. As the Prague Now guide informs us, "the Romanian Embassy seats in this palace". It does indeed and it is proclaimed by a circular badge above the grand entrance: 'Romania Ambasad'. The mighty wooden door, with vertical rows of silver buttons and a silver knocker, has never been opened in the dozens of times we have passed it over the decade or two in which we have followed our past selves in search of the astonishment of our first encounter with Nerudova.

We continue downhill, past the Institute of International Relations where our older son worked for several years. We once attended a lecture that he was chairing and introduced ourselves as his ancestors. It was a strange experience to penetrate one of the buildings, look out through windows, and see the outside from that outside of the outside that is inside.

With little warning, the street widens into Malostranská Square. St Nicholas Church divides that wonderful space into the part we can see now and the part we could see from the café when the Polish bus driver had an argument with an ancient wall. We confirm that the scar is still there, resist the temptation to have another drink, and board the 22 tram which will take us back homewards.

But only as far as Námestí míru.

POST-LUDES

# A Principle Upheld

Why do we dismount from the tram at Námestí míru? To have a further helping of pizza in search of a fifth season? To engage with St Ludmilla's spires, reflecting on the fact that we are now close to the target of our own distant gaze projected from the balcony near the Castle? To visit the dusky spaces of The Beer Factory? Or even to enter the Vinorhady Theatre which we have hitherto seen only from the outside?

No, no, no, and no.

We dismount at at Námestí míru in order to uphold the (ig) noble principle of CBA.

The reader with the retentive powers of Jorge Luis Borges' *Funes the Memorius* will recall that the first stage of our outward journey from our flat to the tram stop at Ruská – was downhill. It must surely follow that the final step of our return journey – from Ruská to Norská – will be uphill. How can we avoid this undesirable end to an otherwise delightful journey through Prague to the Castle? We can do so by varying the final section of our return journey. That variation is provided by the number 16 tram which passes through Námestí míru. Hence our otherwise inexplicable, premature descent from the 22 at that stop.

Courtesy of the excellence of the Prague transport system, the interval between leaving the 22 and entering the 16 is brief. We welcome this brevity because we are now in travelling, not in looking, mode, though Peace Square is objectively unchanged. The 16, which differs from the 22 only in virtue of the number and the destination printed on its forehead, transports us via Sumavská, Vinorhadská vodárna, and Perunova to the junction between Korunní and Chorvatská. The journey is not long enough for us to settle into street-sipping, though Francouszká and Korunní deserve our respectful attention.

We cannot, however, forgo another admiring glance at the water-tower where time (a clock) and eternity (angels) intersect. Nor can we avoid glimpses of the Zizkov Tower that give us an opportunity to renew or refine our grumbles, observing that the structure is a denial of transcendence. It does not even scrape the sky, only pokes it.

What matters is that the tram is doing the heavy lifting for us, our own bodies being the heavy lifteds. The final stage of our return to Norská is therefore downhill: a steepish descent down Chorvatská. This road begins with the Coffee Corner which was for a while one of my favourite writing spots. What I wrote there I cannot remember, a fact which reminds me of how little I retain of the many thousands, and indeed tens of thousands, of hours I have spent scribbling and typing. Perhaps this amnesia is less disturbing than might be expected because the writer's attention should be focused on the screen or the page, excluding the world beyond the edges of either, irrespective of whether that world is in Prague or Stockport. Philosophers are trying to grasp a general elsewhere, an everywhere, that is not clearly differentiated from nowhere. And even non-philosophers – essayists, story-tellers – must take hold of places and seasons from the standpoint of a seasonless nowhere. They can describe a freezing winter's day just as well, or just as badly, when they are writing in Summer as in Winter. The snow they describe is made of characters – ink and pixels – and not flakes. And summer light is re-ignited by means of inky darkness.

Our descent is otherwise without prompts to reflection. Well, not entirely. There is the reminder to resist any jokes about the first side-road we encounter which is labelled 'Dycková'. And there is our admiration of the large villas either side of Chorvatská, that are part of the 19th century efflorescence of this quarter of Prague – Vinorhady – that was until 1922 a city in itself and the fourth biggest in Bohemia. Hence the Neo-renaissance, Pseudo Baroque, Neo-gothic, and Art Nouveau buildings soliciting our flaneurial admiration.

And, if the weather is suitable, we cannot resist an inspection of one of our favourite manhole covers. It looks like a giant copper coin. At its heart is a shield displaying three castle towers and beneath them a brick oval entrance with open gates (whose metal reinforcements I once confused with chicken legs – but that is confidential) revealing a portcullis. Beneath this in turn is a detached arm holding a sword. In the inner of the two circles that enclose this picture is the inscription *Prazská kanalizace* (Prague Sewer). The details, down to the acute accent on the second 'a' of Praszká, to which I have done little justice, are exquisite.

Near the bottom of Chorvatská, we pause to look at – and occasionally photograph – our own street, Norská, that lies ahead and below. We usually focus on the beautiful domed, spired, and finialed apartment block that we admired on our way out. Thus, we return to our flat.

One key gives us permission to enter the block of flats and a second allows us to open the door of our own apartment on the fourth floor. The lift between the two doors enables us to respect The Principle that has governed our expedition.

From the sunlit lounge – we recall it as always sunlit – we look across Norská to the little figure on the building directly opposite, dressed in a mediaeval tunic, leggings, pointed slippers, and a floppy hat over his Plantagenet hair. His feet are pressed against the cream-washed wall and his outstretched arms are supporting a small ornate balcony. In his face, turned to one side, it is possible to see the stress of physical effort. This little character, whom we acknowledged on our way out, has come to be a marker of the exuberance and imagination that made possible the city we have travelled through. Praha Matka Mest: Prague Mother of Cities.[193]

We are home.

Time for a drink.

# A Principle Undermined

*The Journey to the Gym: Vrsovice námesti-Cechovo námesti-Koh-I-Noor-Slavia*

It is 6 a.m. and we are already awake and about. The toilet lid has performed its terse, unwelcome *Aubade*, greeting the city and the new day. We are dressed for our first appointment: with the gymnasium in Slavia a few stops on the 22 tram in the direction opposite to that of the journey to the Castle.

Appropriately dressed, we gather up the necessaries in shoulder bags. They are the same as we need for our sessions at the Village gym at home so I can look up and transcribe them from a list sello-taped to the shelf just above this computer screen: head phones; connector; i-POD; key and lock for the changing room; swipe card to enter the gym; reading glasses; pen and notebook lest my mind serves up something I want to save before it dissolves into my past; a book to read (while waiting for Mrs. T. who has longer sessions); wallet; and Ricola (herbal candy). The note is wrinkled from being a survivor of a coffee stain that confers a pleasant antiquity upon it.

# Ruská to Slavia

After a false start or two -and some false stops triggered by our being unable to remember whether we really have done things we have done automatically - we leave the flat, descend the echoey, uncarpeted stone stairs, tug at the recalcitrant main door, and enter the street. It is dark and cold because it is Winter. (In other seasons, we usually choose the alternative of a walk in the park.) We reach Moskevská and cross to the other side, taking note of the warning written in thick print on the road: *Pozor tram.* Thus, do we avoid a turning of the tables where a tram we might wish to catch catches us instead.

We have a choice of vehicles. By a happy (at least for one of us) coincidence the alternative to the 22 tram is a 7. This prompts a sharing of thoughts about the extraordinary ratio 22/7, otherwise known as Pi.

Pi, as everyone knows, is a transcendental number. Confidentially, it is not the root of a non-zero polynomial with rational coefficients. Closer to home, is the fact that it cannot be translated into a decimal with a finite number of places: 3.14159 etc. is the beginning of a journey without end, though computerized calculations have followed it to many trillions of digits. Closer still, is the fact that it represents the ratio between the perfect straight line diameter and the circumference of a perfect circle – neither of which exists. By this means, we come to the relationship between straight and curved space, which naturally leads to a consideration of the presence and absence of a gravitational field, the fundamental identity of inertial and gravitational mass, and the difference between the strain of walking uphill and the pleasure of walking down.

Such mansplaining so early in the day is a form of spousal abuse – notwithstanding its relevance to our seeking out in the gym precisely the kind of effort we had shunned in our pilgrimage to the Castle. It is therefore fortunate that the tram arrives, that we board, and are in adjacent rows of seats occupied by citizens heading for an early start for what looks largely to be manual work, the residual grunt and groan of analogue labour in a digital world, a world in which even the erasure of script has been outsourced from the rubber at the end of a pencil to a delete button. In this early hour we are not offered seats by glum passengers nor, as the tram is half empty, do we need such an offer. There is an unsurprising absence of Italians.

The first step of our journey takes us to *Vrsovice námestí.* *En route*, we pass a Drogerie, and are reminded of a recent episode which required us to purchase a range of cleansing materials. We had pushed a buggy, containing one of our grandchildren, through an instance, indeed a generous helping, of ("Please don't use this term" – Mrs. T.) dog-fruit. It was evident that the beast of origin had none of the problems that caused so much suffering for Luther-on-the-Loo. There followed a clean-up that could not be faulted on thoroughness: offending material was tracked down to the last furrow on the tyres.

The operation began with spraying, proceeded to the application of a stiff-haired, long-handled dishwashing brush, continued with baby-wipes, and was completed with dry tissues. The materials were all purchased on the spot to deal with the crisis. The laundering lasted at least 15 minutes. As we cleaned our hands with anti-septic gel and confirmed that our shoes were not coated with material of the kind scraped off the buggy, we became conscious that, although a physical crowd had not gathered, a virtual one in the form of increasingly frequent curious glances, had totted itself up. Not quite an Event, then, and certainly not Street Theatre, nor material for a column in a local newspaper, or even an entry in a quotidian diary. Ahead of us, after all, lay the need to explain our lateness, the strong smell of disinfectant, and an inspection of our work – trouble with a small t.

It prompted a reflection on a small manifestation of the development of civility in this, the Mother of Cities. Only a few years earlier, the price of an odourless return from a street-tasting was similar to the price of freedom: constant vigilance. Prague was identified by one observer as 'the dog-poo capital of Europe'[194] – a fact you would not have found in the Lonely Planet Guide. Now such missteps are rare. This may have been the result of more expensive fines rather than an increasing social conscience on the part of the dogs. And there have been the activities of Václav the Czech Superhero in Superman tights who pelts dog walkers with the stuff donated to the surfaces of the city by the backsides of their beasts.[195]

Which is not to deny that there remains much work to be done to persuade citizens to pre-empt the undesirable consequences of their dog's walking the streets. I do not have up-to-date figures for Prague 10 (the site of the buggy incident) but, according to an 'award-winning' editor and reporter, information from the City Hall office in Prague 8 suggests that "registered dogs will produce more than 180 tons of poop in that neighbourhood that year" (2020).[196]

This is neither the time nor the place to address this issue but it might be interesting at some time in the future to discuss a) how these figures were arrived at; b) how accurate they are; and c) whose job description included responsibility for compiling them. For those who want to get a firmer grasp on the quantity in question, and to dally longer in this capillary of civic history, the amount corresponds to 14 full loads of a Tatra 815 Truck.[197] There is no good reason for thinking that fewer such trucks would be required to accommodate the output of the pets domiciled in Prague 10. By this means 'dog, faeces arising from' would have earned its place in the Index to this book – for alphabetical reasons rubbing shoulders with 'Defenestration, First'– if it had had one.

The speed of this admittedly incomplete revolution reminds us of another one equally surprising: the banning of smoking in public places in Prague from World Non-Smoking Day 31st March 2017. The surprise is that the law was passed in a country with a libertarian tendency and that it should have been obeyed by a citizenry with an instinctive suspicion of and resentment of the State.

The ban is the final step in a long journey from my first experience of being 'on the Continent' as a hitchhiker in the 1960s when the most compelling impressions and enduring memories were provided by the scent of *Gauloises, Gitanes* and *Disque Bleu*. It provides an opportunity to recall how shoppers entering Tesco Extra in Kodanská are met by a notice printed on the glass door forbidding the following: ice-cream eaters, dog walkers, skaters, cameras, toters of guns – and smokers.

We pass the Gothic church of St. Nicholas, once the centre of Vrsovice. On the opposite side of the road is the Vrsovice Chateau, which is approached by sweeping staircases linked by a promenade. It was originally an imposing and ornate silk factory, but this early 19th century neo-Renaissance building is now a home for elderly people for whom the stone staircases must seem less of an orna-ment than a barrier to escape. It offers a compendious view of St. Nicholas' church, of the square, and of acres of Prague, afforded to elderly citizens who may view it with perhaps blurred, perhaps uncomprehending, eyes.

Just before the tram leaves Vrsovice square, we pass the Hus' House, a place where much that is worthy of comment converges. The church[198] was constructed in 1930 in less than a year and it was one of the first structures in Prague to be built from pre-stressed concrete and brick panels. Its foundation stone was transported from a castle in Sézimo Ústi in South Bohemia where Jan Hus had first preached the ideas that sent those long-lasting ripples across Europe. It has an extraordinary pencil-like tower, nearly 100 feet high. The inevitable cross is placed on top of a box-like room with windows in all directions, which support a structure shaped like the chalice used in the eucharist. The design is intended to signify a ship's lantern or a lighthouse pointing the way to eternity. Whether this speaks to the glum commuters in the 22 tram is a matter of considerable doubt.

Even more surprising than the structure of the church is the additional functions it took on. These included a theatre, which could accommodate almost 300 people, with space for an orchestra, dressing rooms, and make up. (Make up!) The theatre was so successful that it may have been responsible for the temporary closing of Vinorhady theatre a short distance away. In the 1960s, it was itself closed by the communists who did not approve of a theatre so closely entangled with religion. What is surprising is that the communist disapproval had not been anticipated by the tut-tutting of the faithful.

Our next stop is puzzlingly entitled *Cechovo námesti*. I had thought it was rather cheeky that a square in a distant suburb should call itself Czech Square. However, it means 'Chekhov Square' – as I should have appreciated from the fact that a road on the eastern side of the square is named Tolsteho, after the writer's fellow literary giant. Some mystery remains, however, because on the map the square is Svatopluk Cech Square, named presumably after the 9th century monarch Svatopluk. Svatopluk was responsible for expanding Moravia to its greatest extent. He was born nearly 1,200 years before we acquired our habit of passing through the square on our way to the gym. His reign was a rather confusing story involving vanished kingdoms including Carinthia, factions such as the Wilheminers, and characters such as Charles the Fat who was notoriously lethargic and inept.[199] The medic in me suspects he may have suffered from myxoedema before the collective introspection of the human body had revealed the thyroid and understood its function.

Rather than fret over this inconsistency, it is perhaps more fruitful to turn our gaze to another church that, like the Hus Congregational House, is intended to point the way to eternity; for *Cechovo námesti* is dominated by a Roman Catholic Church dedicated to St. Wenceslaus – a name that will doubtless ring a bell.

Described as 'a Constructivist Masterpiece' (me, neither – until a few years ago), it was built in 1930 to commemorate the 1000th anniversary of the Saint's death. Whether he would have approved of this reinforced concrete construction erected 52,000 Wednesdays after he took his last breath is not clear, as he has not been available for comment for a millennium. It is possible that he might have found it less shocking than the architecture of other churches erected in his name over the preceding centuries.[200] The sense of space within it more than makes up for the barren impression given by the low-rise, oblong (indeed ob-very-long) wall that faces one at the top of the steps up to the church, the thin rectangular 80 m high bell tower lighthouse, and the succession of stacked boxes leading to a cylindrical nave. The large clocks on the four sides of the tower do a little to redeem the geometrical starkness.

Now is not, however, the time for sightseeing and judging the sights that are seen. Six a.m. on a tram full of hardworking citizens – where some are coughing, others dozing, and most, as noted, look glum – commuting through neon-lit empty roads is not a point in space and time from which to mobilize the sensibilities of a tourist. Few flaneurs are up at this hour; fewer still heading towards a gym. Which may be a good thing in view of what lies between us and our destination.

For we are about to enter a Prague that is remote from any imagined version of 'Prague', and a theme we have touched on before, as Somewhere gives way to the necessary Anywhere required to support Somewhere, and its fluorescent lights are the opposite of the lambent, mysterious, alchemical, evening warmth of Golden Lane. This should come no more of a surprise than that the face requires an entire body to ensure its animation: it could not function without humble interstitial tissue and kit-like kidneys and bladders. Which is why cities have more in common than they have differences.

Perhaps the most striking mark of our descent from the cultural heights of Magic Prague – evident as we swing towards the exotically named *Koh-I-Noor* – is that graffiti here are not unwelcome stains but an alleviation of grimed concrete. One or two are quite skillfully executed, especially those that advertise a hairdressing facility called Edward Scissorhands. There is a multicoloured portrait of this humanoid who has scissor blades instead of hands.

I refrain from repeating (my) much repeated jokes about spin-off horror movies such as 'Edward Scissorhands Picks His Nose' or 'Edward Scissorhands Scratches His Anus' – somewhere between Gothic and Go-thick. And it is probably too early in the day to dwell on the extraordinary nature of scissors – merging enantiomorphic, chiral opposites whose chiasmic blades magnify the power of the thumb and index finger to apply pressure on material and whose sharp edges translate precision into incision. Or even to ponder on its more easygoing technological cousin – the tweezer that pulls off the magic trick of making the pincer grip of the thumb and index finger at once more powerful and more precise.

Sufficient, perhaps, to recall, as we sweep round the corner, something that Lord Tennyson once said: that "he knew the quantity of every English vowel except those in the word scissors". And the explanation he gave for it: that "each vowel is enclosed and made of uncertain quantity by two consonants".[201] What can one say except "Eat your heart out Nezval!" at such a word and the device – that closes in on itself, cunningly exploiting the principle of the lever, to divide that which has to be separated in order that paper and fabric should be shaped according to the heart's desire – to which it refers?

As we swing into our final straight, the mysterious relationship between words and the world, and the even more mysterious relationship between words and words that look at words, not to speak of the inexpressible guile of the implements that magnify our powers and assist our interaction with the material world – our temporary friend and our permanent enemy – should be sufficient to set aside any gloom that might be instilled in us by a vast street flanked by endless mid-rise functional flats for persons of very moderate means set between forlorn relics of industry.

There is consolation in thinking of this place as an 'opposite pole' highlighting the distances from the panoramas ignited by excited gazes seen from the Castle. Somewhere in the background of this contrast is a reminder of the poignant recollections we have as we grope in the seasonless loft for Christmas decorations and see fairy lights next to surfboards, and baubles only a few feet from wet-suits and sand-dusted spades. The spindrift from incoming waves of memory momentarily reminds the winter interior of the outermost spaces of seaside summer, the December loft, that makes us stoop and crawl, of the vast open of the July beach where we ran towards the Atlantic Ocean. The sense of Lost Summer is greater when the search in the loft is undertaken by two septuagenarians and the children they ran with across the beach are long grown up, with children of their own.

Our turn into the street – Vrsovická – is marked by a vast building which gives the tram stop its name – Koh-i-Nor. The building has been described as 'an industrial gem'.[202] 'Gem' is perhaps generous: it looks like a deserted mill in Huddersfield or Rochdale. The picture I have on the screen in front of me enables me to do something I never even attempted from the tram: count the windows. There are 120 in four layers of 30, each set in brown and yellow walls.

In this factory, the brothers Jindrich and Sigmund Waldes established a multi-million-pound business making buttons, in particular snap fasteners, press studs, or poppers, that became internationally famous. Their logo – of a smiling woman wearing a Koh-i-Noor fastener like a monocle – became a global icon. The image is still present on a crumbling side wall, looking like a transfer in black ink. All over the world, blouses, trousers, jackets and coats, and the many elements of such polyliths, have been held to a state of order and decency by items manufactured in this now derelict building. It is an innocent pleasure to think of trillions of tingle-moments of satisfaction as snappers snapped or poppers popped, instants spread over space and time, rooms, buildings, cities, and countries, as bodies were clothed and unclothed. For a moment the dead building glows with its past life.

The life of the two extraordinarily talented and cultured Jewish brothers began to unravel tragically with the Nazi invasion of 1938. It ended for one in New York and for the other in Havana *en route* from Dachau to his brother, where he died suddenly – probably of a heart attack.

And so, we arrive at *Slavia*, our final stop. Nothing could illustrate the contingency of names more clearly. The distance between Slavia and Café Slavia is one measure of the distance between the Prague of the map and the Prague of the mind. The Slavia of the football team has hovered in the outermost penumbra of my (faint) football consciousness.

# Eden

We enter a vast shopping complex named after the Eden funfair that preceded it.

In the Prague of Thomas Masaryk, the funfair had a 5-kilometer roller coaster that was a wonder of its age. Next to it was a giant, spidery structure supporting whirling baskets so that those who had been terrified by a succession of helpless descents could round off the afternoon's experiences with the contrapuntal terror of centrifugal force. When I researched the device on the internet, I was shepherded past poignant, sepia images of an era innocent of the coming catastrophes of Nazism and Communism, towards merchandise for Slavia FC and opportunistic adverts for new treatments for fungal toe-nail infections with unattractive pictures of corroded keratin.

No further distractions must delay our passage into the Eden Centre that, in addition to a vast Tesco, has 100 'outlets' – I think that means shops. Most of them at this early hour are closed, Tesco being a striking exception. Although we are in pursuit of exercise, we have no choice but the assisted ascent of one of many escalators. We glide past a bright red Maserati racing car, seemingly unembarrassed by being unexplained, and reach the large, shiny space of the upper floor encircled by cafés and populated with largely empty tables and chairs.

At the end of this space is the gym whose name – Form Factory Fitness Centre – seems to be in English. Its website – and by association the Centre itself – has at the time of writing garnered a vast number of micro-accolades in the form of 'likes': 16,552 in total. The idea of 'a like' – an intentional relationship between a conscious subject and an object or an experience – as a discrete item, scissored from general approval by a noun that looks sideways to a transient imaginary community or audience of web-based judges nodding their heads in agreement or shaking them in dissent, should stop us in our tracks. The chorus of likes is a ghostly reconstruction of a society that has been pulled apart as it re-directs its attentions from those who are present to those who are absent from here but present on a screen. But we are too busy being particular human beings to reflect on the curious, tangled nature of human consciousness generating an international currency of quantified, even quantized, approval. Be that as it may, a further 'Like' – perhaps the 16,553$^{rd}$ – now hangs on our experiences of the next hour and a half. It would be a gratuitous dramatization to describe the additional 'like' as 'hanging by a thread' – and one that could be cut by something as trivial as an unwelcome at the entrance or the failure of the conversation between our electronic entry cards and the turnstile. Nothing occurs for us to dislike.

Our journey within Prague from Magic Prague to Anywhere or Nowhere-in-Particular is completed by our entry into this House of over 16,000 Likes. Our mental downsizing to what philosophers call 'the specious present' will now continue as our bodies swell to fill more of our minds.

Mrs. T. and I part company to enter our separate changing areas with our usual salutation: *Je vous verrai dans l' abime de l'enfer.*

The *enfer* in question is the gym with its balance aids, treadmills, rowing machines, punch bags, dumb-bells, squatting structures *(sic)*, ellipticals, stairs, stretching zones, rubber ropes, polymetric boxes... Though I can speak first-hand only for the Male space, the changing rooms are most certainly Anywhere. I hardly need describe the benches on which we may sit while swapping shoes for trainers and the lockers in which our street clothes and valuables are kept safe from the forelimbs and subsequently the pockets of thieves, and the keys that remind us that the lockers are not active but passive lockees that are locked.

The changing room prompts reflection on why exercise that costs quite a bit of money and involves a lot of bother is valued more than exercise that is a feature of otherwise purposeful activity and is free of charge. How lifting weights in the gym will be welcomed while lifting the shopping bags we shall fill in Tesco after our session will be resented, though the gravitational challenge and its capacity to strengthen muscles is the same. How we might have resented rushing back for something forgotten, when the rushing was associated with a tachycardia in as good a standing as that which we seek on the treadmill. Nipping back to get something is, after all, the gym by other means – if the nipping is nippy enough. But we are disinclined to think in this rational way. I remember an amused conversation on this very point in New York State – two years and thousands of miles away – with a fellow visitor to a university. My interlocutor remarked on our choice of the lift to get to the gym, and we had a shared wryness. I am arrested, as I enter the pandemonium of the gym proper, by the thought – shared with Mrs. T. and, earlier in this work, with you, gentle reader – that my recollection of this event in USA alights so securely on a landing ground so remote, that it's like a swallow from Egypt touching down on the same eaves in Gloucester in successive years.

And so we begin, with a routine that has behind it only the force of a habit that seems to have acquired itself and seasoned with a soupcon of folk biology. Soon there is panting, rapid beating of the heart, and the first signal of complaint from muscles that normally keep well in the background as a mere platform for the otherwise engaged person. The respiratory tract that has failed so dismally to articulate more than the odd mispronounced greeting in Czech is given over to fluent puffing and panting, prompting the owner of the body to reflect on the very mechanism of respiration and the law first articulated by Robert Boyle not very long after the Battle of Bilá Hora in a country – England – of which the combatants knew little. As the volume of the chest increased, so the pressure of its gaseous contents fell, thus offering an invitation to the air that surrounded the gymnast's body to enter said body. His oxygen-hungry flesh consequently wolfed down the air of a precinct of a Prague which is known to few. Meanwhile, his Purkinje fibres ensured that the increased input into his cardiac ventricles from the atria was successfully harvested and transformed into output of oxygenated blood delivering their precious element to the muscles that were propelling him in whatever direction his carnal self-improvement required. Meanwhile, his other Purkinje fibres (in the cerebellum) helped maintain his balance on the moving surface. And those minute conduits, that Purkinje had been the first to see with his artificially sharpened gaze, pooled their nano-squirts of coolant into visible trickles coursing down his flushed face and into runnels making their way out of the unkempt shrubbery of his armpits on to his trunk and limbs. All added up to sensations that are deeply familiar, being older than any thoughts he has had, any world-self-slices he can recall.

He searches for his pulse and is surprised by the animal-warm movement in the stillness of his wrist. He is struck less by its rapidity than by the sullen, incommunicative tone of the soft thuds against his fingertips. Unlike breathing, which (as discussed with Jan Halák) seems always to be in the littoral zone between something one does and something that happens, the pulse seems to belong to the world of objective events, more remote than the length of his arm from the beating heart at the centre of his being. He is sometimes struck by the strangeness of the process of making measurements on himself. Occasionally he recalls how Galileo, carrying the torch lit by Brahe and Kepler, timed the pendulum swinging in the church with his pulse; and how Galileo's physician later timed his pulse using a pendulum whose regularity had been established by a pulse.

Notwithstanding all these miracles enacted by a body being exercised by the person whose relationship to it is somewhere between ownership ('my body') and identity ('I'), RT can be a little bored as he goes through his routine.

And so, he thinks some thoughts.

Not infrequently, his thoughts take themselves on a virtual trip to the Castle along the route that is now well-known to us. When, as is often the case, the trip shrivels to a mere recitation of names, he digs a little deeper and thinks about himself in the gym back in Stockport and of the fact that the Slavia gym self and the Stockport gym self think of each other and think also of the fact that they do – that they can – think of each other. The connectedness of consciousness becomes a *leitmotif.*

Treading a treadmill rather than walking the streets, lifting weights rather than a bag of shopping, or rowing a rowing machine rather than steering a boat down a river, and other such seemingly purposeless busyness of the body, have the serious purpose of seeking a future state of the flesh that is engaged in these activities. We pursue this goal with equal vigour in our native country, as we populate the carnal future with counterfactuals headed off. It is a strikingly intimate exercise of our free will: curating our own bodies, creating a more enduring or reliable platform for the future exercise of our agency, and postponing the inevitable ontological re-badging that will transform the gymnast into a carcass to be eaten by fire or dissolved in the rain. That this is possible in a place almost identical with the gym in Stockport highlights the seasonless, nowhere place where we seek futures defined by the most carnal of abstract possibilities – the state of our bodies next week, next month, next year (if there is one).

Thus, the report from *l'abime de l'enfer*. And, yes, we would have added our 'Like' – earned by the nice smile and a *Zatím* from the receptionist – to the other 16,552, had we not lacked the technology to record it.

# Bilá Hora: 1620 and All That

We board the tram, our bodies transformed by our efforts, to return to Norská. The tram's ultimate destination – Bilá Hora – printed on its forehead, piques our curiosity. The knowledge that we shall soon be leaving Prague explains why this piquing has happened to a curiosity hitherto unpiqued by this item. We decide to devote the last afternoon of one of our many visits to translating the place-name into an experience, by transporting our sensorium to the place it denotes.

This time we pass through Pohorelec, giving Brahe and Kepler only a brief glance to make sure their images have not been stolen. The remainder of the journey is along the kind of road with which we are already familiar: a suburban to outer urban, midiskirts to outskirts, highway. It is straight and necessarily wide in order that it can accommodate tramlines between fat lanes of traffic going to and from the centre. Not much changes in the nine stops – Malovanká, Drinopol, U kastanu, Breznovsky Kláster, Ricanova, Vypich, Oboro Hvevda, Mally Breznov – that separate Pohorelec from Bilá Hora. For the most part, the route is flanked by blocky medium-rise cream or white apartment buildings and the shops and occasional cafés that serve them. The beautiful green spaces near here are just out of sight and we are for the most part unaware of them. (Prague never misses an opportunity to turn a space into a park.)

One tram-stop – Vypich – stands out. It does so not because it is handy for the largest Kauffland hypermarket in the Czech Republic, or its proximity to a hospital important enough for one of its buildings to be crowned by a heliport, but because it was once close to the vast tented cities that accommodated the quintennial Spartakiads – mass public gym performances, incorporating dance, music, and poetry, unique to what was then Czechoslovakia. It is impossible to resist a brief, virtual hop-off at this point.[203]

Spartakiads were at first banned under Communism but were revived in 1955 "to document the joyous life of building the…people's democratic Czechoslovak Republic" and to provide a climax to the celebration of the tenth anniversary of the liberation of the Czech Republic by the Red Army. The 1960 Spartakiad was particularly impressive, with almost 1.5 million (this is not a typo) competitors participating at different venues over the city. Compositions included 'Fairy Tale' for children aged 6-8, 'A Joyous Spring' for 8-11 year olds, the unfortunately named Red Balls for girls 12-14, 'Be Ready to Work and Defend Your Country' for mixed 12-14 year-olds, 'Light Fires in the Mountains' for mature teenagers, and for adults 'Alongside the Working People, We Guard the Way Forward' which included verses by a faded Surrealist whose name is already familiar to us – none other than Viteslav Nezval.

Imagine the panic-stricken preparations, worries over shoes and costumes, the fear of minor illness, the rows between parents and children, in the run-up to the moments when each of the participants becomes a small pixel in a vast, unfolding picture addressed to the mediators of the collective conscience of the nation – of history, of the future, of the God that (thank God) failed.

The tram is now slowing down and swinging into the circular track that marks the terminus where it can turn round. We have arrived at our destination: Bilá Hora.

Well, yes and no. The Battle of Bilá Hora or The White Mountain did not take place next to the tram stop of that name. If the combatants had been travelling to the field of battle by public transport, they would have been better advised to dismount at the Vypich tram-stop; otherwise – given the brevity of the conflict – they would have missed out on the action. Further historical inquiry locates the actual battlefield in front of the Hevdna Renaissance Summer Palace built in 1534 by Frederick I (possibly with a little help from others).

The palace is situated in the beautiful forest park of Obora Hevdna which we had overlooked from the blinkered gaze afforded by the tram. A late reminder, perhaps, of the limits of a head-in-a-tram, distracted from within or by other heads, as an organ of perception: like all modes of assisted transport, it overlooks at least as much as it sees. There is only so much one can see at a time.

It is here, at any rate, that the Battle is re-enacted each year. The organizers do not want to celebrate war and militarism they hasten to reassure others; rather "They want people to understand the role of Bohemia in the broader context of European history" – adding that "At the same time, they want to support tourism with interesting events".[204] The merchandise, the merchandise.

And so, to the Battle, the outcome of the build-up of tension within Bohemia between Protestant and Catholic factions. For some 40 years, "the Habsburgs had been trying to claw back power across their various provinces, using religion as a definition of loyalty".[205] The increasing domination of the Protestants, who had been granted the right to practise their own faith by Rudolf II, angered the Catholic Habsburg Emperor Ferdinand I who did his best to assert power through restricting court appointments, titles, and positions in government to Catholics. His anger was further inflamed by a defenestration prompted by his prohibition of the construction of Protestant chapels on land deemed to be royal property.

This is variously named the Second or the Third defenestration; for the present we shall rest content with noting that it is the third defenestration to be registered on our tram trip, the other two being the disposal of the councillors from the New Town Hall by a Hussite mob, and the probable murder of Jan Masaryk.

This Second Defenestration took place in Prague castle on May 23rd, 1618. Representatives of Ferdinand – hardline Catholics and possible authors of a letter diminishing the rights of Protestants to practise their faith – were tossed out of a window by the protestant delegates whom they were meeting. The consequences were not immediately as deadly as in the case of the First Defenestration. The emissaries survived a 70-foot fall from a third floor.

There are two rival explanations of their extraordinary luck.

The Catholic explanation centres around the Virgin Mary and her swift action: she caught the delegates in mid-flight, something of a feat as three well-upholstered gentlemen must have been quite a handful and a challenge that even the nearest contemporary executor of such miracles Chase – one of the Paw Patrol Pups – might not have pulled off.[206] The Protestant account is less romantic but has the attraction of plausibility: the impact of the defenestrates with the ground was mitigated by a dung heap on which they landed. As a self-declared secular humanist [207] I incline to what we may call the 'Dungist' or Coprological rather than the Marian or Mariological interpretation of the salvation of Ferdinand's men. After all, it seems unlikely that, even had the Virgin Mary been an assiduous attendee at the gym, she would have been able to respond with sufficient speed and mobilize the necessary motor power and fancy footwork to gather the three gentlemen to her bosom in their unexpected hour of need.

At any rate the relatively happy outcome of the defenestration – quite unlike the sickening transformation of persons into carcasses of the earlier defenestration from the Town Hall – makes a comic take acceptable. One of the defenestrated was later ennobled by the Emperor and received a title that reflected the descent rather than the soft landing: The Baron of Highfall.[208]

As we know, however, that was not the happy outcome we might hope for: it triggered a Europe-wide catastrophe. The defenestration focused a lot of free-floating, transcendentally validated ire, with God kept busy being on everyone's side. After two years of preparation fueled by seething rage, the Catholic Habsburgs advanced on the capital of Protestant Bohemia. The total number of combatants and civilian camp followers amounted to 60,000 people – equaling the entire population of Prague at that time.

It was on November 8th 1620 that Team Habsburg arrived at Bilá Hora, where Team Bohemia had paused their retreat. There was some initial resistance from the home team but, after the loss of 2,000 men, the army – demoralized, uncommitted, and most importantly underpaid – suddenly disintegrated. The Battle had lasted just two hours, less than the duration of a return journey between the termini of the 22 tram.

The horror of the Thirty Years' War triggered by Bilá Hora may have hidden the importance of a battle which seems to have consisted largely of the losing side running away.[209] But it was the most decisive event in Czech history, a hinge moment equal in consequence to Hastings, plus Agincourt, plus the Armada, plus Waterloo. It determined the future of the Kingdom of Bohemia for the next 300 years. Protestantism and the Czech language and culture were marginalized, nearly 10 per cent of the population left Bohemia, there was a vast transfer of wealth and power from protestant nobles to incoming or indigenous Catholics, the Protestant church was decapitated, and many Baroque Catholic churches – including our much-loved St. Nicholas – were built. The portentous consequences extended into the rest of Europe and indeed the history of the world, with the ripples doubtlessly affecting our beloved Stockport.

The Virgin Mary, by the way, was richly rewarded for her mid-air Paw Patrol rescue operation. Not only did everything go the way we might imagine she had hoped, but there was also one event she would not have allowed herself to dream of. The Habsburg King honoured her with the (presumably honorary) title of Commander-in-Chief of his army[210] – admittedly to deal with a bitter rivalry between two of his own leading generals.

Mary did not of course anticipate the end of her triumph – and the toppling of her pillar in Old Town Square in 1919 – with the coming of the secular Republic, followed in short order by Nazism and Communism; nor a Prague in which the footfall in Tesco or other outlets, far exceeded that in any churches, with the latter becoming predominantly backdrops for selfies or the venues for concerts in which Vivaldi's Four Seasons and Mozart's *Eine kleine Nachtmusik* would be repeated *ad nauseam*.

Thus, the connections between the world we live in and two action-packed hours a couple of tram stops away from this spot four hundred years ago.

This is the point at which we begin to take our leave of Prague.

# Leaving Prague

The two syllables of 'goodbye' last about a second. Leaving Prague, however, takes a little longer. We haven't really left Prague until we have arrived at The Other Place.

Departure begins with packing the possessions we brought with us, and for the most part used during our stay, adding items purchased in the city, such as aperients, a plastic dinosaur, a novel about a man executed (the ultimate P45) by his Tudor king employer, and other imperfect mementoes to supplement our imperfect memories. Packing brings with it a surprise at how the contents of our suitcases seem, like us, to have gained weight and volume. The cases are zipped shut against the resistance of their contents, stickers commemorating our incoming flight are unstuck, and ribbons are re-attached to give them a distinctive identity to ensure that we welcome the right pieces when we arrive at Manchester.

A last look round combines utilitarian check with misty-eyed farewell to a much-loved *pied a terre*. As we get older, the truism that we are not getting any younger presses its truth upon us: farewells are spiked with the fear that this time might be the last time.

We exit, lock inner and outer doors, demit into the street, and complete our short journey to the 22 tram, accompanied by the *sotto voce* rumble of our wheelies. The tram takes us to *Náměstí míru* where we have a Last Lunch at Grosseto – our Pizza on the Piazza.

We descend that escalator, which is the longest in Prague, or is it in the Czech Republic, or is it in Europe, reminding ourselves that (as the reader knows) we knew the answer to this once. As a result of our overground perambulations, the names of the metro that mark our progress to the 119 bus, have added more petals to the mental images of the places to which they refer. The synaptic connection between underground and overground has become even smoother of late because escalation now ascends all the way to the surface. As for the 119 journey, it gets shorter each time: scarcely have we registered the Cube than we are swinging from the airport Cargo depot to the Terminus 1 of Václav Havel Airport, hanging on to our wheelies.

We are among those lucky individuals whose papers are almost invariably in order and pass through the various security checks swiftly. This means that we have to wait longer for our plane. The length of our wait, however, is primarily explained by our neurotic fear of missing our flight, of being caught out by a sudden transition from 'Wait in Lounge' to 'Final Call for Boarding'.

We reminisce a little, but we pass more time in a manner that seems like a betrayal of the city we are leaving: reading to-day's *Guardian* (much prized after so many days of making do with yesterday's); continuing to follow the fate of the Tudor grandee to decapitation; catching up on emails (as if that were possible); and working on something that suddenly seems pressing now that the return to UK is imminent.

The queueing, when we are summoned to our gate, strengthens our sense of being nowhere in particular, of a progressive dilution of a Prague of the mind, especially at the point where individual uncertainties fatten the queue into milling, the most unattractive form of togetherness. The miller's tale is one of humbling – at being one-of-many – mitigated by brief solidarities sealed with co-grumbling or eyes raised to a heaven that for most of the millers is void of transcendental entities, benign purpose, or anything else that would allay the suspicion that much of life free of suffering may consist of mere hanging about. The purpose the members of the queue have in common – of loading their bodies into the plane in order that they might be shipped to Manchester – conceals the profound disparity of where the flight fits into their different lives, the coming from and the going to, what pasts had anticipated the journeys and what futures will remember or forget them. The sense of common purpose, that is, is an illusion, though the uneasy sense that we are 'interchangeable' remains.[211]

The final stage of the stop-and-start queue, where we pass down the caterpillar (with its flinty-frost floor) fastened on the entry to the plane, prepares us to be nowhere in particular. The identification of our seats as 22A and 22B signals the triumph of denotation over connotation. The standard instructions and other announcements reinforce the anywhere-sense as do the universal engine noises that climax towards take off, and an ascent that always disappoints by not delivering us a view of the city and the opportunity to complete our farewell.

All of which motivates the purchase of alcoholic drinks. These, alas, hasten the passage from patchy reminiscence or attentive reading to dreamless or dream-impoverished sleep. In between these states there is a doziness and an endeavour to glimpse memories of an already-distant Prague through a lattice of bodily sensations as experienced in Grébovka: head fizzing on the border between outside and inside, neck on verge of stiffness, pressure on shoulders, the continuity of the back with the backside, legs aware of their own bent state, feet in whispered dialogue with socks, socked feet in sterner dialogue with shoes, and shoes in insentient interaction with the extracorporeal world. It adds up to a reassurance that the body being propelled from city to city is fundamentally unchanged by this transition. Unlike the thoughts about it, that are located nowhere at all – not even in Prague when the body is in Prague – this entity occupies a universal space shared with the streets, parks, pubs, and buildings of Prague.

We awake to a circling descent round the great metropolis of Manchester reduced in the darkness, and flattened by our altitude, to a fragmented orange stain, its streets to parallel rows of suspension points. Continuing descent unpacks the houses from rubble to dwellings, and the traffic expands from lines of aphids to individual vehicles large enough to house passengers.

We touch down, spared the crash for which we always brace ourselves, and experience a seemingly panic-stricken deceleration in which the brakes are assisted by mechanical spoilers increasing the aerodynamic drag of the wings which revives a worn-out metaphor employing the dog Pluto whose skidding to a halt is assisted by its erected ears.

There is an agonizingly slow disembarkation, as if the plane were constipated. Disembarked, we follow corridors we are inclined to describe as 'endless', to another queue of queues, folded a dozen times by barriers. We show our passports to a profession-ally unsmiling functionary of the state who seems insufficiently concerned by the discrepancy between the antique face that faces him and the younger portrait on the document. Beneficiaries of our earlier foresight, we proceed to baggage reclaim to wait for the beribboned cases.

The choreography – in the plane as ranks disciplined by seats, subsequently clotting into a crowd that just falls short of jostling, and unspooling into a fat thread filing through the final barriers – is another stately familiar, highly structured reminder of our individual unimportance. The reminder, of course, does not cut ice: we are never 'lost' in the crowd because *we* are always here-most-here while it is others who are over there where they add up to mere numbers. They are not even lost.

United with our cases, we pass through an exit that warns us we cannot turn back and pause to shop for essentials before catching a taxi. We are relieved that at this hour we are not sub-jected to the confident but evidence-lean opinions of the driver about matters with which we do not have the energy to disagree. The driver is paid – his tip reduced by his reluctance to assist his elderly passengers with their cases – and we walk up the drive.

We reach the front door. The key that enables us to enter our house in England (we had, after all, locked the door) is next on the ring to the key with which we locked our flat in Czechia. The permissions are side-by-side, ring-mates that rattle together, though the doors they unlock are separated by 750 or so tram, bus, airplane, and taxi miles. Had we been less tired we might have paused to contemplate this collapsing of distances, and to teach these distances folded up in our doziness to wake up, and to be startled by what are, after all, startling manifestations of the manner in which we have formatted and indeed transformed the physical space into which we were born and in which our ultimate ancestor generated the possibility of a human world where 'together' and 'apart' are not translatable into the distances and proximities in the physical world brought into being by the Big Bang. We pacify the burglar alarm with a wave of a magic button cancelling what had been set by our outgoing wave.

We have arrived at The Other Place – the second place in the world where we are not visitors. We are relieved that it has not, as on a previous occasion, been ransacked by burglars who, keyless, had broken the side door. On that occasion we had been relieved, rather than insulted, that they had ignored the manuscripts and box files and the published works of RT that had filled the study.

In our absence, our dwelling has acquired its own, faintly ecclesiastical, scent. We register changes, processes that have got on with themselves in the weeks we have been away. Unwatered flowers have drooped. A coffee on my desk – abandoned in the rush of departure – has acquired a skin. Rooms, reflecting the conditions in the greater outside, are chilly. A door that had hitherto been silent emits a brief, ironical call of surprise. There are more intimate markers of what is erroneously called the passage of time,[212] among them an unexplained bruise on my arm which has changed its spectral frequency and bluish has been replaced by jaundice yellow. Conspicuously unchanged are the cirrus clouds behind the Castle on the cover of Granta next to the coffee on my desk, the wistful smile of Alexander Dubcek, his pale blue tie, and the reflections in the Vltava.

It would be remiss to forget one return – in early March 2020 – when, with great reluctance, we cut short our stay in Prague for reasons that do not need spelling out. We arrived home in twilight and discovered that in our three-week[213] absence the daffodils had exploded into full wattage. They were leaning forward, as if returning our attention. Each, individually a masterpiece, was not diminished by so many others into mere members of a crowd. Their pouting trumpets synaesthetically echoed memories of other members of the brass section: exclamations of forsythia, modest primroses, and yellowed-billed blackbirds picking up on songs discontinued the previous July. The cold March air making their notes glisten, seemed to prophesy the sunshine to come. The blazing thisness of the daffodils, poised between colour and meaning, stood for hope, for the possibility of a new beginning glowing through an end. By their transforming light, perhaps, we might see the Stockport *Wunderkammer* for what it is.

The chill, tiredness, and a desire for closure propelled us to bed, after the usual preparation which included a tinkle without the pistol shot with which this tale began, and a Lutheran deposition perhaps remotely triggered by the pizza from Grosseto many hours ago and 700 miles away. The bodies that had propelled themselves and been propelled to and through Prague now laid themselves down and fell asleep, dreaming perhaps of that city, or perhaps oblivious of Magic Prague and, equally, of Magic Stockport.

CODA

What should they know of Stockport
who only Stockport know?[214]

# (Even More) Scattered Reflections

Readers who have suspected from the outset that the author may have had designs on them, baiting their attention under false pretences, will by now have had their suspicions fulfilled beyond doubt. The designs are philosophical and the philosopher in question is one who, after too many books with too many pages, may feel that any revelation that philosophy may have to offer will not be the conclusion of an argument. It may, however, be the reward of a patient picking away at the patina that covers the world when we come to know it, or think we know it, too well.

In support of this project of thinking about the world and his place in it, The Philosopher has recruited a city that he has had the good fortune to visit on many occasions. A city to which he had been denied off-line access for nearly two years by Covid, has been made available to him through his own, unreliable, memory and the more reliable collective memory accessed through the Internet whose alchemical transformations of space and time and its extension of the reach of individual consciousness that Rudolf and his circle of magicians could not have even imagined.

As we think of the impact Prague had on us we forget the impact we might have made on the city: the spoor of our perambulations, and our many kinds of footprints. We were overheard by involuntary audiences, blocked other's views straining to see things that we, too, are looking at, exchanged glances, greetings, or comments with strangers, were a dull puzzle to passers-by, were snapped up accidentally by snapshots, added to the length of queues, contributed to the fullness of trams, made a small addition to a low buzz in the theatre before the curtain rose, filled bins, added to the congestion of the sewage system, annoyed or pleased a waiter by the size of our tips or tone of voice, made our contribution to the city's economy by buying bread, wine, souvenirs, and tickets for this and that.

We set ripples in motion and had no idea where they ended. Who knows what impact the after-warmth of my sitting on a tram seat sipped by a successor bottom might have had on the bottom owner's mood?[215] (A question that does not seek an answer.) And think of that trouser whisperer near the Castle, whose journey of many thousands of miles from the Far East to what he would justifiably call the Middle West delivered our enhanced sense of the quietness of the city. Such are the errant ways of causation, highlighted when someone's vision of the world is blurred by dense fog, courtesy of a kettle chivvying water to the status of solvent of instant coffee, misting his glasses.

The contrail left by our passage through a city is as unimaginable as the posthumous existence we will have in the minds of those who encountered us in our lives. We all of us can think of individuals who are reduced in our intermittent recollections to a single thing they said. I recall the first consultant I worked for when I was a houseman. He was not a dedicated follower of the advances of medical science. He held an electrocardiogram (upside down) while informing me that the three most useless things in the world were "fog at sea, hair on a man's arse, and the ECG".

Be that as it may, it will be evident that behind any attempt to harvest Prague in sentences - that while they may be written out street-straight across the page are necessarily curled in the minds of anyone who reads them – there is an agenda that can scarcely be described as 'hidden'. It is the wish to say something about the relationship between a mind and its world through observing that between a visitor and a city. At the heart of this relationship are the forgetfulness and ignorance necessary to make it possible for the city to deliver itself to a particular moment in a particular life.

Forgetfulness is easily dealt with. If nothing were overlooked in panoramas, there would be no overview. If nothing were lost of streets, interiors, conversations, faces, patterns of sunlight, memory would be chaos, a purée of mutually buried particulars. And ignorance? If there were no barriers to knowledge, there would be no knowns to stop at – just as a purely transparent world would be invisible. Thus, a city: closed doors, windows curtained by reflections or shuttered by blinds or other barriers, faces that are opaque, bodies whose sensations cannot be guessed at, discourse that makes sense only in a world to which one has limited access, by the torchlight of guesses, prejudices, and unsound extrapolation from unregulated experiences. The thoughts that seem to part closed curtains, to open doors, to interpret the expressions on faces, are to some degree self-deceived.

And this ignorance is exacerbated by an inattention to the surrounding world as one walks down a street, or enters a café, a church, a lecture room, a hallway, a lounge, or a bedroom. For travellers have more baggage than they pass through security or collect at reclaim. They enter a foreign land trailing clouds of preoccupations and have long-term, medium-term, and brief purposes, that have little or nothing to do with the city to which they have travelled. Indeed, they *are* baggage, a fact felt most acutely when one is walking through a much-admired quarter in the eye of a quarrel, harried by a deadline, or invaded by a stomach over-filled with Grosseto's Four Seasons. Thus, is there knitted a sleeve for consciousness that muffles the streets and extinguishes the past that generated those streets. An EasyJet flight on an angel with a contrail does not liberate us from the tangled state of being a human being.

If we are self-deceived and insist on saying that we 'visited Prague' rather than 'visited a minute sample of Prague with a small slice of oneself' it is because we are accustomed to referring to vast entities as if we could get our heads round them. Of course, there are even more blatant cases of epistemic cheek, of cognitive over-reach, than 'Prague'. I am used to referring to 'the universe' and characterizing it in this way and that and citing an equation such as $E=mc2$ as if my gaze could cast a torchlight on its totality. Insofar as there is a 'Prague', it is a Prague of the mind, a unity unpacked in a million predicates, experiences, spoken and unspoken, thought out loud, and kept to one's self.

Grounds for despair? No, for joy.

I owe you an explanation. It can be summarized in two words: Magic Stockport.

# Magic Stockport

Dr. Johnson said many things during his long life but one thing he did not say was that "when a man is tired of Stockport, he is tired of life". Nevertheless, he would have been justified in saying so. Which brings us to a scandal that has haunted our pilgrimage to and around Prague. It is not that behind curtained windows, closed doors, in cafés, in the lucent space that is the head-packed night tram, are hundreds of thousands of people living millions of ordinary, rather than magic, hours. No; the scandal is that we feel that the ordinariness of life in Prague is a scandal. Or more precisely that we cannot see that life in Prague is nothing of the kind – as is evident when we look at it closely or think past the surface features which our hurry obliges us to skate past. And so, also, life in Stockport.

It is a fundamental mistake to assume that home is nothing to write home about.

I could, of course, try to set the cities in competition. I could pit Prague Castle against the iconic Stockport railway viaduct (completed in 1842, composed of 11,000,000 bricks, 34 metres above the Mersey, and 500 metres long amounting to the largest brick-built structure in Western Europe[216]) or St. Nicholas' Church against the Hat Works Museum (ranked 8th of 58 things to do in Stockport). Alternatively, I might put the Frogtastic Art Trail (18 large plastic frogs with little top-hatted froglets sitting on their backs[217]) into the ring against David Czerny's thought-provoking cock-a-snookery scattered through his native city. Or, less ambitiously, I could highlight the way the sound of the traffic on the wet M60 heard from the Redrock car park rather precisely echoes the audio recording by the Marks brothers of the Brusnice stream busying off to its mother-river, the Vltava. Or, less ambitiously still, line up the eye-lash extension shops in Stockport ('Lash Revolution') against the Absintherie of Prague or, Stockport's 'Thai Massage' outlets against the ones that seemed to be ubiquitous in Prague prompting us to remind ourselves that 'Thai' is pronounced 'Tai' not 'Thigh'. Or mobilize something that Prague could not match: a sign for a mountain footpath (yes, the Pennine Way) located next to a café in Stockport Market.

And then there is the comma on the forehead of an omnibus – "Sorry, out of service" – apologizing for not being available for the ride. The comma carries a pause between the bus's broadcast sorrow and that for which it is sorry. While I had seen it before, it was perhaps the afterglow of Prague that made me see it for the strange thing that it was; or prompted me to be self-teased into the anteroom of thought. I might reference the cluster of wind turbines that are less than 25 miles from Stockport, somersaulting with gymnastic ecstasy, harvesting fire out of the air, order out of chaos. Or, if that seems too desperate, finally, I might mobilize some rather remarkable bas reliefs, applied to the concrete side wall of a now defunct British Home Stores.

They gather up the spirit of city from 1239 to 1978 in five panels. In Panel 1 the city is represented by two soldiers, one dated 1239 and the other 1260, armed with shields for defence and swords for attack. Panel 2 brings on a praying divine (1334) and a scholar

(1439) with a scroll and drink. On Panel 3, we are introduced to a soldier – who in view of his date (1642) must have been on active service - and a civic worthy (1772). Richard Cobden – a 19th century liberal politician advocating free trade and world peace – and 'The Cheshire Farmer' (a stout person rather than a pub selling stout, with a fine big-buttoned coat and a sheep at his feet), represent the next phase of the city. And the final panel (1978) celebrates British Home Stores and is jam-packed with all the hard- and soft-ware – from pans to pants – that it sold before it was itself sold. Throughout, there is a lavish supply of lions, standing on their hind-legs, warming their front paws in the solar heat of generic pomp.

Even armed with such firepower, fostering a competition between the two cities would be a mistake, not just because the outcome would be a foregone conclusion but because it misses a fundamental point. It is time to reach towards that point: to see the treasure buried in plain sight. To rise above particular evidence of magic, which is anyway vulnerable to extinction – as when a Frogtastic frog is reduced to a load to be carried to the re-cycling centre or a surrealist poetry reading becomes the destination of an irritated or otherwise bothered hurry. Even this could be reignited by reflecting on the fact that I was thinking, as I passed the frog, about the etymology of 'poppycock', a word that entered my consciousness without knocking, and reminding myself that it had reached me via the Dutch *poppehak* meaning 'dollop of excrement' (with the term 'pap' referring to excrement that is as soft as 'porridge'), having coming via USA, where the Dutch had arrived in the 17th century talking nineteen to the dozen. Or that I was fresh from breakfasting on a boiled egg cupped in a holder that wished me Good Morning from the mouth of Felix the Cat and that I would shortly (and not for the first time in my life) be thanked by a paper bag.[218]

And now is the time to recall that episode in the Summer Palace (a.k.a Královsky letohrádek) when Mrs. T. found it necessary to dismount from the tram to respond to a call of nature – one of the increasing number of occasions when, with increasing age, the body, which is supposed to deliver on the agenda of the person, puts down agenda items of its own. While the author was waiting for the business to be concluded he had, as is his wont, a thought. On this occasion the thought circled round the claim that the "And the end of all our exploring/ Will be to arrive where we started/ And to know the place for the first time".[219] And the starting place in question is – well, Stockport. Magic Stockport. Stockport made magic through the journey to Prague. Made unfamiliar at least through an itinerary that has placed it – not the Castle – at the end of the journey. If the hardest place to imagine is the place you are in, it is harder still if you live there. Let us therefore look at Stockport from a distance and imagine how it might be recalled by a man 700 miles away waiting for his wife in the Royal Summer Palace.

More specifically, let us imagine not an entire quarter of the city, nor a street, or even a house, but a room. But which room? The answer comes via the crash of a third toilet seat, whose call illuminates Magic Stockport with the light of Magic Prague. The room brought into unaccustomed spotlight is what used to be called 'The Smallest Room':

> Although often overlooked because of its size, the smallest room in the house should never be underestimated. Most of us are now fortunate enough to live in homes…

with a downstairs cloakroom which allows guests to use our facilities without ever stepping foot on our stairs.[220]

It is just such a facility that is the subject of what follows: a Cabinet of Curiosities that might have astonished even that world-ranking collector of such curiosities, the Emperor of Bohemia Rudolf II, who has stalked us through Prague, popping up here and there. And, as we have already noted, it is a feast of lessons for Surrealists who would pretend to astonish us with the chance meeting between an umbrella and a sewing machine on a dissecting table, reminding them to pay attention to the world around them. Notably, to these seasonless, somehow placeless places in Stockport where the extraordinary is presented, courtesy of familiarity, in the guise of the ordinary.

Truthfully, behind this is a search for consolation. Each time we return from Prague, we know that there remains one less visit from our lifetime's total. And this stands for something larger: regret at our finitude. I suspect that there are a few people in this world who have had more than enough of Raymond Tallis, but he can't get enough of himself.

What follows then is, so far as it understands itself, a determined attempt to deliver on the Summer Palace Promise. As such it is (also) an incidental reminder of the greatest of all miracles: the connectedness of ourselves....

# A Wunderkammer or the House of the Sneezing Thurible.[221]

The holiness of minute particulars.[222]

The first thing that might strike the occupant, who sits and looks about him with the eyes of a visitor, is that the room is, among many other things, an art gallery. The upper half of the reddish walls is lavishly hung with pictures. A photograph of workmen in caps and overalls, sitting in a row on a girder hundreds of feet above the New York streets, broadcasting their aplomb by smoking, opening food boxes, or reading a newspaper, has landed from another planet. The moment is approximately 3,300 miles and a century away. The photograph has a natural companion in an aerial view of Manhattan encompassing the Chrysler Building, Brooklyn Bridge, and other landmarks, also constructed by workers whose workplace would be a place of terror for others.

This short thread of coherence is not sustained. A commissioned photograph of Polzeath Beach and Pentire Head in Cornwall; a map of the London Underground (where Highbury and Islington station connects with Námestí míru station by a link unknown to public transport but known the reader); an acrylic painting, by a deceased colleague, of a tree in his garden; reproductions of water colours of London's St Paul's Cathedral in the snow and of St. Michael's Mount Cornwall seen through drizzle; and a copy of Caspar

David Friedrich's 'The Wanderer Above the Mists' – these are united by raw 'and'. They belong to the order of aggregation rather than coherence, a realm where separation dominates over unity.

The rawness is underlined by the contents of a white painted straw basket on the carpeted floor two feet beneath the mountain peak on which the Wanderer is standing, contemplating who knows what. His frock coat, ordinary shoes, and lack of Gortex, totally unsuitable for the unforgiving crags on which he stands, suggest that he might in due course be seeking the assistance of the Mountain Rescue. The basket also contains a photograph of waiters in dinner jackets serving two men sitting on a girder above New York City with a very expensive meal on crisp linen, seeming to continue an already established theme. But it is stacked next to a portrait of a cloven-footed Cornwall by the Cornish artist John Miller as The Land of Saints or 'Cornubia' which name it shares with a ship, a town in Australia, and a genus of mites.[223]

Just to rub in the triumph of randomness, where *bric* knows nothing of *brac*, nor knick of knack, 'Cornubia' is half-concealing a copy of The Onion ('The Finest News Reporting') already referred to when we were at the Royal Summer Palace. It is in turn partly concealed by a three-year-old issue of France magazine.

The basket is just a few feet away from the Canal and Rivers Trust Calendar where the picture for September portrays 'Community Celebrations at the popular Angel Canal Festival'. This is no Spartakiad, but an event, nonetheless. The picture is dominated by a smiling bearded, turbaned man, wearing a silk garment of hi-vis yellow, standing in the foredeck of a boat. From his neck hangs a lanyard in turn adorned by a plastic smiling emoji. He is engaged in the innocent pastime of creating vast suds like cellophane, out of soapy water stretched between two sticks, that magically turn to huge bubbles. He is smiling with pleasure at his magic making and at being multiply photographed by people who are themselves in the photograph. Its message is 'Making Life Better by Water'. Behind him is a display of more resilient bubbles, otherwise known as balloons, tugging at their strings.

Just a foot below Caspar David Friedrich's mist-conquering Wanderer is a large, framed set of sterling coins placed on a baize background. The coins don't look like manhole covers in Lilliput, but they license the metaphor. (And what is this book if not an opportunity to get a few metaphors off my chest?) They include most of the denominations of the pre-decimal era. There is the defiant, jaw-jutting head of Mr. Churchill, a portcullis echoing the Prague coat of arms, a monarch from the distant time when the occupant of the throne had a beard, a galleon in full sail, a rose surrounded by thistles, helmeted Britannia armed with a shield and a giant toasting fork, any number of lions, and a wren. At the centre of the display is the half-crown that, to my childhood self, represented the limit of imaginable riches.

It is difficult not to think of the long, winding journeys these items have taken – stopping at grubby pockets housing handkerchiefs and scraps of paper, enclosed in sweaty hands, purses, wallets, handbags, piggy banks, slot machines, cash registers ingeniously registering cash, hidden drawers, backs of sofas – before reaching this retirement home, following farthings, half pennies, and half-crowns into numismatic history, and subsequently relying for their value on the contemporary currency used to purchase them as souvenirs of an earlier age. The duration of their post-circulatory existence is measured in an accumulation of blue-grey fluff round their edges, creating a connection of which they are innocent with the time-brewed patina on the bronze arms of a certain poet commemorated on Petrina several hundred miles from this spot.

We have so far avoided the Big Beasts of The Smallest Room whose presence is scarcely accidental. It is time to correct this.

There is, first and of course, the pale mustard sink whose most prominent part is a porcelain basin. It has two taps with the temperature of the water they offer hinted in red and blue circles, a universal language, that trades on the assumption that we all associate red with heat and blue with cold, a cross-modal correspondence justified perhaps by the appearance of some skin in different conditions.[224] The black plug is restrained by a lead goosed by silver spheres half way in size between ball bearings and suspension points.

None of this will come as a surprise to a visitor. Nor will the toiletries scattered haphazardly on the little shelf between the taps and thus handy for the hands of the handwasher. Garnier Hand Repair billed to nourish and soothe the skin of the item in question – thus meta-feeding the hand that feeds it – is separated from Carex Derma Clean (claimed to deliver fatal blows to a tantalizing 99.9% of germs) by a nail brush with a transparent plastic handle, fashioned out of the stuff of boiled sweets, and sporting a Prussian hairdo. And then there is a bloated tube of toothpaste whose cap replicates the form of an Orthodox priest's kamilavka – almost certainly by accident. This little discovery pre-empts any disappointment I might have felt at the absence (because it is upstairs) of Heel Balm that would have given me the opportunity to pun on the healing of a surface that had been repeatedly struck by the paved surfaces of the Bohemian capital.

The temptation at this moment to discuss the washing that takes place in the basin is strong but not overwhelming. What strength the temptation has derives from its philosophical connection with our ambiguous nature as embodied subjects. The hands washing each other are both agents and the objects of each other's agency, rubbed rubbers rubbing rubbed rubbers. And while there is no such vertiginous reciprocity in the case of washing our face, there is something special about the primary agent of our agency – our hands – laundering that part of our bodily surface which, more than any other, is associated with the identity of the agent. Behind the question as to why our hands can wash themselves while they require a towel or some other absorbent surface to dry themselves is the ghost of those two interlocutors who talked of embodiment in Prague's Café Mistral and the possibility of an agenda item for our next meeting.

The basin is supported on a plinth concealing the technology necessary to access the distant reservoirs – in the principality of Wales, I believe, in the case of Stockport – that have harvested and stored the rain that will become tap water. Between the plinth and the toilet (of which more presently), there is a brush with a steel handle stored in a steel quiver, a waste bin that opens its mouth in a silent scream when you stamp on its single foot, Duck Deep Action Gel which like Carex also claims to kill 99.9% of germs (and we hope that the surviving 0.1% will not return the compliment by killing us), and a tipped-over weighing machine, seemingly permanently in disgrace for always giving unwelcome answers. On the top of the toilet, there is more Carex, hand gel (killing 99.9% etc.), and a glass full of 'soft cotton' buds whose many purposes, in addition to extracting from the ears the secretions by which they deafen themselves, need not be spelt out here.[225]

Set into the wall is a dispenser with a white toilet roll. Close inspection of its seemingly plain, exquisitely thin, rashers of paper reveals a pattern, a honeycomb of hexagons of such modest altitude that they would not tower over goose pimples, a microscopic expression of the frozen exuberance of rococo, confirming to the followers of Adolf Loos that this toilet is a crime scene of superfluous ornament. The impression is reinforced when, as the roll is stripped down to a cardboard cylinder, we catch a glimpse of hearts on the holder. What "if design govern in a thing so small"?[226] What indeed? Nevertheless, in view of what we know about him, we shall be disinclined to take lessons from Herr Loos on the aesthetic morality of toilet paper.

Every now and then a certain joke crosses your author's mind. It makes a frail connection with the country 700 miles away when it was seen through the lens of Soviet occupation as an Eastern European state. "Why" asks the innocent proletarian, "given that paper is so scarce – do we have the criminal luxury of toilet paper that is doubled to wipe our loyal Marxist-Leninist bottoms?"– "Because we are always obliged to send Moscow a copy of anything we have done". Pause for laughter that comes late or not at all.

The toilet roll *in situ* can serve the secondary purpose of signaling, through the neat envelope-like folding of the free end, the spoor of the cleaning lady indicating that she has done her work. Next to it is a white stalk on a stand on which toilet rolls are stacked in anticipation of the future need to absterge the podex.

And so, and not before time, we come to the artefact that gives the room its name and central purpose: the garrulous toilet that, if it is not swallowing excrement and swilling it down with after-swigs, is noisily refilling its reserves. Its chatter competes with the steady muttering of the fan that is automatically switched on with the electric light when the toilet is entered, in rather tactless anticipation of the expected pong. And, on the principle of belt-and-braces, the toilet carries a cannister of 'Glade' which warrants attention.

We have already guessed that Mrs. Luther would have happily given up the holiest brand of incense from the most impeccable of sources emitted from the most wonderfully crafted thurible, shaken into sacred spaces by men closer to God than their congregations, for a few squirts, mist-cones of 'Glade', disseminated by an index finger pressing on the top of the can, purchased in a supermarket to combat the colonic malodour emitted by her husband in his struggles with his recalcitrant gut.

Glade – 'a fragrance infused with essential oils' - is 'Designed to fight tough odours'. (The toughness of odours is a difficult abstraction, even when one is creating one. But it would not do to suggest that the paying customers were associated with a stench.) The scent it projects into the air, when pressure applied to the nozzle prompts a succession of brief, formalized sneezes, is certainly more subtle than its olfactory adversary – perhaps too subtle. The name is hand-written, and the 'L' of glade has a tail that sweeps under the next three letters, changes from black to blue, and as it doubles back over 'd' and 'e' awakens into blue that flies off in the form of a shape that is a petal, a butterfly, or a bird. Connotation-heavy image of a land far from the whiff of the dunny.

Quite a different tone is struck on the back of the cannister. It is covered with warnings – and 'Varnings' because the instructions are handily repeated in Swedish in case, as a result of defaecation, one finds that one has changed nationality. Such upsets may have been commonplace in the enchanted world of the court of King Rudolf. The gravest of the varnings, a few inches away from the promise of 'Pure Clean Linen', is that 'Solvent Abuse Can Kill Instantly'. It is bracketed by iconic punctuation marks made from idealized lightning flashes.

It is chastening to reflect that every line of the small print on the can has been crawled over with more attention than Paul Valéry gave to *La Jeune Parque* in the five years that it took him to compose this poem of 500 lines.[227] The convergent minds of lawyers making the product lawyer-proof may represent the highest wattage of human consciousness, though it was remote in its intention from the dream that motivated the author of *La Jeune Parque*:

> I remember how the fundamental idea behind the composition [of the poem] intoxicated me and that I did not conceive of a more admirable work than the drama of the generation of a work.[228]

The prose on the Glade can is a reminder, if any were needed, that it would take a lifetime to create an adequate *catalogue raisonné* of the items in this small treasure house created out of shared or joined agency, to unpack the consciousness has gone into developing them, and to map the cognitive terrain from which they have emerged. But we have not yet finished with this *Wunderkammer*. For, as is often the case, the toilet has a small library; more precisely, there is a shelf which contains a range of books, as eclectic as those in my father's library, whose fate, like that of many books most of the time and most books all of the time, is to be unread.

Their names and the higgle to which they belong says all that needs to be said: *1001 paintings you must see before you die; Secret Britain. The Hidden Bits of Our History; 50 Ways to Kill a Slug; One for Sorrow. Old-Fashioned Lore; Old Wives' Lore for Gardiners; Teach Yourself Czech* (why did *this* self prove unteachable?); *I Wandered Lonely as a Cloud and Other Poems You Half-Remembered from School; The Bedside Guardian 2011; Red Herrings and White Elephants. The Origin of Phrases We Use Every Day; Pub Walks in Cheshire; Taken for a Ride* (a novel); and *Nellie Longarms Will Get You If You Don't Watch Out.* Straddling *1001 paintings you must see before you die; Secret Britain and 50 Ways to Kill a Slug* is a small box of BORIS Butt Wipes -- 'Number 10's choice for Number 2's' – on which there is a portrait of a man, for whom lying is inseparable from breathing, with a *vol-au-vent* turd plonked on his calculatedly uncultivated shock of blonde hair.

There is a brown wooden cupboard built into the shelf. When we open its doors, we discover Night Nurse; Tissues; soap; Right Guard; Anti-Bacterial Handwash (99.9% etc.); Grapefruit and Ginger Room Spray. Perched on top of the cupboard are: six brass pots and bowls from Northern Nigeria; a brass handbell – from who knows where – with a handle in the form of an anchor round which a rope snakes in a manner for reasons that are entirely obscure. Behind them are three postcards adding to the gallery already noted: 'The Convalescent' by Gwen John ca 1910s to 1920s, which portrays a long, thin young lady in a blue dress reading a letter with a facial expression in which the bad or sad news in her hand and the malaise of her body converge; A Portrait of Caspar John (the future First Sea Lord) – a beautiful youth – painted by Augustus John who was his father and the brother of Gwen John; and 'Los Cigarillos Paris' an art nouveau smoking nymph – the work of the most energetic artistic promoter of the myth of the Czech nation, Alphonse Mucha, whose museum is in Old Town Square and whose body is in Vysehrad cemetery.

This return to Prague may seem an appropriate place to pause our inventory, so that we need not dwell on a small alarm clock that, long past its last tick, has alarmed no-one for years; the Stop Cock which sounds like celibacy by edict; the slim radiator painted a light primrose, very unlike the heavy black-grey ones at school which we were warned not to sit on for fear of piles; and the orange carpet on which are blurred roses, large and small, scattered in something that is on the verge of a pattern, with among them heraldic patches which I am inclined to call motifs, and tiny spots that could have been plagiarized from a rash – all adding up, against prior expectation perhaps, to a pleasing appearance that complements the pleasure of the sitter's bare feet tasting the softness of the carpet's pile.

So, there we have it: "The chance meeting of a sewing machine and an umbrella on an operating table" has been outshone by the (sur)reality of the non-accidental meeting of Carex and Cornwall, Glade and the Wanderer above the mists, and – well you know the rest. And here is another chance meeting. Having just re-discovered my signed copy of Octavio Paz's essays translated by Michael Schmidt, I am reading it while I await the clemency of my gut, and a happy conjugation of peristaltic waves, and encounter a paragraph singled out by my biro-stroke of decades ago:

Recently Gunther Grass was putting us on our guard, re-calling the pseudoradical frivolity of German intellectuals in the Weimar Republic. While there was democracy in Germany, they never ceased to scoff at it as an illusion and a bourgeois plot, but when, fatally, Hitler came, they fled – not to Moscow but to New York, doubtless to pursue there with increased ardor their critique of bourgeois society.[229]

I find myself back on the tram, travelling smoothly between occasional jerks along Národní trídá, wagging my finger at Viteslav Nezval whose contempt for the democracy of Czechoslovakia's First Republic led him to embrace the Communism that exiled his muse to a grey place equidistant from his accordion and the stars.

I wake up to what is not just a toilet but 'a toilet complex' (cf. you know what) – contemplating my return from Prague, be-ing reminded of the paradoxes of agency, such that that which is nearest at hand (one's own body) may be less under control than distant places in the shared world, and becoming aware of the low continuous hum of the fan, rhyming with the head-hiss, not tinny enough to be tinnitus, that weaves the sketch of an acoustic halo round my head, reminding me (for example) of the soft spray of rain near Legii Most and how it in turn took me to the idea of the streets of Vienna as they were walked by Heimito von Doderer's characters.

The objects that surround me on the toilet are the products of the convergence of so much consciousness, of the conscious-nesses of strangers unknown to each other, scattered over space and time, cities and centuries. As I grip the notebook – where I add to the inventory of the riches that surround me and recall that notes on earlier pages were inscribed in a street in Prague, in a café, or in the study at Norská – I note the shadow cast by my thumb – the same thumb as I used to thank those few drivers who stopped to allow us to cross the road. I reflect on different kinds of light: the light of the lamp and the light of the mind radiated by the dark webs of inscription. I would like to think that these words may outlast this thumb.

# A Meta-Preface: A Battle of the Genres

> Loud-breathing and wind-breaking, Winnie the dog lay near the old lady's stool on a cushion embroidered with a Berber aiming a rifle at a lion.[230]

> ... the linking of two realities that by all appearances have nothing to link them, in a setting that by all appearances does not fit them.[231]

> One may as well begin with Helen's letter to her sister.[232]

At this juncture, I should say "I rest my case" and free you to get on with your life. But the philosopher in me cannot let things go. If this suggests a distrust in the ghost on the other side of the page, that distrust begins on this side with the attitude to himself of the man talking to you. If philosophers are thinkers who tell people things they know already, they do so as an excuse for telling themselves those same things. By this means, taken for granted reality will be untaken for granted and, thus granted reality.

The miracle at the heart of Prague – the transformation of thoughts into voices and voices into buildings so that visions are realized as spires and bridges, and century speaks to century – is also a miracle at the heart of Stockport, even though it is instantiated in a viaduct rather than a castle, a parish church in a suburb rather than a cathedral, or the ingenious aerosol in the *Wunderkammer* of a humble toilet in a modest house rather than a 1000-year-old jeweled crown.

Before I say goodbye, it may be worth reflecting on the nature of this present work, to pre-empt the justified impatience of the reader for whom it may seem neither one thing nor the other. It is the product of the quarrel between two books – one of philosophy and another of reminiscence, itself reflecting a deeper quarrel between looking and thinking. It...

But I have used up enough of your time. Thank you for your attention – "the rarest and purest form of generosity".[233] The embodied subject that goes under the name of Raymond Tallis will resume circling round himself with a notebook, placing moments in cryogenic storage, breaking off from time to time to dream of returning to Prague to arrive there for the first time.

## Notes and References

1.  Arthur Conan Doyle 'A Case of Identity' in *The Adventures of Sherlock Holmes* Project Gutenberg eBook.
    Most recent update May 20th, 2019. (eBook #1661).

2.  Erwin Mortier *While the Gods were Sleeping* translated by Paul Vincent (London: The Pushkin Press, 2014).

3.  Louis McNeice 'Snow'. *The Collected Poems of Louis McNeice* (Oxford: Oxford University Press, 1967).

4.  Richard Powers *Generosity* (London: Atlantic Books, 2010).

5.  Derek Sayers *Prague. Capital of the Twentieth Century. A Surrealist History* (Princeton: Princeton University Press, 2015).

6.  See, for example, Derek Sayers excellent *The Coasts of Bohemia. A Czech History* (Princeton: Princeton University Press, 1998). This complements his *Prague. Capital of the Twentieth Century.* Ivan Klima *The Spirit of Prague and Other Essays.* (London: Granta, 1995) is another must-read.

7.  JL Austin 'Other Minds' in *Philosophical Papers* Second Edition Edited by J.O. Urmson and G.J. Warnock (Oxford: Oxford University Press, 1970), p.76.

8.  In this connection, Larry Woolf's *Inventing Eastern Europe. The Map of Civilization in the Mind of the Enlightenment,* (Stanford University Press, 1994) sounds like a book I ought to read.

9.  Raymond Tallis 'Certain Thoughts Arising out of being Pointed out by my Two-Year-Old Son' *Granta* 11 1984 pp.15-18.

10. Slawomir Mrozek 'A Letter' *Granta* 11 1984 pp.13-15.
    In 1953, at the height of the Stalinist terror in Poland, Mrozek argued vigorously for the death sentence for three priests who had been groundlessly accused of treason. A decade later he fled into exile having become disillusioned with Communism.

11. The Jan v Jan argument is covered with scrupulous fairness to all parties in the Wikipedia article 'Jan of Holesov' (Last edited 28th May 2021).

12. This is not my phrase, but I cannot remember whose it is. I hope to be able to track the origin of this perfect description in time for future editions of this work. (Two hopes springing contemporaneously.)

13. See Note 12.

14. As discussed in 'Reimagining the Wheel' in Raymond Tallis *Epimethean Imaginings. Philosophical and Other Meditations on Everyday Light* (Durham: Agenda, 2015).

15. The history of the wheelie is given *con amore* in 'Retrowow', an online information source for readers who want to know more about, and to relish, the fashion, styles, and cultural histories of the 50s, 60s, 70s, and 80s. Such trips down Amnesia Lane be come more precious with time.

16. On this basis, it might be thought that the most accurate, indeed honest, title for this work would be 'A Self-Reflecting Embodied Subject Visits Prague' but I suspect that this would lack box-office appeal. So, *Prague 22* it is.

17. I should have avoided the word 'monstrosity'. Since I heard it used mockingly by the wonderfully opinionated architecture critic Jonathan Meades, it has echoed in my own head, inviting me to 'just listen to yourself'.

18. I am grateful to Julian Spalding for this characterization.

19. Brandon Donnelly 'The paneláks of Prague' October 2nd, 2020. Blogpost.

20. For a comprehensive account of the hostility and a decisive rebuttal of the arguments that underpin it, see Benjamin Tallis

'Panel Studies: Public Lies & Private Lives in Paneláks and Sídlistes'. Posted May 2015 in *CEE Architecture & Urbanism. Longer Essays.*

21. Theodore Dalrymple 'Trash Studies. Great Britain: The Litter Bin of Europe' *City Journal* Autumn 2016.

22. Jackie Craven 'Biography of Adolf Loos, Belle Epoque Architect and Rebel' *ThoughtCo* August 20, 2019.

23. 'Graffiti in the Czech Republic. A Symbol of Freedom' Zachary Goldhirsch Global Studies Atavist buglobalstudies.atavist.com/graffitiinCzechRepublic. (No apparent date).

24. William Mann wrote admiringly about the Beatles many times, beginning with his famous article in *The Times* 'What songs the Beatles sang' 27th December 1963.

25. Adolf Loos' *Ornament and Crime* is discussed in Jimena Canales and Andrew Deutscher 'Criminal Skins: Tattoos and Modern Architecture in the work of Adolf Loos' *Architectural History* 2005 48: 235-256.

26. Karel Hynek Mácha 'May' translated by Edith Pargeter. The translation is on a page created by Borek Lupomesky.

27. Compellingly described in Derek *Sayers The Coast of Bohemia* op cit pp.25-28.

28. Sayers ibid p.25.

29. John Maynard Keynes *The Economic Consequences of the Peace* excerpted in *Essays in Persuasion* The Collected Writings of John Maynard Keynes Volume IX (London: Macmillan, 1972).

30. *The Sudetenland: Stolen Suffering.* YouTube video Simon Whistler and M. Morris. *GeoGraphics.*

31. Beautifully encapsulated in 'The History of the Villa Grébovka' published by the Central and Eastern European Law Initiative.

32. Owen Feltham 'Of Dreams' (1628) in *English Prose*. Chosen and

arranged by William Peacock. Volume 1 (Oxford: Oxford University Press, 1921), p.512.

33. 'The Novelist and the Witch Doctor. Unpacking Vladimir Nabokov's Case Against Freud' *The History of Literature* 112 Podglomerate (with Josh Ferris).

34. It is expressed by Father Zossima on his death bed in *The Brothers Karamazov*.

35. Ivan Klima *The Spirit of Prague* op cit p.61.

36. I cannot find the hashtag sign on the keyboard of this computer which I bought in Prague. There are some quirks among the QUERTY.

37. The difficult relationship between the habits of the universe, the laws of nature, and the laws of science are teased out in Raymond Tallis *Freedom. An Impossible Reality* (Newcastle: Agenda, 2021).

38. I have obtained these poignant details from 'Námestí Míru, the Peace Movement, Peace & Resistance' in 'The Prague Trail for Peace and Non-Violent Resistance initiated by the Czech Quakers'. Written by Ondréj Skovasja and translated by Liz Colin. Undated but accessed 25th April 2021.

39. 'Will Religion Become Extinct in the Czech Republic?' *Expats.cz* Dave Park 22/06/2016. A more recent study, however, suggests that about 1 in 5 Czechs believe in God. 'Is the Czech Republic the Most Atheistic Country? A Recent Study Casts Doubts' Raymond Johnson *Expats.cz* 5th November 2021. Before the faithful start dancing in the streets, it should be noted that 28% of the good citizens of Prague believe in astrology and horoscopes.

40. Thomas Carlyle *On Heroes and Hero Worship* (London: Chapman & Hall, 1872). Carlyle was a Calvinist without a theology. Make of that what you will.

41. Narrated in 'The Vinorhady Theatre' by someone combining modesty and its opposite describing him/herself as 'Local Expert' November 28, 2015. If mediaeval Coventry is a surprising presence in a 20th century Prague theatre, it may be because a naked, beautiful lady is always box office.

42. The wicked events are set out in *The Trap*, a Czech film released in 2020 and described in an article by Daniela Lazarová: 'Film about tragic fate of great Czech actress highlights communist atrocities in the 1950s'. Radio Prague International 2/13/2020.

43. 'Charles IV voted most influential figure in Czech history' *Kafkadesk* 2nd December 2019. The survey in question is worth a pause. The top three figures voted the most influential in Czech history are Charles IV (20%), Thomas Masaryk (19%) and Václav Havel (18%) – all seemingly rational, at least arguable, choices, though Jan Hus (4%) might have challenged the methodology of the survey. The fourth place awarded to Karel Gott, who at 16% was feeling Havel's collar, would have strengthened Hus' case for a re-run.

44. Sayers op cit p.34. It is an opportunity again to acknowledge *The Coasts of Bohemia* as a rich source for much of the history that is reported in these pages.

45. IP Pavlova *metroweb.cz* 19th March 2012.

46. Daniel P. Todes *Ivan Pavlov. A Russian Life in Science* (Oxford: Oxford University Press, 2014).

47. From Pavlov's notebooks, cited in Todes ibid.

48. See the self-citation in Note 33 to Raymond Tallis *Freedom. An Impossible Reality* (Newcastle: Agenda, 2021).

49. James M. Barrie 'Courage' The Rectoral Address at St. Andrews University, Canada May 3rd, 1922. *The Literature Network*.

50. Rem Koolhaas quoted in Peter Campbell 'Why Does it Take So Long

to Mend an Escalator?' *London Review of Books* 7th March 2002.

51. Koolhaas ibid.

52. For the curious, the title is *Seeing Ourselves. Reclaiming Humanity from God and Science* (Newcastle: Agenda, 2020).

53. Quoted in Derek Sayers *The Coasts of Bohemia* op cit p.35.

54. Mach never wrote this down, but it was attributed to him by his friend the physicist Philip Frank who fled from Prague when the Germans invaded the city.

55. Quoted in Ignazio Cuifolini and John Wheeler *Gravitation and Inertia: 101* (Princeton: Princeton Series in Physics, 1991) p.387.

56. Ibid p.387.

57. Quoted in Special Issue: 'Thought Experiments in the History of Philosophy of Science' Michael T. Stuart and Yiftach Fehige 'Motivating the History of the Philosophy of Thought Experiments' *Journal of the International Society of the History and Philosophy of Science* Vol 11 Spring 2021 pp. 212-221 p.214.

58. There are innumerable accounts of this sudden intuition. One of the best, because most accessible, is in Walter Isaacson *Einstein: His Life and Universe* (New York: Simon & Schuster, 2007), pp.145-9.

59. The happy ending may not have been an ending at all. There are interpretations of Einstein's General Theory according to which space and time *are* absolute and not mere relations between items. The tram-rider has discussed this in Raymond Tallis *Of Time and Lamentation. Reflections on Transience* (Newcastle: Agenda, 2017, 2019), Section 10.3.3 '(Many) Relations or (One) Substance?' pp. 444-450.

60. Isaacson op cit p.164.

61. This is the narrator's self-description in Isaac Babel's *Red Cavalry,*

a collection of short stories. (London: Pushkin Press, 2015).

62. Jan Patocka *Body, Community, Language, World.* Translated by Erázim Kohák Edited by James Dodd (Chicago and LaSalle, Illinois: Open Court Publishing, 1998), p.155.

63. Jan Halák 'Merleau-Ponty on Embodied Subjectivity from the Perspective of Subject-Object Circularity' *Acta Universitatis Carolinae Kinanthropologica* 52:2 (2016), 26-40.

64. WV Quine 'Two Dogmas of Empiricism' *The Philosophical Review* 60 1951: 20-43.

65. Jonathan Hale 'Merleau-Ponty's "Body Schema" *bodyoftheory* posted February 8th, 2021.

66. Jan Halák 'Embodied higher cognition: insights from Merleau-Ponty's interpretation of motor intentionality' *Phenomenology and the Cognitive Sciences* (2023) 22: 369-397.

67. Ibid p.371.

68. Ibid. p.371.

69. Discussed in Steven Pinker *Rationality. What it is, why it seems scarce, why it matters* (London, Penguin: Allan Lane, 2021).

70. W. van Orman Quine *From Stimulus to Science.* (Harvard: MIT Press, 1995), p.16.

71. Jan Halák 'Embodied Higher Cognition' op. cit. p.393-4.

72. The books in question are *A Conversation with Martin Heidegger* (London: Palgrave, 2002) and *The Enduring Significance of Parmenides* (London: Bloomsbury Continuum Studies in Ancient Philosophy, 2007).

73. Sayers op cit p.35.

74. 'Dancing House' *Wikipedia* last edited 11th February 2021 18:55.

75. Calum MacDonald *The Assassination of Reinhard Heydrich* (Edinburgh: Birlinn, 2007), p.218.

76. 'The Nightmare Prague Horror Bar' advertised in 'Prague

Attractions'.

77. harryf68 Stafford, United Kingdom. January 2020.

78. 'Elishka Krásnohorská' *Encyclopaedia of Prague 2.*
    Cultural Heritage.

79. 'Song' from *An Anthology of Modern Bohemia* (2015, Open Source)
    translated by Paul Selver, a prolific translator of Czech literature
    into English. Thank you, Mr. Selver. 'Cheskian' is an obsolete term
    for Czech.

80. Thomas Nashe 'A Litany in a Time of Plague'.

81. 'Church of Our Lady of the Snows' *Prague.net*

82. The story is told in 'Our Lady of the Snows' James Fitzhenry,
    *roman-catholic-saints.com* Marian Calendar August 5th.
    Year not given.

83. Walter Benjamin's 'Theses on the Philosophy of History' in
    *Illuminations* Edited with an Introduction by Hannah Arendt and
    translated by Harry Zohn (London: Fontana, 1973), pp. 259-60.

84. Beginning with *Enemies of Hope. A Critique of Contemporary
    Pessimism* (London: Macmillan, 1997; 1999) and more succinctly
    in 'Fifty Shades of Black. The Malignant Pessimism of John Gray'
    *Philosophy Now* Issue 127 August/September 2018, pp.54-5.

85. One of my favourites is Hans Rosling *Factfulness. Ten Reasons Why
    We're Wrong About the World – and How Things Are Better Than
    You Think* (London: Hodder & Stoughton, 2018).

86. Ernest Renan 'What is a Nation?' Lecture at the Sorbonne March
    11th, 1882.

87. I am grateful to two lovely articles for filling out my very scanty
    knowledge of Purkinje: Icilio Cavera, Jean-Michel Guillon, and
    Henry H. Holzgrefe 'Reminiscing about Jan Evangelista Purkinje:
    a pioneer of modern experimental physiology' *Advances in
    Physiology Education* 41:528-538 2017; and Venita Jay 'The

Extraordinary Career of Dr Purkinje' *Archives of Pathology and Laboratory Medicine* (2000) 124: 662-3.

88. Quoted in Jay ibid p.662.

89. Discussed in Raymond Tallis 'Ambodiment' in *Circling Round Explicitness* (forthcoming – I hope).

90. Quoted in Cavera et al op cit p.530.

91. Ibid p.531.

92. Ibid p.533.

93. Ibid p.538.

94. Michael Zantovsky *Havel. A Life* (London: Atlantic, 2014).

95. This is not quite correct. In his biography Zantovsky lists as the contents of Havel's blue bag: 'four shirts, underwear, toiletries, a sweater, pyjamas, slippers, and a copy of the Czech translation… of Ken Kesey's *One Flew Over the Cuckoo's Nest*' (Ibid, p.213). I have hidden this correction away in the endnotes because so much that follows is justified by the reference to aperients. I am relying on the haste of readers, sweeping them past the little numbers in the text, for this to be overlooked.

96. Frederick Gowland Hopkins quoted in Jeffrey Tze-Fei Wong 'Emergence of Life: from functional RNA selection to natural selection and beyond'. *Frontiers of Bioscience* 19: 1117-1150 June 1st, 2014, p.1118.

97. Which is why the body has loomed large in my philosophical writing. I have devoted books to the hand, to hunger, to the head, and even to the indicative role of the index finger.

98. This comes from *Molloy* where a character is described as having "a thin red mouth that looked as if it was raw from trying to shit its own tongue". Samuel Beckett (1958) *Three Novels. Molloy, Malone Dies, The Unnamable* (New York: Grove Press), p.145.

99. The non-identity of mind (consciousness, person, etc.) and brain

has been a longstanding preoccupation of the author. For a recent iteration, see Raymond Tallis *Seeing Ourselves. Reclaiming Humanity from God and Science.* Op cit.

100. Quoted in *Ethical Dative* April 13th, 2021. The article is signed by 'JMN'.

101. Henry Bergson *Laughter: An Essay on the Meaning of the Comic* Project Gutenberg posted July 26th, 2009.

102. S. Takano and D.R. Sands 'Influence of body position on defaecation: a prospective study of the "The Thinker" position' *Techniques in Coloproctology* 2016 February 20 (2) 117 -121.

103. August Rodin, quoted in the publication Saturday Night Toronto December 1st, 1917.

104. Examined at length in Danielle Mead Skjelver 'German Hercules. Impact of Scatology on the Image of Martin Luther as a Man, 1483-1546' Thesis University College University of Maryland. Undated.

105. Nina Martyris 'The Other Reformation: How Martin Luther Changed Our Beer Too' *The Salt* October 31, 2017, p.1.

106. Ibid p.3.

107. The whirligig of time brings in his revenges. There has been a recent revival of *gruit*-based beer. *Herbal Brewery* recommends that we 'experience beer with a botanical twist' Accessed 15th November 2021

108. Ibid p.5.

109. I have been reliably informed from several sources that this pun is even more ill-advised than other puns in this work.

110. Anonymous 'Toilet where Luther strained to produce the Reformation' *The Sydney Morning Herald* October 25th, 2004.

111. Philip Larkin in an interview with Miriam Gross 'A voice for our time' *The Observer* 16th December 1977. Reprinted in *Required Writing. Miscellaneous Pieces* 1955-1982. (New York: Farrar,

Strauss & Giroux, 1983).

112. René Descartes *The Philosophical Works* Volume 1 translated by Elizabeth S. Haldane and G.R. Ross (Cambridge: Cambridge University Press, 1967), p.192.

113. Ascribed variously to St. Augustine of Hippo and to St. Bernard of Clairvaux. The latter's exemplary misogyny licensed the infliction of physical, psychological, social, and political misery on countless women over many centuries.

114. Jonathan Swift 'The Lady's Dressing Room'.

115. It is ascribed to Father Ronald Knox but my attempts to discover when or where he made this observation have been unsuccessful.

116. The story is recounted in many places, including 'The Swan' by *The Lutheran Press* (Undated). Luther referred to himself as the swan which Hus prophesied.

117. Richard Cavendish 'The Treaty of Westphalia' *History Today* Volume 48 Issue 10 October 1998.

118. For the full argument see Raymond Tallis "The 'p' word. Does it matter if philosophy does not make progress?" *Philosophy Now* April/May 2016. It doesn't by the way. If philosophy is pointless, it is pointless only in the sense that being in love, being awake, and being alive are pointless.

119. Arthur Schopenhauer described newspapers as "the second hand of history".

120. Erich Heller *The Disinherited Mind. Essays in Modern German Literature and Thought* (London: Penguin, 1961), p.177.

121. "After the Second World War, he became the official cultural agent of the communist regime and the quality of his work deteriorated". (Viteslav Nezval. Poems by the Famous Poets all.poetry.com/ Viteslav Nezval). You bet.

122. The original rant is to be found in Raymond Tallis

*In Defence of Realism* (London: Edward Arnold, 1988), pp.104-108.

123. Louis Aragon 'Red Front' quoted in Maurice Nadeau
*The History of Surrealism* (trans. Richard Howard)
London: Pelican, 1973, p.316.

124. Tallis, *In Defence of Realism* op cit p. 104.

125. A more balanced assessment of Aragon is available on-line:
Ciaran Conliffe 'Louis Aragon, Surrealist Poet, and Communist'
*HeadStuff* June 12th 2019.

126. Josie Griffiths 'Royal Family always carry a handbag or clutch'
*Sun Newspaper* 15:26 11th May 2021 Update 15:30 11th May 2021.

127. The line was discovered through a chance encounter between
the mind of André Breton and Comte de Lautréamont' s
*Chants de Maldoror.*

128. *The Rough Guide to Prague* quoted in 'The Unbearable Lightness
of Brutalism Ignored. Czech Architecture in the Politics of Material
memory in Post Communism' *Torn Curtain* Jan 30th, 2013.

129. Walter Benjamin 'Experience and Poverty' 1933. First published
1933 in *Die Welt in Wort Gesammelte Schriften* 11; 213-219
Translated by Rodney Livingstone.

130. I cannot find the origin of this figure. '20 Best Prague Cafés
by Neighborhood' 2023 Local's Guide, *Just a Pack*,
says that 'are tons of cafés in Prague'.
Attentive readers may remember that that unit – tons – was
employed to quantify the amount of history
associated with the New Town Hall, whence the First Defenestration took place.

131. Slavenka Drakulic *Café Europa. Life After Communism*
(Abacus Books: London, 1996).

132. Derek Sayers *The Coasts of Bohemia* op cit. p.9.

133. George Steiner 'The Idea of Europe' first published in *The Liberal*

*Magazine* in 2004. It was published in hard covers, in 2015 (London: Duckworth Overlook Press).

134. Simone de Beauvoir quoted in Carole Seymour-Jones *A Dangerous Liaison* (London: Century, 2008) p.335.

135. Steiner op cit.

136. These details are gleaned from Michael Zantovsky's magnificent biography cited earlier.

137. His Café Slavia dreams were unlikely to be of political power. He was an accidental leader of his country, though that position was earned existentially.

138. This is spelled out in merciless detail in Sartre's *chef d'oeuvre* whose English translation is *Being and Nothingness. An Essay on Phenomenological Ontology* translated by Hazel Barnes (London: Methuen, 1943). It seems unlikely, however, that if the waiter dismounted from his role as waiter, discussed his life or even phenomenological ontology, with the philosopher, forgetting all that contingent business of serving coffee, Sartre would be best pleased. Bad Faith, at least as much as love or money, makes the world go round.

139. Dagobert D. Runes. He was a Ukrainian-born writer who spent most of his life in faraway places, making his home in USA. A correspondent of Einstein and many other leading intellectual figures and founder of the Philosophical Library, he lived a life devoted to the dissemination of thought.

140. Malcolm Lowry *Under the Volcano* (London: Penguin Modern Classics, 2000).

141. 'Green Devil's Absinth Bar and Shop' www.greendevils.cz.

142. John Keats 'Fancy'.

143. Heinrich Heine 'The Palm and the Pine'.

144. Heimito von Doderer *The Demons* translated by

Richard and Clara Winston  (London: Quartet Books, 1993.

145. H.C. Robbins Landon *Mozart's Last Year*
     (London: Thames & Hudson, 1988; 1998), p.97.

146. 'Most Legii' Prague Boats.Cz

147. Ibid.

148. This and other details have been derived from 'John of Nepomuk'
     *Wikipedia* and "'Who is St. John of Nepomuk?' St John of Nepo-
     muk, Our Patron Saint St John of Nepomuk Catholic Church and
     School, Yukon (Building, Bridging, Being)." The latter article is also
     a vehicle for advertisements for Daylight Donuts, Yukon, Chuck
     Gooch Broker ('Call Chuck Today') and Yanda & Son Funeral Home
     and Cremation Services.

149. Philip Larkin 'Annus Mirabilis' in *The High Windows*
     (London: Faber, 1974).

150. Joe Moran *If You Should Fail. A Book of Solace*
     (London: Penguin Viking 2020), p.79.

151. 'Stalin's statue site reveals chilling remains of Prague labour camp'
     Robert Tait *Observer* Sunday 28th March 2021.

152. *Humankind. A Hopeful History* (Rutger Bregman London:
     Bloomsbury, 2021), p.113. Or, as he put it in an earlier book, "For
     roughly 99% of the world's history, 99% of humanity was poor,
     hungry, dirty, afraid…sick". *Utopia for Realists and How we Can Get
     There* translated from the Dutch by Elizabeth Manton
     (London: Bloomsbury, 2017), p.1.

153. Raymond Tallis *The Kingdom of Infinite Space. A Fantastical
     Journey Around Your Head* (London: Atlantic Books, 2008).

154. The computer programme warns me that this language 'may
     offend your readers'.

155. Triggers another warning.

156. These figures are given on a notice in both Czech and English next

to the monument.

157. 'Memorial to the victims of Communism unveiled in Prague' Radio Prague International 5th May 2002.

158. Vaclav Havel 'The power of the powerless' in *The Power of the Powerless. Citizens against the State in Central-Eastern Europe* edited by John Keane Introduction by Steven Lukes (London: Hutchinson, 1985).

159. The details that follow are taken from an entertaining review 'Relive *The Good Soldier Schweik* at Prague Restaurant U Kalicka' by Marianne Crone March 9th, 2014, Prague Travel Tips.

160. I am indebted to 'The History of the Church and Our Lady Victorious and the Prague Infant Jesus' published by Kláster Prazského Jezulatka Karmelitská 9. (Undated).

161. John Knox's dismissal of an image of the Virgin Mary - he threw it into the river on which he was rowing as a galley slave - is described in Thomas Carlyle op cit p.136.

162. Michael Zantovsky op cit p.167.

163. Thomas Carlyle op. cit. p.123.

164. The facts have been obtained from Vladimír Kelnar 'Kostel Sv Mikuláse' Arcibiskupstvi Prázsky 16th March 2012. Very much worth a read.

165. Steven Pinker *Rationality. What It Is. Why It Seems Scarce* (London: Allen Lane, 2021) p.124.

166. The information that follows has been drawn from *Prague.eu. Prague City Tourism.*

167. P.G. Wodehouse 'Jeeves Takes Charge' in *Carry on Jeeves*. Project Guttenberg p.17.

168. Samuel Taylor Coleridge. 1828 addition to *The Eolian Harp*. In Ernest Hartley (ed). *The Poems of Samuel Taylor Coleridge* (Oxford: Oxford University Press, 1921).

169. 'Prague Guide FM' 'Self-Guided Tours with Tram 22'.

170. TS Eliot 'Little Gidding'. *The Selected Poems of TS Eliot* (London: Faber and Faber, 2009).

171. 100 Spires City Tours. Prague Castle Promotional Video. The guide introduces herself as Valerie.

172. Zantovsky op cit p.345.

173. Zantovsky ibid p.129.

174. None more cunning, perhaps, than those that led an intelligent, visionary, poet (T.S. Eliot) to write a poem – 'Gerontion', from which this line is taken - in which brilliant images share page-room with dimwitted and poisonous anti-Semitism and other manifestations of a shaven-headed xenophobia to which Eliot was prone.

175. I owe many of these details to a charming and witty little video: 'Novy Svet Prague. One of Prague's Hidden Gems' .

176. Jesse and Jonah Marks 'The Touch of Sound. Authentic Sound Recordings from Around the World'.

177. *Magic Prague* Angelo Maria Ripellino translated by David Newton Marinelli (London: Picador, 1995), p.67.

178. Tycho Brahe Died from Pee, Not Poison' Megan Gannon *Live Science* November 16th, 2012.

179. Kepler's self-penned epitaph.

180. Raymond Tallis 'The realistic novel versus the cinema' *Critical Quarterly* 1985-86 Volume 27 (2) pp. 57-65.

181. Both quotations taken from 'A picture is worth a thousand words' – a characteristic Wikipedia labour of love.

182. Joseph Roth *The White Cities. Reports from France* 1925-1939. Translated by Michael Hofmann (London: Granta Books, 2004), p.77. Another example served up by a random walk around my own bookshelves:

   Berlin is a city that is forever in the process of becoming, never being, and so lives more powerfully in the imagination. Long before setting eyes on it, the stranger feels its aching absences as much as its brazen presence: the sense of lives lived, dreams realized, and evils executed with an intensity so shocking that they rent the air and shook its fabric. Rory Maclean *Berlin. Imagine a City* (London; Weidenfeld and Nicolson, 2015), p.2.

183. These and other details are taken from 'Czernin Palace' issued by the Ministry of Foreign Affairs of the Czech Republic.

184. For an attempt at a more complete story, see Raymond Tallis 'Bringing the Laws on Side' in *Freedom. An Impossible Reality* (Newcastle: Agenda 2021).

185. The tale that follows is taken from 'Drahomíra and the gateway to Hell' an article by Baba Studio with Raymond Johnson *Magic Prague*. Undated.

186. Zantovsky op cit p.328-9.

187. William James *The Principles of Psychology* 1890 p.488. It is usually cited as an example of 'blank sheet' psychology of the mind, prior to an attack on such a view.

188. Zantovsky op cit. p.344.

189. Rainer Maria Rilke *Duino Elegies* translated by J.B. Leishman (New York W.W. Norton, 1963)

190. Pablo Neruda 'Walking Around' translated by Robert Peake "I am tired of being a man" posted on 20th December 2010. There is a lovely short video on Mr. Peake's website in praise of Buttons.

191. A phrase I have often used in ignorance of the strange journey it has taken to its meaning. There are two candidates. The first path goes via 'as tight as a rat's arse', where an extremity of tightness is expressed through the narrowness of the rodent's anal sphincter. And why 'tight'? Perhaps 'as tight as a tick' – filled with alcoholic beverages as completely as a tic is filled with blood. The

second path goes via rats who were fond of the contents of open vats but realized that they could enjoy them without drowning if they simply swished their tails through the liquor and licked the stuff off. I am grateful to Howard Makin for guidance through this tangle of ancient meaning.

192. I am indebted not only to many happy memories but also to the description of Nerudova in 'Prague-Now'.

193. This was the motto on the Prague coat of arms between 1918, when the Republic of Czechoslovakia was established, and 1991 when it was changed to PRAGA CAPUT REI PUBLICAE – 'Prague Capital of the Republic' – which may have more literal truth but seems rather pedestrian by comparison.

194. 'Crusader polices dog poo capital' *The Star* October 10th, 2011.

195. 'Czech superhero launches war on Dog Poo' Daniel Sperling *Digital Spy* 09/10/2011. A compelling video is available showing the pursuit of a dog owner by the superhero.

196. Samantha Tatro *expat.cz* 'Despite Improvements, dog poo still a problem' 14th August 2020.

197. Tatro op cit.

198. The information has been provided by Hus' House (Vrsovice) Wikipedia 16th August 2021.

199. 'Svatopluk I - King of Great Moravia (871-894). Lostice Czech Republic. Historic Figures.' On Waymarking.com. 'The Legend of the Three Twigs' is worth an e-visit, but not on a dark winter morning.

200. Anonymous 'Church of St Wenceslas' www.farnostvrosovice.cz Accessed 16th August 2021.

201. R.P. Blackmur 'Tennyson's Scissors: 1912-1950' *The Kenyon Review* Winter 1952 Volume 14 No 1, pp.1-26.

202. The details that follow are drawn from Rob Cameron 'Koh-i-Noor – a tale of two brothers, a famous painting, and the Holocaust'.

Radio Prague International 29th July 2011.

203. Spartakiads are described in loving detail in a hefty Wikipedia article from which the information in what follows has been drawn.

204. www.expats.cz Bilá Hora upoutavka 2020.

205. Peter H. Wilson interviewed by Radio Prague International 'The Battle of White Mountain – arguably the most decisive battle of the Thirty Years War'.

206. I owe this information about Chase of *Paw Patrol* to Jay Makin-Tallis who  introduced me to the television series.

207.  In, for example, Raymond Tallis *Seeing Ourselves. Reclaiming Humanity from God and Science* op cit.

208. 'Defenestrations of Prague' *Wikipedia.*

209. Peter H. Wilson op. cit.

210. C.V. Wedgewood *The Thirty Years' War* (London: Pelican Books), p.113.

211. See Jean-Paul Sartre 'Series: The Queue' in *Critique of Dialectical Reason. Theory of Practical Ensembles* Translated by Alan Sheridan-Smith. Edited by Jonathan Rée (London: Verso, 1982, p.259).

212. See Raymond Tallis Of *Time and Lamentation. Reflections on Transience* (Newcastle: Agenda, 2017/2019), Section 2.2.3 for a tussle with this idea.

213. 'Three-week' is the result of the auto-correction of 'three week'. It has drawn my attention to the strange idea of 21 days as an adjectival inflection of an absence.

214. With apologies to Rudyard Kipling and his 'The English Flag'.

215. It is impossible to resist quoting Einstein's reassurance to the great mathematician Marcel Grossman who had assisted him to make the transition from special to general relativity. Grossman loathed sitting on a toilet seat that was still warm from his 'pre-sitter'.

Einstein reassured him that what had been left behind was merely heat and it was therefore impersonal. I am confident of the truth of this story but have already spent too much time trying to locate the source of it.

216. Historic England Research Records Stockport Railway Viaduct.

217. 'Frogtastic Art Trail' Stockport's Giant Leap. *Totally Stockport.* Undated.

218. An example borrowed from Raymond Tallis 'On Being Thanked by a Paper Bag' *Philosophy Now* 107 April/May 2015 pp.48-9.

219. TS Eliot *Four Quartets.* 'Little Gidding' . The alert reader will note the difference between the lines recalled when RT was waiting by the Summer Palace and those cited now. He did not have access to his library outside of the public toilet. The intellectual sentiment, however, remains the same.

220. 'The Smallest Room in the House' 'plumbworld'. 'Big Brands, small prices. Bathroom blogposts for everything you might need brought to you by the Plumbworld Team.'

221. Since this chapter was written, the *Kammer* in question has had a major makeover and, as of the time of writing, few of the items celebrated in its paragraphs are in place. Nevertheless, the room still draws on a vast sea of joined human consciousness, sedimented in artefacts. The *Wunderkammer* principle, that is to say, is remains operative within its four walls.

222. William Blake 'Jerusalem'.

223. Thank you, yet again, 'Wikipedia' for the article on 'Cornubia'.

224. Goerg van Dorn 'Is Red Warmer than Blue? What Colours Can Tell You' *The Conversation* April 1st, 2014. While this colour code is followed in Japan and Australia, there are certain African countries where blue signifies hot and red cold.

225. *Ackermans Magazine* Live Your Best Life '8 Uses for Cotton Buds'

22nd May 2018

226. With insincere apologies to Robert Frost for this slight modification to his poem 'Design'.

227. He began it in 1912, when he was asked by André Gide to revise some of his earlier poems for publication. He completed it in 1917.

228. Paul Valéry *Fragments des Mémoires d'un Poéme* XXXVII quoted in G.W. von Ireland 'Notes on the Composition of La Jeune Parque *Zeitschrift für französische Sprache* Bd.72.H. 1 / 2 1962.

229. Octavio Paz *On Poets and Others* translated by Michael Schmidt (London: Paladin, 1992), p.126.

230. Saul Bellow *The Adventures of Augie March* (New York: Viking Press, 1953).

231. Max Ernst – on the nature of a surrealist painting. I cannot trace the origin of this passage.

232. The opening sentence of E.M. Forster's *Howard's End* (London: Penguin Classics).

233. Simone Weil Letter April 13th, 1942, to Joe Bousquet, a poet. Bousquet was paralyzed, and left bedfast and in permanent pain, as a result of an injury received in the First World War.

I am enormously grateful to Anja Steinbauer and Rick Lewis without whom *Prague 22: A Philosopher Takes A Tram Through A City* would not have seen the light of day. Thank you for everything you have done to make it possible for this book to be published, for your work on the text, and for the beautiful cover which I am sure will entice many readers. And thanks also to Andrea Bölinger for being so generous with her time and expertise in assisting with the process of getting the manuscript ready for publication.